Turning the Century

Centennial Essays on Ibsen

Other books from Norvik Press

Paul Binding: *With Vine-Leaves in His Hair. The Role of the Artist in Ibsen's Plays*
Robin Young: *Time's Disinherited Children. Childhood, Regression and Sacrifice in the Plays of Henrik Ibsen*

Anglo-Scandinavian Cross-Currents (ed. Inga-Stina Ewbank, Olav Lausand & Bjørn Tysdahl)
Aspects of Modern Swedish Literature (revised edition, ed. Irene Scobbie)
A Century of Swedish Narrative (ed. Sarah Death & Helena Forsås-Scott)
English and Nordic Modernisms (ed. Bjørn Tysdahl, Mats Jansson, Jakob Lothe & Steen Klitgård Povlsen)
European and Nordic Modernisms (ed. Mats Jansson, Jakob Lothe & Hannu Riikonen)
Gender – Power – Text. Nordic Culture in the Twentieth Century (ed. Helena Forsås-Scott)
Nordic Letters 1870-1910 (ed. Michael Robinson & Janet Garton)
Northern Constellations. New Readings in Nordic Cinema. (ed. C. Claire Thomson)
On the Threshold. New Studies in Nordic Literature (ed. Michael Robinson & Janet Garton)
Ellen Rees: *On the Margins. Nordic Women Modernists of the 1930s*
Michael Robinson: *Studies in Strindberg*
Michael Robinson: *Strindberg and Genre*
Freddie Rokem: *Strindberg's Secret Codes*

Knut Hamsun: *Selected Letters*, Vols I and II (ed. & trans. by Harald Næss & James MacFarlane)
Erik and Amalie Skram: *Caught in the Enchanter's Net. Selected Letters* (ed. & trans. Janet Garton)
Edith Södergran: *The Poet who Created Herself. Selected Letters* (ed. & trans. by Silvester Mazzarella)

Victoria Benedictsson: *Money* (translated by Sarah Death)
Hjalmar Bergman: *Memoirs of a Dead Man* (translated by Neil Smith)
Jens Bjørneboe: *Moment of Freedom* (translated by Esther Greenleaf Mürer)
Jens Bjørneboe: *Powderhouse* (translated by Esther Greenleaf Mürer)
Jens Bjørneboe: *The Silence* (translated by Esther Greenleaf Mürer)
Hans Børli: *We Own the Forests and Other Poems* (translated by Louis Muinzer)
Camilla Collett: *The District Governor's Daughters* (translated by Kirsten Seaver)
Gunnar Ekelöf: *Modus Vivendi* (edited and translated by Erik Thygesen)
Kerstin Ekman: *Witches' Rings* (translated by Linda Schenck)
Kerstin Ekman: *The Spring* (translated by Linda Schenck)
Kerstin Ekman: *The Angel House* (translated by Sarah Death)
Kerstin Ekman: *City of Light* (translated by Linda Schenck)
Jørgen-Frantz Jacobsen: *Barbara* (translated by George Johnston)
P. C. Jersild: *A Living Soul* (translated by Rika Lesser)
Runar Schildt: *The Meat-Grinder and Other Stories* (translated by Anna-Lisa & Martin Murrell)
Hjalmar Söderberg: *Martin Birck's Youth* (translated by Tom Ellett)
Hjalmar Söderberg: *Short Stories* (translated by Carl Lofmark)
Hanne Marie Svendsen: *Under the Sun* (translated by Marina Allemano)

Turning the Century

Centennial Essays on Ibsen

edited by

Michael Robinson

Norvik Press
2006

A catalogue record for this book is available from the British Library.

ISBN 13: 978 1870041 64 5

First published 2006

Norvik Press was established in 1984 with financial support from the University of East Anglia, the Danish Ministry for Cultural Affairs, the Norwegian Cultural Department and the Swedish Institute.

Managing Editors: Janet Garton, Michael Robinson, Neil Smith and C. Claire Thomson.

Cover illustration: Henrik Ibsen, by Gustav Lerum (1898).
Courtesy of Gyldendal Norsk Forlag

Cover design: Richard Johnson
Layout: Neil Smith
Printed in Great Britain by Page Bros. (Norwich) Ltd, UK.

In memoriam

Inga-Stina Ewbank

(1932-2004)

Contents

Introduction

Few in England when Ibsen died in 1906 would have anticipated the spectacular translation of Henrik Ibsen into 'Henry Gibson' over the course of the following century when he and his plays became not the object of opprobrium but central to a vital strain in twentieth-century British acting, as well as to the development of drama in English. The same period has witnessed his naturalisation by syllabus with the teaching of his plays in both schools and universities, and Ibsen remains the most prominent of non-British dramatists on the contemporary stage where, during his centenary year, productions have ranged from such regulars as *A Doll's House* and *Hedda Gabler* to *Pillars of Society* and *Little Eyolf* (both these last to great critical acclaim).

The essays published here have all previously appeared in the journal *Scandinavica* since its foundation in 1962. Not surprisingly, the collection reflects trends in recent Ibsen scholarship over the past forty-five years during which what was often an overriding concern with social issues has given way to a recognition of the poetic complexity of Ibsen's prose as a medium for the realistic portrayal of contemporary life, the links between even these dramas with folkloric and mythic structures, both Christian and pagan, and, above all perhaps, with the probing of the astonishing complexity with which Ibsen has endowed the inner lives of his characters, a complexity that often seems both to require and recall the strategies of psychoanalytical discourse in its analysis.

The essays, which have been selected to cover a range of topics and as many of the individual plays as possible, are given here as originally published apart from the correction of a few inadvertencies and printing errors in the originals. My thanks are due especially to Neil Smith for the patience and skill with which he digitalised so many back numbers of *Scandinavica*, a journal which was edited for many years by one of England's foremost Ibsen scholars, and in whose watch the plays were never regarded as parochially English but always as both Scandinavian and European.

Michael Robinson
Norwich, November 2006

General Studies

England's Ibsen, or Performing Ibsen's Dramas of Contemporary Life Today[1]

Michael Robinson

Ladies, gentlemen, colleagues, friends, it is a great honour to have been invited to deliver the first Popperwell lecture of the new millennium, and a great pleasure too. When I was in the Faculty of Modern and Medieval Languages here in Cambridge, researching and writing what became my study of Strindberg and Autobiography, Ronald Popperwell sought in numerous deft and practical ways to support my work, and to keep me, or at least my studies, in some kind of order. Indeed, in a very real sense he continues to do so. Part of my current research project is housed in ten box files that I inherited from Dr Popperwell (don't ask me how), on the spines of which it is still possible to decipher the titles of Hamsun's novels, written in pencil in Ronald's hand. At one time, they had presumably contained the notes for his projected monograph on Hamsun, a work on which he had been engaged since the late 1950s but which, sadly, he did not live to complete. This was a serious loss to Hamsun scholarship in general, and to Scandinavian Studies in Britain in particular.

I am not sure what Ronald Popperwell would make of the fact that Strindberg has now supplanted Hamsun in those boxes, but that is something else I shall not pursue now. Indeed, it is neither about Hamsun nor (for once) Strindberg that I propose to speak today but about Ibsen, and more specifically, England's Ibsen and how he might be performed. I would begin by recalling that on several Wednesday afternoons last year I interviewed a number of students who had applied for a place in the School of English and American Studies at the University of East Anglia, where I teach. They had all studied English at A level; consequently – if perversely – they had all been required to read Ibsen's *A Doll's House* as one of their set texts. From what I could gather, the translation most of them had used was not a very reliable one; but that was obviously not a major concern since it did not seem to matter greatly to any of them that Ibsen had been a nineteenth-century dramatist who wrote in Norwegian, so comprehensive had the process of his assimilation or domestication to English and England been – what James McFarlane used to call 'naturalisation by syllabus'. And nor, of course, did any of these aspiring students remark the irony that this process had been achieved in a country where the initial reception of his plays had been so vituperatively hostile; in fact, Ibsen and *A Doll's House* seemed to have struck almost all of them as irremediably passé.

But annexing Ibsen for England is hardly a new phenomena. In his introduction to the volume devoted to Ibsen in the Critical Heritage Series, for example, its editor, Michael Egan, justified the exclusion of virtually all non-Anglo-Saxon criticism from his anthology of reviews, letters and essays on the grounds that 'Ibsen's impact ... was felt throughout the English-speaking world in his lifetime owing to the speed and efficiency of translation, and to this extent he functioned in effect as a contemporary English and American playwright'.[2] So Anglo-Centric a view is all the more bizarre given the extent to which Ibsen was so profoundly European in his concerns, in his residences, in his impact. As the anonymous reviewer of Egan's book in the *TLS* (but the prose is unmistakably that of James McFarlane) remarked on its publication in 1972:

> Never before, and rarely since, has the publication of a book or the staging of a play been such an expressly European event as was the case with Ibsen's works in the 1890s. Within a few short months of the publication in Copenhagen in December 1892 of *The Master Builder*, for example, translations had been published in German (three), English (two, one of which was in America), French, Italian and Russian. Moreover, within a year of its composition it had been staged in Berlin, Trondheim, Leipzig, Åbo, Christiania, Stockholm, London, Chicago and Rome, with Paris following very shortly afterwards.[3]

There is, of course, a sense in which we all talk 'Ibsen' as the *lingua franca* of the theatre wherever realism is the dominant theatrical convention, as it continues almost invariably to be throughout Western theatre, film and television. Furthermore, the Ibsen we speak is often strongly, sometimes fatally, inflected with English since he is better known throughout the world in translation rather than in the original language, and many of these translations have themselves been made not from Ibsen's original Norwegian but from German or (increasingly) English. As Kristian Smidt points out, in his recently published book *Ibsen Translated*,[4] most, if not all, of the numerous Chinese versions of *A Doll's House* have been translated from English and the situation is similar in Bangladesh. It is therefore all the more important to heed Inga-Stina Ewbank's warning that in domesticating Ibsen and reading him only from the perspective of English literature, we overlook 'a profound and ineluctable alienness: an otherness which we support, or "naturalise", at the risk of losing his uniqueness and turning him into a Henry Gibson'.[5] What a fate indeed for a dramatist who once declared, in a letter from Rome to Magdalene Thoresen, dated 3 December 1865, that he did not wish to return to Norway with his recently born son because, he fervently insisted, his son 'shall never, if I can help it, belong to a people whose aim is to become Englishmen rather than human beings.'[6]

With this in mind, it is worth pondering the English Ibsen who sometimes appears either a very parochial, even marginal figure or (as my interviewees seemed to find him) hopelessly outmoded, or both. Certainly, the plays may seem so to be if one reads them merely as period pieces, or if they are staged museologically with the prescribed Victorian parlour set in which the play is easily submerged within the impedimenta of circumstantial, ethnographical detail. Indeed, Ibsen's plays with contemporary settings seem at times almost to conspire to support this approach with devices that (in Roy Fuller's words) 'clump across the stage / As obvious as wigs'.[7] In dialogue that sometimes seems to replicate the catechistic style of Augier or Dumas *fils*, the melodramatic skeleton of the well-made-play is frequently visible in the lineaments of these social dramas with their climactic act endings, avalanches, revelatory letters, and pistol shots. Chekhov's observation that the economy of effective theatre permits the introduction of no superfluous elements, and that consequently, if someone mentions a pistol in Act One it must be fired, usually to fatal effect, in Act 3 or 5, applies to Ibsen as well, and there can be few performances of *Ghosts* at which even the most naïve spectator does not realise that the first act discussion concerning the rights and wrongs of insuring the new orphanage means that it will, with terrible consequence, have burnt down before the play ends. In fact there is a nice irony here since it is customary now to dismiss as conventional plays that began by offending precisely by the way in which they transgressed dramatic convention. For what offended the first audiences of *Ghosts*, who were otherwise familiar with the incidence on stage – or at least in the study – of incest in plays as various as *Oedipus*, *Phaedra* or *The Cenci*, was not only that it occurred in a furnished space resembling their own front rooms, peopled by men and women dressed like themselves, but also (and perhaps most crucially) performing such obscenities in a play that closely resembled those of Scribe and Sardou, Augier, Labiche and Dumas *fils*. But where the latter generally served up what Henry James called 'the time-honoured bread sauce of the happy ending',[8] Ibsen manifestly did not. Where the former reassured their audiences, the latter disturbed and challenged them.

But before considering how Ibsen might continue to challenge and disturb, I would like briefly to reflect on this adopted English Ibsen as a basis for thinking through some of the contradictions we confront in continuing to perform a dramatist who sought (in his own words, to the Swedish actor and director August Lindberg who was staging the European première of *Ghosts*) 'to make the spectator feel as if he were actually sitting, listening, and looking at events happening in real life'.[9] Consequently it is Ibsen as the dramatist of contemporary life on whom I shall concentrate, rather than the author of the poetic dramas *Peer Gynt* and *Brand* or the earlier history plays, partial though all such distinctions into genres, styles or periods ultimately are.

The leading – and most articulate – early supporters of Ibsen in Britain were the man-of-letters Edmund Gosse, the critic and translator, William Archer, and the emerging dramatist, Bernard Shaw, although a case might also be made for the initial importance of Philip Wicksteed, the Dante scholar who, in *Four Lectures on Henrik Ibsen* of 1892, wrote one of the most positive and informed early accounts of Ibsen's work rather than for Shaw, whose *Quintessence of Ibsenism* reveals, in its successive editions, the process whereby he built up the partial myth of his own central role in the Ibsen wars. (Incidentally, Wicksteed was a Unitarian minister and is reputed to have taken quotations from Peer Gynt as the text for his sermons).[10] Archer's advocacy and translations and Shaw's theatre criticism and *The Quintessence of Ibsenism* (1891) defined Ibsen's reception in England in a number of significant ways. Archer's enthusiasm for the sober realism of the contemporary dramas in prose prejudiced him against identifying Ibsen with radical contemporary movements, whether aesthetic or social, and led him to foreground the dour realist – thus he abhorred the introduction of the tarantella into *A Doll's House* as an unnecessary concession to theatricality on Ibsen's part almost as much as other critics abhorred Nora's behaviour in leaving her husband and abandoning her children. Meanwhile I simplify only in part in saying that Shaw saw Ibsen as the passionate moral reformer of a corrupt society and enlisted him in his own ongoing struggle with the forces of British conservatism – an easy enough thing to do given the outraged response of those on the political right to Ibsen's plays.[11] Even though it might be argued that Shaw in fact read – or came to read – Ibsen with rather more perception than is often assumed, it was Ibsen as the castigator of social ills and the all-pervasive hypocrisy of the public lie in the middle, 'sociological' plays rather than the poet or probing psychologist whom he sought to emulate in *Widower's Houses* (1892) or *Mrs Warren's Profession* (1893), and with whom he is generally perceived to identify.

But as Kirsten Shepherd-Barr has demonstrated in her recent study of *Ibsen and Early Modernist Theatre*,[12] once entrenched in the English theatre, this – what one might crudely term – theatrically conservative Ibsen remained the norm – not least, perhaps, because of Shaw's standing and influence – whereas elsewhere, for example in France, a more experimental dramatist, whose affinity was with an emerging modernist theatre rather than with nineteenth-century realism, was almost immediately to be seen in the Symbolist experiments of Lugné-Poë. Lugné-Poë not only staged *Peer Gynt* with Alfred Jarry as one of the trolls – the manuscript of *Ubu Roi* tucked safely away in an inside pocket (no Eilert Løvborg, he) – but also *Rosmersholm*, *The Lady from the Sea* and *The Master Builder*, in all of which it was the novelty of the staging and the challenge this presented to prevailing artistic criteria rather than the social issues these plays raised that immediately concerned the plays' first French public.

Swings and roundabouts, one may feel; London's loss was Paris's gain, and vice versa. But neither theatre achieved the balance implicit in Ibsen's own comment on his later dramaturgy when he observes that

> [i]t was not really my intention in this play (he is referring specifically to *Hedda Gabler*) to deal with so-called problems. What I principally wanted to do was to depict human beings, human emotions, and human destinies, upon a groundwork of certain of social conditions and principles of the present day.[13]

Nevertheless, hard on the heels of Lugné-Poë came a series of theatrical innovators who, in helping to define the nature of modernism in the theatre, seemed throughout Europe to do so by challenging the naturalistic style to which Ibsen's so-called realistic plays seemed unalterably wedded.[14] But whereas directors like Max Reinhardt in his Berlin Kammerspiele production of *Ghosts* with expressively simple stage designs by Edvard Munch that sought to capture the predominant mood and themes of the play rather than reproduce precisely a middle-class Norwegian interior, Meyerhold with Vera Kommisarjevskaya as Hedda Gabler in St Petersburg, and Gordon Craig, who intended his staging of *Rosmersholm* with Eleonora Duse in Florence to create what he called 'a place which harmonises with the thoughts of the poet' and to convey 'the drift of the words',[15] all sought to achieve something beyond what was immediately to be seen in the conventional impedimenta of the box set, in England what James Agate rather wonderfully called Ibsen's 'dingy parlours covered with penitential gloom' continued to be the norm. Whereas directors like Reinhardt and Craig would all have agreed with the theatrical reformer Georg Fuchs who argued in 1906 (the same year as all these productions, incidentally) that 'the meticulous reproduction of a specific environment, which is revealed to the spectator at the rise of the curtain, [might exist] for his eye and for his consciousness only so long as the action itself has not yet taken possession of him. [And that f]rom the moment when he is carried away by the acting, that detailed illustrative setting disappears from his consciousness, and if in the further course of the play it ever bobs up again, it is either to annoy him or to indicate to him that the performance has begun to drag',[16] Ibsen in England continued to be staged amidst a clutter of circumstantial detail. It is hardly surprising, then, that as long ago as 11 July 1921, the *Daily Telegraph* should have remarked that an audience of *A Doll's House* 'can feel nothing but a detached interest in it as a great piece of drama that was once something like life.'

There is a paradox here, a double one in fact. Firstly, academic criticism of Ibsen in England can celebrate some remarkable achievements since the days of Archer and Shaw, precisely in the appreciation of his theatricality. There is, for example, the monumental eight-volume Oxford Ibsen, edited and largely translated by James McFarlane. There is also John Northam's theatrically aware analyses of the prose dramas in terms of the unspoken information projected visually through their specified costume, set-design, properties, make-up and lighting in *Ibsen's Dramatic Method* (1953).[17] And lastly, but not least, if I may annex her contributions for England, there are Inga-Stina Ewbank's several studies of what she calls 'the verbal tissue' of Ibsen's plays, which demonstrate how he fashions a 'metaphorical language to probe depths of mind not available to ordinary rational discourse'.[18] This language is not what William Butler Yeats once dismissed as 'spilt poetry' but prose put to work in as dense and complex a manner as verse, and it is therefore hardly surprising that, in her various collaborations with Peter Hall and John Barton, Inga-Stina Ewbank should also have produced some of the most sensitive and performable English versions of Ibsen's plays.

Secondly, one needs to acknowledge the way in which English-language writers from Henry James to David Hare have also found inspiration in his dramaturgy. Confronted by the vision of Elizabeth Robins as Hilde Wangel in *The Master Builder*, James was forced to concede that there was more to Ibsen than what he once called 'the mere dead rattle of the surface of life' and to appreciate in the same actress's performance as Hedda Gabler that there was both beauty and profundity in his stagecraft. This may not have helped James practically in his own disastrous flirtation with the theatre, but reading Ibsen carefully undoubtedly contributed to his masterful control of dialogue and scenic structure in novels like *The Spoils of Poynton* and *What Maisie Knew*. In a play like *Plenty*, meanwhile, in which public hypocrisy is associated with the private neurosis of his female protagonist, Susan Traherne, David Hare follows numerous other dramatists (of whom Arthur Miller is perhaps the most notable) in writing what Raymond Williams termed 'Liberal tragedy'. And one might add to this short list James Joyce who, in 1915, 'proved' that Ibsen was superior to Shakespeare and greater than Strindberg.[19]

But notwithstanding the insights of these writers and critics, or indeed Ibsen's own deconstruction of the realist project in *The Wild Duck*, it is predominantly the dramatist as the careful photographer of society who remains the English Ibsen. Which is not to say that some of what Ibsen gave to the English theatre it did not hold in common with theatres elsewhere. For here, too, he was at the heart of the modern independent theatre movement, and J. T. Grein's staging of *Ghosts* at the Independent Theatre in 1891 is a defining theatrical moment in England as were the productions of the same play by Antoine and Brahm in Paris and Berlin. Meanwhile, from the moment that naturalism dictated the determining influence of the environment on the characters, it became necessary to incorporate each significant, verisimilar detail into a whole in which all the elements of a production – setting, lighting, acting, costumes, etc. – are integrated – a practice Ibsen's plays made mandatory. In short, following Ibsen, unified production values became the norm, even in England.

Likewise, although many other dramatists who followed Ibsen did not always grasp the dual function of his apparently realistic detail and consequently 'filled their scripts with exuberant stage directions and their stages with puppets',[20] this new dramatic language – what Ibsen called 'the much more difficult art of prose' – combined natural speech rhythms employed in a supple, precise and resonant way with visual stage images to produce a truly modern poetry of the theatre. Most important of all, perhaps, in England as elsewhere, Ibsen's theatre demanded and fostered a new style of acting, in which an intense inwardness was combined with a pellucid matter-of-factness.[21] Precisely what this entails in the way of a new and more complex attitude on the part of the actor towards the script and the analysis of character has been frequently described, most recently by Gay Gibson Cima in her persuasive study of 'Ibsen and the Critical Actor',[22] but in fact Henry James had already noted how Ibsen would always 'remain intensely dear to the actor and actress. [Because h]e cuts them out work to which the artistic nature in them joyously responds – work difficult and interesting, full of stuff and opportunity'.[23] Generations of English actors have proved him right, even if they have sometimes eschewed the fragmentary, inconsistent, discontinuous aspects of identity that in Ibsen replaces the older Victorian conception of character as something seamless, unified and consistent and embraced a theatre of characters that focuses essentially on the quirks and foibles of the eccentric 'personality', more Miss Havisham perhaps than Gunhild Borkman. For Ibsen's characters 'are split and vacillating... scraps of humanity... patched together as is the human soul' like those defined by Strindberg in the Preface to *Miss Julie*,[24] and they are animated by the same 'secret stirrings that [normally] go unnoticed in the remote parts of the mind, the incalculable chaos of impressions... [the] untrodden, trackless journeyings by brain and heart strange workings of the nerves, the whisper of the blood, the entreaty of the bone, all the unconscious life of the mind' that Knut Hamsun wrote of in 1890, shortly before embarking on his novel *Hunger*.[25]

But while England may have made Ibsen what Michael Billington has called one of the strongest cards in its theatrical suit,[26] a pillar in what is often and rightly thought of as an actor's theatre, there is perhaps a subtle difference to the way in which these characters are apprehended here and elsewhere. In the first place, this may be due to an approach which is essentially novelistic; the character is excavated from the text in pursuit of what James again, writing of *Hedda Gabler*, described as 'the portrait of a nature' rather than (say) as a figure in an existentialist theatre of situation in which it is not

> 'character' as the sum total of psychological traits' that sets the performance agenda but a concern to reveal the inner governing shape of the play as a whole, where the characters are ultimately defined by the dramatic situation and 'the choices it affords (or denies) them.'[27] Or, in James McFarlane's words, the world of a play like this 'is a thing of characteristically Ibsenist construction...not a loose assemblage of characters that are, but a tightly woven mesh of things done or intended, a shifting pattern of events, a series of encounters and conflicts and defeats in a world where life is a relentless living on or loving off others.[28]

Thus Ibsen's dramas of contemporary life present us with a lattice work of interacting figures and there is consequently a danger in approaching them as exclusively the excavation of character whether, like Raymond Williams, one concludes that in a play like *Rosmersholm*, 'The refinement of the characters... is a fictional refinement; [where] the degree of attention to motive and behaviour is that of the psychological novel',[29] or sees them as merely a series of case histories since, after all, the piecemeal discovery of a shifting, unstable, and initially falsely perceived and incoherent past by a retrospective technique that brings what is buried to the surface is common both to the form of Ibsen's plays and Freud's analytical practice. Indeed, like Freud's patients, Ibsen's characters also suffer from reminiscences, and in some respects, and in various ways too complex to unravel here, Nora, Mrs Alving, Rebekka West, Hedda Gabler and both Ellida and Hilde Wangel have a great deal in common with the female subjects of Freud and Breuer's *Studies on Hysteria* of 1895 or the 'Dora' of Freud's fragment of a case history of 1905. But these characters are also very much more than mere case studies, and while Freud's extraordinary reading of Rebekka West in *Rosmersholm* may lead to the discovery of layers in the text otherwise overlooked – or repressed – by less hermeneutically disposed and suspicious readers, one has in practice to agree with one of the most memorable of recent English-language Heddas, Janet Suzman, who observes: 'You cannot act concepts or abstractions or theories. Freud may well have been right about Rebecca West's Oedipus complex, but you can't *act* an Oedipus complex.'[30]

I would add, though, that while one may criticise the temerity of Freud's psychoanalytical reading of Rebekka West in his essay on 'Some Character-Types Met with in Psychoanalytic Work' (1916),[31] where he analyses the fictional Rebekka as if she were one of his living patients, the very fact that his approach seems plausible at all testifies to Ibsen's achievement in endowing a fictional character with the complexity of lived experience, of rendering on stage what George Eliot, for example, sought to achieve in prose fiction, when she strove for 'as full a vision of the medium in which [a] character moves as of the character itself'.[32] Indeed, as those committed to the psychoanalytic project were to discover, it is not so much that

Ibsen's characters resemble their patients, but living people who appear to accord with a template previously fashioned by Ibsen. It was, after all, Ibsen who influenced Freud, not Freud Ibsen. Standing proud on a shelf in the entrance hall of Freud's consulting rooms at 19 Berggasse in Vienna where they are the first thing to meet the visitor's eye in what is now the Freud Museum, is a German edition of Ibsen's works. Ibsen clearly takes precedence, as a letter from Jung to Freud confirms: 'Every properly analysable case,' Jung remarks, of a new patient, 'has something aesthetically beautiful about it, particularly this one, which is an exact copy of Ibsen's *Lady from the Sea*. The build-up of the drama and the thickening of the plot are identical with Ibsen's'.[33]

In speaking of England's Ibsen and women at the turn of the century one must remark, too, the close identification there of his plays with the New Woman. How Ibsen provided actresses like Elizabeth Robins or the first English Nora, Janet Achurch, with a series of roles in which they could recognise and articulate themselves as women is now a familiar story. He empowered these actresses both personally and professionally in roles where they were at once changing performance style and values and performing social change: 'For [such an] actress, the exercise of her interpretative intelligence, her engagement with textuality rather than simply with the immediacy of physical spectacle, meant that she exceeded containment within the visual perspective of the stage'.[34] Robins and Achurch found in Ibsen both a real theatrical and a potential social liberation; they could identify with characters who seemed to speak 'their' words and articulate their own desires, unlike the generally vapid or openly repressive roles which they were otherwise ordinarily condemned to play. Artistically, then, these actresses participated in the work of a dramatist who seemed to regard them as 'fellow creators' (the phrase is Robins'); they shared in the creation of a 'New Drama', as challenging to the conventions of the age in theatrical terms as the New Woman was to social convention.

But this identification of Ibsen in England with the movement for women's emancipation not only reinforced the image of the issue-driven dramatist promoted by Shaw, it also encouraged the notion that Ibsen is a dramatist whose admittedly complex but ultimately fathomable characters are constricted by the terms of the age in which the plays are set. Thus, once he was no longer excoriated as a purveyor of filth but accepted as a master builder of great plays, the English Ibsen fell foul of the seeming paradox of the successful realist, who in the very act of portraying his period signals his own future obsolescence. 'My intention,' Ibsen said of *Ghosts*, 'was to try and give the reader [sic] the impression of experiencing a piece of reality'.[35] But once achieved, this realism as realism which reproduces the impression of life at a specific historical moment, becomes history, becomes not the eternally relevant but the ephemeral, and the more faithful subsequent productions are to the blueprint of the original the greater the risk they run of petrifaction. 'If my existence has been of any importance,' Ibsen once observed, 'the reason is that there is a kinship between me and the times';[36] but in that case, the greater the emphasis we place on realism, the more we are compelled to see Ibsen's characters as figures immersed in the minutiae and felt-experience of their, not our, moment in history.

Consequently, as the Norwegian 1880s and 1890s recede (and the specifics of place rendered them already in some respects 'unreal' to Ibsen's contemporaries elsewhere in Europe), there comes an increasing need to pare away the circumstantial surface detail and uncover the inner landscape underlying the play's realistic super-structure as, for example, Ingmar Bergman has sought to do, in his productions of *Hedda Gabler* and *A Doll's House*.

For what one often encounters in England's Ibsen are productions in which the well-wrought theatrical architecture of the plays becomes one with the outer stability of the society these plays in fact excoriate, the two combining to offer the illusion of stability in an uncertain world. The danger is therefore that 'the anarchist who scandalised all Europe and who was fiercely denounced in the publications of the respectable bourgeoisie... [will have] been transformed into a benignant moralist' and a 'sturdy champion of bourgeois values',[37] whereas what characterises many of the most successful recent productions of these plays – it characterises recent Ibsen criticism too – is a recognition not so much of their photographic accuracy, which in any case frequently suggested something more than a character appeared to be saying or doing (as Peter Hall has pointed out, in a recent *Festschrift* for Inga-Stina Ewbank, 'Ibsen lived in the white-hot revolution of Naturalism so that if someone actually lit a lamp on the stage, or drew a curtain, it was so unusual that it had a metaphorical meaning').[38] Rather, we need to place the emphasis on their inherent theatricality. Like her nineteenth-century sisters Carmen and Violetta Valéry, Nora in *A Doll's House* is performing a role, or rather, many roles. There is in fact a play within the play in *A Doll's House*.[39] The masquerade in which Nora appears as a Neapolitan's fisherman's daughter dancing the tarantella which so horrified Archer, is directed by her husband, Torvald, with Dr Rank as an accompanist and Mrs Linde for audience. Briefly, at the end of Act Two, we are presented with a theatrical ensemble on stage, doubling the theatrical illusion and playing upon the metaphors of role play and performance which are at the heart of the drama which is Nora's marriage. As has frequently been noted (after all, the symbolism is obvious enough), the denouement comes only after Nora has divested herself of her 'fancy dress' in favour of her everyday clothes; but this marriage has been a masquerade all along. Torvald has played the singular role of the titillated male voyeur who indulges in the secret pleasure he derives from the spectacle of his wife but Nora, who excels in precisely the one art in which women were taken by a generally held opinion of the time to surpass men, is a consummate actress and has given a succession of stage performances of almost infinite variety as (among others) the lark, the gambler, the squirrel, the doll, the spendthrift, the flirt, the carefree wife and mother, the girlfriend, the self-sacrificer and, most recently, as a woman in travail awaiting deliverance by an act of heroism on the part of her male companion. But this is a role that Torvald, who has spent their marriage directing Nora in the parts he wishes her to perform and who is himself unwittingly trapped in the socially imposed role of being a man, a husband, is manifestly unable to play – just as he is unable to accept what is implicit in Nora's behaviour, in the evidence it provides of a free and flexible selfhood that contradicts Victorian ideas about the self in general and of a woman's self as something circumscribed by being a wife and mother in particular. In Ingmar

Bergman's production of *A Doll's House*, as first performed at the Royal Dramatic Theatre, Stockholm, Nora acts her role – without any of the detailed staging that Ibsen specifies in his stage directions – on an almost bare rectangular performance space, surrounded throughout the play by her fellow performers who, when not involved in the action on stage themselves, are seated watchfully on chairs placed around the acting area, from where they observe her as she seeks to break out of the moribund world of masks and roles in which she has been imprisoned by her father and then her husband; seeks in fact to break not only out of the artificial theatrical walls of her doll's house, but also out of the box-set within which the play was originally confined.

There is therefore perhaps not so great a disjunction between what are normally taken to be Ibsen's monumental architectural structures and the metatheatricality of the non-realistic theatres of Jarry, the later Strindberg, Brecht or Genet, which are generally seen to be in flight from the realism over which Ibsen presides. If Bergman's production confirms that in *A Doll's House* life is not artless but a forum in which games are played and roles enacted, a similar histrionic dimension is to be found throughout the sequence of prose dramas with their frequently self-dramatising characters like Hjalmar in *The Wild Duck*, John Gabriel Borkman, Thomas Stockman in *An Enemy of the People* or, indeed, Hedda Gabler who, in another Bergman production, also remains on stage throughout the play, observed by the audience even when the text does not specify her presence on stage, as she sits in what, following Ibsen's stage directions, is normally depicted as the inner sanctum to which she retreats at various points of the play, but which is now placed side wall to wall with the drawing room where the action takes place, so that she is now always to be seen reacting to the conversations of the other characters in the adjoining room. This Hedda also studies herself repeatedly in the mirror, as the actress – both character and performer – observes her own performance and before which, at the end of the play, she points the pistol to her head and squeezes the trigger. Thus Hedda, who believes she is performing in a romantic tragedy opposite the Byronic Løvborg with vine leaves in his hair, discovers she plays a dubious role alongside the red-haired Mlle Diana in what has become a tawdry farce.

Such a production not only reveals a generally unobserved theatricality in Ibsen's play, it also indicates how we may tackle the problem of the circumstantial realism that otherwise seems to weigh a play like *Hedda Gabler* down. If these plays are understood as theatre pieces about life seen as already theatricalized, with as much in common with *Peer Gynt* as with the social dramas of Dumas *fils*, Henry Becque, or Gerhart Hauptmann, we can appreciate their inherent theatricality rather than their superficial likeness to nineteenth-century life. They become not still lives, images of the past frozen in a moment of time, but profound explorations of experience as it unfolds in time, 'great reckonings in little rooms'.

To do this may seem to violate Ibsen's own intentions for their staging. But in the first place, and bearing in mind the affinity which Ibsen's contemporaries believed there was between hysteria and histrionics, so theatrical an approach is not at odds with the realism of a text like *Hedda Gabler* that is motivated, according to Ibsen himself, by hysteria; rather it defines its place within a recognisable late nineteenth-century discourse. According to Georgette Déga, one of the few female interns who worked with Charcot at the celebrated mental asylum of La Salpêtrière in Paris, 'Theatricality is part and parcel of all women's lives and originates... in the dissonance produced in [their] psychic lives by their being assigned, in all social classes, inferior roles to play' (she might be summarising Nora's situation in *A Doll's House* in fact). Similarly, while observing the violent chorea to which his female patients were prone, the Doctor and alienist Harry Campbell wrote in 1891 (*Hedda Gabler* had appeared the previous year) of how

> The movements of these wild dances imperceptibly shade off into the co-ordinate movements of the hysterical fit... Hence it is possible that the love of dancing, so peculiarly strong among women, is the outcome of a nervous organisation affording a suitable soil for hysteria.[40]

Consequently the wild dance music that Hedda plays immediately before her suicide or Nora's desperate tarantella in *A Doll's House*, which Archer believed strained credibility beyond break point, emerge as both finely theatrical and realistic. And in case we are tempted smugly to equate an outmoded view with an antiquated dramaturgy it is worth recalling that only in 1987 the *Diagnostic and Statistical Manual of Mental Disorders* officially renamed what had previously been known as 'hysterical personality disorder' as 'histrionic personality disorder'.[41] In this context I would therefore highlight one English (and partly Irish) Ibsen of the last decade, namely Deborah Warner's production of *Hedda Gabler* with Fiona Shaw in the title role, first performed at the Abbey Theatre, Dublin, and subsequently adapted for English television. Here it was the symptomatic language of Shaw's body that spoke as eloquently as anything she said, in a discourse that recalled the symptomology of Hedda's close contemporaries 'Anna O' and 'Dora', and Shaw is in fact on record as having built the role upon her memories of the hysterical fits to which her grandmother was prone when she was confined within an old Victorian corset.

But secondly, and perhaps more persuasively, Ibsen is no exception to the general rule that there always has been a tension between the play on the page and its staging. If Bergman's productions seek to negotiate the limits he believes that Ibsen the Master Builder has placed there himself in his elaborate, prescriptive stage directions – 'closing doors, leaving no other alternatives', as Bergman puts it – this only echoes a comment made in 1898 by one of the greatest of Ibsen's early stage interpreters, the actor Emil Poulson, who observed:

> It is said that [Ibsen] works out his plays in his head, down to the minutest detail; only when everything is completely finished is the play written down. Thus he lives with his characters in the most intimate relationship – knows every feature of their faces, every intonation in their voices, virtually every fold in their garments. How then can he expect to see precisely this image reproduced on the stage? Every moment will be a struggle between the actor's picture and his own – a continual effort on the actor's part to erase the picture that has been stamped on Ibsen's mind for so long.[42]

Notes

1. Apart from a number of impromptu remarks at the outset, and with the addition of the appropriate scholarly apparatus, this is the text of the last Popperwell Memorial Lecture, delivered at the University of Cambridge to a non-specialist audience on 25 October 2000. The lecture was established on an annual basis in 1985, in memory of Dr Ronald Popperwell who was, from 1953, University Lecturer in Norwegian in the Faculty of Modern and Medieval Languages. *Scandinavica* published the first of these lectures, by Harald Næss on 'Knut Hamsun and Growth of the Soil', in May 1986. The lectures are jointly hosted by the Faculty and his Cambridge college, Clare Hall.
2. See the unpaginated 'Preface' to Michael Egan, ed., Ibsen: *The Critical Heritage*, London: Routledge and Kegan Paul, 1972.
3. 'Anglo-American Ibsenists', *TLS*, 26 May 1972, p. 601.
4. Kristian Smidt, *Ibsen Translated*, Oslo: Solum Forlag, 2000, pp. 7, 115.
5. 'Ibsen on the English Stage', in Errol Durbach, ed., *Ibsen and the Theatre*, London: The Macmillan Press, 1980, p. 31.
6. See Francis Bull, Halvdan Koht and Didrik Arup Seip, eds, *Henrik Ibsen: Samlede Verker (Hundreårsutgave)*, vol. 16, Oslo, 1940, p. 119.
7. 'Ibsen' in *Collected Poems 1936-1961*, London: Andre Deutsch, 1962, p. 148.
8. Quoted in Egan, p. 13.
9. Letter dated 2 August 1883, cited from Evert Sprinchorn, ed., *Ibsen: Letters and Speeches*, London: MacGibbon & Key, 1965, p. 222.
10. The importance of the Unitarian minister and Dante scholar, Philip H. Wicksteed, in the early reception of Ibsen in England is stressed by Egan (pp. 19, 21). See also Philip H. Wicksteed, *Four Lectures on Henrik Ibsen*, London: Swan Sonnenschein & Co., 1892.
11. For a detailed account of Shaw's complex relationship with both Ibsen's plays and the 'Ibsenism' he promoted, see J. L. Wisenthal's introductory essay to *Shaw And Ibsen: Bernard Shaw's The Quintessence of Ibsenism and Related Writings*, Toronto: University of Toronto Press, 1979, pp. 3-73.
12. Kirsten Shepherd-Barr, *Ibsen and Early Modernist Theatre, 1890-1900*, Westport, Conn.: Greenwood Press, 1997.
13. In a letter to Count Moritz Prozor, 4 December 1890. Sprinchorn, ed., p. 297.
14. My argument here follows closely that of Frederick J. Marker and Lise-Lone Marker in their essay 'Ibsen and the Director: From Traditionalism to Travesty in Recent European Theatre', *Contemporary Approaches to Ibsen*, VII, eds. Bjørn Hemmer and Vigdis Ystad, Oslo: Norwegian University Press, 1991, pp. 39-49. Like everyone who studies the stage history of Ibsen's plays I am greatly indebted not only to this essay but also to the Markers' book, *Ibsen's Lively Art: A Performance Study of the Major Plays*, Cambridge: Cambridge University Press, 1989, as the accounts of *A Doll's House* and *Hedda Gabler* below will demonstrate.
15. Cited by the Markers (p. 41) from Denis Bablet, *Edward Gordon Craig*, London: Routledge, 1966, pp. 87-88. It was Craig's designs for *Rosmersholm* that prompted Duse's celebrated remark, quoted by Isadora Duncan in *My Life*, London: Gollancz, 1928, p. 218: 'Only through Gordon Craig ... will we poor actors find release from this monstrosity, this charnel-house, which is the theatre today.'
16. Georg Fuchs, *Revolution in the Theatre: Conclusions Concerning the Munich Artist's Theatre*, Condensed and Adapted from the German by Constance Connor Kuhn, Port Washington, N. Y.: Kennikat Press, 1972, p. 74.
17. John Northam, *Ibsen's Dramatic Method*, London: Faber and Faber, 1953.
18. 'Ibsen's Dramatic Language as a Link between his "Realism" and his "Symbolism"',

Contemporary Approaches to Ibsen, [I], Oslo: Universitetsforlaget, 1966, p. 116.

19. See Bjørn Tysdahl, *Joyce and Ibsen: A Study in Literary Influence*, Oslo: Norwegian Universities Press, 1968, p. 55.
20. John Northam, *Ibsen's Dramatic Method*, p. 219.
21. See Ewbank in Durbach, ed., p. 35.
22. Initially published as 'Discovering Signs: The Emergence of the Critical Actor in Ibsen', Theatre Journal, 35 (1983), 5-22, Cima's valuable study of the impact of Ibsen's dramatic writing on nineteenth-century acting styles now forms part of her book *Performing Women: Female Characters, Male Playwrights, and the Modern Stage*, Ithaca and London: Cornell University Press, 1993, pp. 20-59.
23. James goes on: 'The opportunity that he gives them is almost always to do the deep and delicate thing - the sort of chance that, in proportion as they are intelligent, they are most on the lookout for.' *The Scenic Art*, London: Rupert Hart-Davis, 1949, pp. 253-254. Cf. Elizabeth Robins' remark in *Ibsen and the Actress*, London, 1928: 'Ibsen could, and usually did, cooperate with his actors' (p. 52) and her insistence, in the face of much contemporary (and subsequent) opinion, on Ibsen's consummate theatricality: 'Ibsen was by training so intensely *un homme du théâtre* that, to an extent I know in no other dramatist, he saw where he could leave some of his greatest effects to be made by the actor, and so left them. [Nevertheless w]hatever direction the individual gift and temper of the actor inclines to, the effects that Ibsen leaves him are Ibsen effects' (pp. 153-154).
24. *Samlade Verk*, Vol. 27, Stockholm: Almqvist & Wicksell, 1984, p. 105. [Transl. MR]
25. Knut Hamsun, 'Fra det ubevidste Sjæleliv', *Samtiden*, 1890, pp. 325ff.
26. Michael Billington, *One Night Stands: A Critic's View of Modern British Theatre*, London: Nick Hern Books, 1993, p. xiv.
27. See the Markers' discussion of character and situation in *Ibsen's Lively Art*, pp. 172-173. James' remarks on *Hedda Gabler*, in which he observes that 'his drama is essentially that supposedly undramatic thing, the picture not of an action but of a condition', were original published in the *New Review*, June 1891, pp. 519-530, and are reprinted by Egan in *The Critical Heritage*, pp. 234-244.
28. 'Introduction' to *The Oxford Ibsen*, Vol. VII, Oxford: Oxford University Press, 1966, p. 18. Reprinted in James McFarlane, *Ibsen & Meaning: Studies, Essays, & Prefaces 1953-1987*, Norwich: Norvik Press, 1989, p. 292.
29. Raymond Williams, *Drama from Ibsen to Eliot*, London: Chatto & Windus, 1952, p. 80. Cf. Georg Lukács, also on *Rosmersholm*, in *The Historical Novel*, translated from the German by Hannah and Stanley Mitchell, London: Merlin Press, 1962: 'the basis of the play is ... that of a novel, full of the undramatic drama of bourgeois life. As drama, therefore, *Rosmersholm* is unproblematic and fragmentary; as a picture of the times it is authentic and true-to-life' (p. 125).
30. Janet Suzman, '*Hedda Gabler*: The Play in Performance', in Durbach, ed., p. 83.
31. See *The Pelican Freud Library*, Vol. 15, Harmondsworth: Penguin Books, 1985, pp. 308-316.
32. J. W. Cross, *George Eliot's Life, as Related in her Letters and Journals*, 3 vols., London, 1885-86, II, p. 361.
33. *The Freud-Jung Letters*, ed. William McGuire, translated by Ralph Manheim and R. F. C. Hull, London: The Hogarth Press and Routledge & Kegan Paul, 1974, p. 92. (Letter dated 10 October 1907.)
34. Gail Marshall, *Actresses on the Victorian Stage: Feminine Performance and the Galatea Myth*, Cambridge: Cambridge University Press, 1998, p. 143.
35. *The Oxford Ibsen*, Vol. 5, Translated and edited by James Walter McFarlane, Oxford: Oxford University Press, 1961, p. 476.

36. From a speech to Danish students in Copenhagen, 3 October 1885. Sprinchorn, ed., p. 250.

37. I am quoting Brian Johnston, *Text and Supertext in Ibsen's Drama*, University Park and London: Pennsylvania State University Press, 1989, p. 64.

38. 'Translating in the Theatre I: Directing as Translating: Sir Peter Hall in interview with Mark Batty', in Shirley Chew and Alistair Stead, eds, *Translating Life: Studies in Transpositional Aesthetics*, Liverpool: Liverpool University Press, 1999, p. 389.

39. On the notion of plays within plays in Ibsen's dramas of contemporary life see Daniel Haakonson, '"The Play-within-the-Play" in Ibsen's Realistic Drama', *Contemporary Approaches to Ibsen: Proceedings of the Second International Ibsen Conference*, 1971, pp. 101-117; Erik Østerud's two essays, 'Henrik Ibsen's Theatre Mask: Tableau, Absorption and Theatricality in *The Wild Duck*' and '*A Doll's House*: Ibsen's Italian Masquerade' in Østerud, *Theatrical and Narrative Space: Studies in Strindberg, Ibsen and J. P. Jacobsen*, Aarhus: Aarhus University Press, 1998, pp. 20-48, 49-67; and Frode Helland, '"Play Within the Play" - Metadrama and Modernity in The Master Builder', *Proceedings. VII International Ibsen Conference*, Center for Ibsen Studies, 1994.

40. The observations by Déga and Campbell are quoted by Elaine Showalter in *Hystories: Hysterical Epidemics and Modern Culture*, London: Picador, 1997, pp. 101-102. For the frequently-made association between women, acting and hysteria, see also Michael Robinson, 'Acting Women: The Performing Self and the Late Nineteenth Century', in Elinor Shaffer, ed., *Knowledge and Performance, Comparative Criticism*, 14, Cambridge University Press, 1992, pp. 3-24.

41. See Showalter, p. 102.

42. Emil Poulson, 'Ibsen og Skuespilleren', in Gerhard Gran, ed., *Henrik Ibsen: Festskrift i Anledning af hans 70de fødselsdag*, Bergen: John Griegs Forlag, 1898, p. 255. Quoted in the translation by Frederick J. and Lise-Lone Marker, 'Ibsen and the Director', p. 49.

Originally published November 2000 (Vol. 39, No. 2).

The Actors' Contribution to Early Ibsen Performances in London

Jan MacDonald

The initial reception of Ibsen's dramas in England was, as is well-known, clouded by issues more allied to moral and social philosophy than to dramatic criticism. From Mrs Lord's translation of *A Doll's House* in 1882, with its Preface on the Rights of Women, to the moral outcry against the first production of *Ghosts* in English in 1891, English reviewers were more concerned with Ibsen as a social prophet than as a dramatic writer. Clement Scott's word 'Ibsenite' came to mean far more than someone who enjoyed Ibsen's plays. To Scott, and to the older critics, it meant 'nasty-minded people who find the discussion of nasty subjects to their taste in exact proportion to their nastiness'.[1] To Herbert Waring, the first Torvald Helmer in Britain, the characteristics of an Ibsenite were, first, a reverence for the 'New Woman', secondly, an intense belief in an intellectual oligarchy as an ideal form of government, thirdly, the appreciation of the possible consequences of heredity, and finally, a yearning after truth and freedom.[2] To Shaw, whose *Quintessence of Ibsenism* has been misunderstood by many critics,[3] it meant one who appreciated the 'realist's' way of looking at society and conventions rather than the restrictive 'idealist's' view.

Ibsenism in England was a vague term which meant a belief in a socialist political philosophy, an opposition to unthinking adherence to social convention, and, as a corollary to the latter, a belief in a new role for women in society. The critics who praised Ibsen's work and the actors who performed in it, to a greater or lesser extent, adhered to this social creed. The controversy of Ibsenism is relevant to this study in so far as it gives one an idea of the social and political views of the actors, and that it reveals an additional hurdle presented to those who performed in the first Ibsen drama to be seen in Britain. To act in an Ibsen play was not only to take an artistic and financial risk but to lay oneself open to social and moral criticism, as Leonard Outram angrily pointed out in a letter to the *Era* (21 March 1891) signed 'Pastor Manders', the part he played in *Ghosts*:

> During the preparation of the piece, in the discussion which arose upon points that are commonly outside the conversation of modest persons, there was felt no shame, nor even embarrassment, for we were dealing not with lewdness but with the material of art.

Although the actors may have been in sympathy with the tenets of Ibsenism – Elizabeth Robins was a powerful advocate of Women's Rights and her propaganda play *Votes for Women* was presented by Granville Barker at the Court in 1907; Janet

Achurch's husband, Charles Charrington, was a leading Fabian, as well as a theatrical director of distinction – they were actors before they were propagandists, and their motives for presenting Ibsen's plays were artistic rather than reformist. In their ironic article for *The New Review*, Achurch and Charrington attempted to answer the charge of didacticism: 'We solemnly and conscientiously affirm and declare that we introduced him [Ibsen] because we thought he was an artist, not because we thought he was a preacher'.[4] Mrs Hugh Bell, a close friend and associate of Elizabeth Robins, commented on her 'revolt from the accepted' and 'her search for the new',[5] but the actress made it clear that the 'revolt', as expressed in her Ibsen productions at any rate, was primarily an attempt to challenge theatrical rather than social conventions: 'If we had been thinking politically, concerning ourselves about the emancipation of women, we would not have given the Ibsen plays the particular kind of whole-hearted enchanted devotion we did give'.[6]

Fortunately for the subsequent high standard of British acting, many of the talented men and women on the stage at this time agreed with William Archer's statement that: 'Ibsen gives his actors incomparable opportunities';[7] and these opportunities were particularly important to intelligent women such as Achurch and Robins, who had tired of vapid leading-lady parts in conventional West End drama. 'No dramatist has ever meant so much to the women of the stage as Henrik Ibsen,' wrote Elizabeth Robins.[8] Herbert Waring found the men's parts equally rewarding:

> It is easier, I think, to get inside the skin of an Ibsen part than any other, for the simple reason that the characterization is so minute and elaborate, the words are so full of suggestion that the actor has infinite scope for the exercise of his best qualities.[9]

Henry James, whose experiences of rehearsals of his own work in the professional theatre were often unhappy, comments on his attendance at a rehearsal of *The Master Builder* in February 1893:

> What is incontestable is the excitement, the amusement, the inspiration of dealing with material, so solid, and so fresh. The very difficulty of it makes it a common cause, as the growing ripeness of preparation makes it a common enthusiasm.[10]

In most instances, the acting of Ibsen's men and women was highly praised, even by those critics most hostile to the plays themselves, but even on the few occasions when the performances were found wanting, e.g. in *The Lady from the Sea* (1891) and in *Rosmersholm* (1891), the earnestness and commitment of the actors are mentioned.

The main subject of this article is the particular demands that Ibsen's dramas made on actors in London in the 1890s, and how they adapted their experience in more conventional roles in an attempt to develop a style suitable for the representation of his characters; but it is first of all necessary to acknowledge the large part played by the actors in getting Ibsen's plays staged at all in the essentially commercial theatrical environment of the period.

With the exception of the Independent Theatre's production of *Ghosts* (1891) and *The Wild Duck* (1894)[11] and Beerbohm Tree's *An Enemy of the People* (1893), the first presentations of Ibsen in Britain were the result of independent action on the part of actors, most notably Janet Achurch and Elizabeth Robins, 'the two high-priestesses of Ibsen'. In an article in *The Listener* (17 July 1952), Sybil Thorndike reports that Elizabeth Robins told her of the abuse she had to suffer in trying to stage Ibsen's work, and of the strength she had drawn from 'a band of actors, men and women brave enough to launch those daring plays on a public fed on very different kind of fare'.

In order to get enough money together to mount *A Doll's House* in 1889, the first significant performance of an Ibsen play in Britain, Janet Achurch and Charles Charrington had to commit themselves to an extended Australian tour for which they were partly paid in advance. The successful run of the play had to be curtailed in order that they might fulfil their touring contract. But despite this artistic and financial success, and the fact that *A Doll's House* had not received the scandalized reviews that were to follow *Ghosts*, commercial managements showed no interest in presenting Ibsen. Two American actresses, Elizabeth Robins and Marion Lea, were however inspired by the production; and two years later, when they acquired the acting rights of *Hedda Gabler* from Heinemann, they set out to find a commercial management who would mount the play : 'We ... tried to persuade them that their indifference and their loathing were equally mistaken. We failed'.[12] The fact that *Hedda Gabler* was 'a woman's play' with no star part for an actor-manager and the feeling that Ibsen appealed only to a minority audience of cranks and faddists were the reasons given for the refusals. Eventually the play was staged by the actresses themselves, and paid for by selling Marion Lea's bracelet and a 'small treasure' belonging to Elizabeth Robins, and by borrowing £300.

A later attempt by Elizabeth Robins and Herbert Waring to mount *The Master Builder* under the auspices of a commercial management was also doomed: 'Oh, it was wild! It was irritatingly obscure. It was dull, it was mad, it would lose money'.[13] Beerbohm Tree expressed an interest in the play, provided certain alterations were made. The scene should be changed to England to make the play less 'provincial', and Solness should be a sculptor. These conditions were naturally unacceptable to Robins and Waring, who eventually found an independent backer, but they made no money from the venture. As Herbert Waring wrote later: 'The study of this part [Solness] was a labour of love to me. As one of the managers, I confess with pain that it was a labour of, or for, nothing else'.[14]

Fortunately, a group which included Sir Frederick Pollock, H. H. Asquith and Lord Haldane partly financed the series of Ibsen matinées at the Opera Comique in 1893, and John Todhunter provided the money for Florence Farr's *Rosmersholm* in 1891. Through their energy in finding backers and their willingness to work hard on difficult, if rewarding, material for virtually no financial gain, the group of actors who were involved in these Ibsen productions made a substantial contribution to the development of British playwriting and acting in the succeeding decade, but constant preoccupation with the business side of the ventures made it difficult to maintain a high artistic standard – as Elizabeth Robins realized when she wrote of the difficulty of 'trying to arrive at a business competence under circumstances when artistic competence and freedom, to increase *that* should have been the main, if not the sole concern'.[15]

Despite the fact that by 1894 the Ibsenite controversy had lost much of its heat, and that the reputations of several actors had been made in Ibsen parts, Henry James wrote to Elizabeth Robins about the possibility of staging *Little Eyolf* in the following terms: 'Is there absolutely no-one in London with a theatre and a mind? I think them over and I confess I see no beckoning portals. I fear Allmers will never be thought an actor-manager's part'.[16] Again Elizabeth Robins was forced to mount the play herself. Although she had offered it to the Independent Theatre Society, the dilatoriness of that body, which had lost much of its impetus on Grein's retiral in 1895, eventually forced her to withdraw the acting rights from the Society and become her own manager again.

The foundation of the New Century Theatre in 1897 by Elizabeth Robins in association with William Archer was a final attempt to stage plays of value without having to resort to offering oneself and one's play to the actor-managers. The scheme depended on subscriptions for a season of four plays, and on donations by the philanthropic. The aim as stated in the Prospectus[17] was to 'provide a means of escape from the influence of commercial conditions'. The New Century had 'an economic, quite as much as an artistic origin'. Although it was made clear that the new group was not 'devoted to any special school or tendency', the first production in May 1897 was *John Gabriel Borkman*, and there were plans, unfortunately never realized, to present *Peer Gynt* in a later series.

To some extent one can understand the reluctance of the actor-managers to become involved with Ibsen. In most instances, although the actors did not make any money from their ventures, they did not lose it, but the appeal was to a minority audience of upper-middle class intellectuals, who could fill a theatre at one or two matinées but could not sustain a long run. The ten matinées of *Hedda Gabler* in 1891 made a net profit of £281, but losses were incurred when it transferred for a month of evening performances at the Vaudeville. Likewise *Little Eyolf* lost £200 on its transfer to the Avenue's evening bill. Shaw appears to have been right when he told Elizabeth Robins that he did not believe in 'Ibsen at night'.[18]

Apart from financial considerations the actor-managers were experienced enough to see that, as it stood, the style of acting used in society drama and in melodrama, however sophisticated, was not suitable for Ibsen's plays. Different demands were being made on their skills; and despite the reputation gained by Achurch, Robins and others by their creations of Ibsen's characters, the more enlightened critics realized that 'it is harder to gain success in interpreting Ibsen's characters than in interpreting the characters of any other dramatist'.[19] Elizabeth Robins believed that it was easier for the young actor, who had not become inhibited by stage conventions and professional tricks to tackle Ibsen, than for the more mature actor:

> With the exception of the very greatest – the great as Duse was great – people who have been a good while on the stage are less likely to show Ibsen at something like his full value than people whose talent is still mobile and comparatively modest, receptive.[20]

As a rule, the most successful actors in Ibsen were young. Janet Achurch was twenty-five when she first played Nora, Charles Fulton was thirty-four when he first appeared in *A Doll's House* and Leonard Outram, the first Pastor Manders, was thirty-six when he created the role. Elizabeth Robins, when she played her first Ibsen part, Martha Bernick in *Pillars of Society*, was twenty-seven.

As soon as an actor, whatever his age, resorted to old stage-tricks in the playing of Ibsen it was at once noticed and commented on. Genevieve Ward failed to give any truth to the character of Mrs Borkman in 1897: 'Nothing would induce her to follow Ibsen's prompting. Her ears were full of the stage directions of all the Sydney Grundy's of the last fifty years'.[21] And Louise Moodie, playing Mrs Solness in 1893, is criticized as follows by the *Daily Telegraph* (21 February 1893):

> Miss Louise Moodie's sound but somewhat antiquated method hardly becomes the character in question, which seems to call for modern and realistic treatment, rather than the sternness and solidity of the old school of tragedy.[22]

Henry James accused her of turning Mrs Solness into 'a stale theatrical category instead of a special person'.[23] Another two relapses into stock-characterization were picked out by A. B. Walkley in Charles Hudson's portrayal of Ulric Brendel in Florence Farr's *Rosmersholm* in 1891: 'Mr Hudson played Ulric as a conventional stage drunkard';[24] and in C. M. Lowne's Borgheim in *Little Eyolf* in 1896, which he turned into 'a walking gentleman part'.[25] When W. H. Vernon, a distinguished Shakespearean actor but very much a member of 'the old school', failed to understand one of his lines in *John Gabriel Borkrnan* (1897) in spite of the efforts of William Archer, Elizabeth Robins and Alfred Sutro to explain it, he said: 'There are any amount of lines in this play that I have to say and don't understand. But don't you worry – that will make no difference'.[26] According to Sutro, it did not; but Shaw's more highly trained dramatic perception picked up the meaningless lines, said without understanding but with 'a sudden access of pathetic sentimentality and an intense consciousness of Ibsen's greatness'.[27] Vernon was not only the actor in the production guilty of resorting to solemn rant when he failed to grasp the meaning of a line, and Shaw deplored this habit: 'It is establishing a funereally unreal tradition which is likely to end in making Ibsen the most portentious of stage bores'. The ability to understand unfamiliar ideas and complex characterization was the most important attribute for an actor in the 1890s if he wanted to tackle an Ibsen role, and it was largely through their intellectual capacity that the leaders of the movement were able to succeed in adapting what they had learned in other types of theatre to their playing of Ibsen's characters.

The plays were confessedly 'difficult' intellectually, and for this reason shaw felt that 'the old school' of actors was quite incapable of playing in them:

> The senior generation of inveterately sentimental actresses, schooled in the old fashion if at all ... quite out of the social and political movement around them ... intellectually *naïve* to the last degree. The new school says to the old, 'You cannot play Ibsen because you are ignoramuses'.[28]

Even among the 'new school', Waring (who played Solness) found that to understand *The Master Builder* took 'long days of laborious study',[29] and was disappointed that, because the translation was slow in coming to the company, there was insufficient time for full critical analysis; yet the *Globe* (21 February 1893) praised him and Elizabeth Robins (Hilda Wangel) as 'two of the cleverest, most spiritedly ambitious of our younger actors'. The delay in receiving the translation was less of a handicap to Elizabeth Robins since she had learned Norwegian in order to read Ibsen's work in the original. A. B. Walkley's review of *Hedda Gabler* complimented that cast on their intellectual grasp of the play:

> The fact that they have got something worth studying, something worth interpreting and straightway from being mere 'professionals' doing a day's work of mumming for a day's wages, they become students and interpreters.[30]

He goes on to describe Elizabeth Robins as 'an intellectual actress of the highest order'. Mrs Patrick Campbell described the peculiar quality of Elizabeth Robins' dramatic gift as 'the swiftness with which she succeeded in sending thought across the footlights; emotion took a second place, personality a third'.[31] It is difficult to know what exactly Mrs Patrick Campbell meant by 'personality'. Was it the ability to impersonate truthfully a dramatic character, or does she refer to that style of acting very prevalent in the 1890s when actors succeeded in shallow society dramas by playing themselves, and so giving flesh to the bare bones of stereotyped characterization? One suspects that the former must be the case, in view of other comments on Elizabeth Robins. It is interesting to see that 'emotion' is mentioned. Among the essential requirements of an Ibsen actor, the ability to portray powerful and intense emotion was second only to an intelligent grasp of the play's meaning. This I return to below.

One of the reasons why a group of younger actors was able to cope with difficult and unusual ideas was that, as a result of the growing respectability of the theatrical profession, a great many of the new generation were considerably better educated than their predecessors. *The Theatre* (1 July 1896), in a profile of Charles Fulton,[32] describes him as 'one of the increasing number of gentleman actors, previously destined for a learned profession, in his case, the law.' But it was an older actress, Mrs Theodore Wright, the creator of Mrs Alving, who had the perfect background for playing Ibsen, according to Shaw. She was a member of the Marx-Aveling circle in London, and was married first to the editor of a radical newspaper, and then to a leading Fabian: 'A lady who had talked over matters with Karl Marx was not to be frightened by Pastor Manders'.[33] Her experience and her intellectual grasp enabled her to fill Ibsen's part satisfactorily, although as far as her stage technique was concerned she was 'unmistakeably a contemporary of Miss Ellen Terry', and her style of playing (she had been a pupil of Mrs Stirling) initially belonged to the older generation.

Although critics of Ibsen's plays frequently declared themselves mystified and puzzled by the works, they equally frequently praised the acting, and one can therefore conclude that their lack of comprehension lay in the unfamiliarity of the ideas of the piece or in their own prejudice, rather than in the actor's failure to communicate the meaning of his part. Intelligence and a sound intellectual grasp of the meaning of the piece was not enough, however, as Florence Farr found in her playing of Rebecca West in *Rosmersholm* in March 1891. None of the critics disputed her perception, but a great many found her performance 'lacking in strength'[34] and 'wanting in that burning passion that would consume every obstacle towards its gratification'.[35] Rose Meller was found inadequate in her portrayal of Ellida in *The Lady from the Sea* for the same reason:

> Miss Rose Meller's performance of the demented Ellida had none of the electric quality that gives a fascination to Miss Elizabeth Robins' interpretation of Hedda Gabler, for Miss Meller not inexcusably makes Ellida a mere congenital idiot instead of an excitable creature of maniacal tendencies.[36]

The great Ibsen actresses, Robins and Achurch, managed to combine satisfactorily an intellectual understanding of the social and moral implications of the role with powerful emotional representation of the individual character. When Elizabeth Robins played Rebecca West in 1893, William Archer described her performance as 'a creation of the rarest subtlety and distinction';[37] and M. A. Franc comments on the 'intense feeling infused into the long scenes'[38] by Robins and Waller. Shaw believed that Elizabeth Robins' greatest quality as an actress was the ability to inject into her Ibsen roles emotion she had experienced in her own life, crediting her with employing the technique that Stanislavsky was to call 'emotion memory'. A short article on Herbert Waring in *The Theatre* repeats the point about intensity of feeling in describing *his* acting style: 'His quiet restrained, authoritative style, allied to an emotional power always ready, but always well under control';[39] whilst Janet Achurch's Nora was 'played with the utmost intelligence, subtlety, intensity and truth'.[40]

Compared to much contemporary drama, Ibsen's characters and dialogue were both true to life and psychologically sound; and one side of the average actor's repertory, the naturalistic drama of the Robertson school, was to prove useful in the playing of Ibsen parts. (The romantic or melodramatic tradition was also of value, as is discussed below.)

Henry Arthur Jones in his inaugural lecture to the Playgoers' Club in 1884[41] outlined both the advantages and the limitations of the Robertson/Bancroft school:

> The essential weakness of that school is found in the fact that it never occupied itself with any greater scheme than a contrast of manners between a vulgar usurping middle class and a decaying aristocracy. The essential strength of that school is found in the improved stage-management, the attention to minor details of accuracy. and the greater air of *vraisemblance* which it has imparted to almost every modern play.

Ibsen's social prose dramas demanded the *vraisemblance* already achieved by the British theatre, while at the same time providing it with themes of moral and social importance. The *vraisemblance* in Ibsen productions was shown less in setting[42] than in characterization, and many critics comment on the psychological truth of the actors' representations. One particularly telling description comes from Elizabeth Robins, writing of the Achurch/Charrington production of *A Doll's House*: 'The unstagey effect of the whole play ... made it, to eyes that first saw it in '89, less like a play than a personal meeting – with people and issues that held us and would not let us go'.[43] Her own clear conception of Hilda Wangel and her identification with the character amazed the interviewer for *The Speaker* (18 February 1893): 'It was curious to see how Miss Robins throughout spoke of Hilda Wangel as a woman whom she knew in the flesh rather than as an imaginary being born of a poet's brain'. And once she had established herself in the character she quickly lost her own mannerisms:

> From beginning to end there is not the faintest trace of Miss Robins ... All the customary tell-tale characteristics have vanished, and in their place is as radiant, vigorous, determined, bouyant a girl as one could well conceive.[44]

She herself believed that Ibsen, while leaving great scope for the actor, demanded that the actor in turn be modest and receptive, and not 'too hopelessly divorced from naturalness'.[45] In his letter to J. T. Grein (20 February 1891) giving permission for the Independent Theatre Society's production of *Ghosts*, Ibsen 'emphasised the importance of "truth to Nature" in the whole interpretation of his play as a point to be meticulously observed';[46] and, on the whole, his English interpreters fulfilled this demand. There is a direct reference to the development of the Robertsonian school to suit the Ibsen plays in W. Davenport Adams's comment on Arthur Elwood, who played Løvborg and who was regarded by the critic as one of the theatre's best younger leading men: 'He is now our best available exponent of reserve force'.[47]

Both Achurch and Robins had had experience of the romantic and heroic form of theatre, still popular and prestigious in England and particularly preva-lent in the playing of Shakespeare and melodrama. Janet Achurch had made her debut in 1883, six years before her appearance as Nora. Apart from a tour with F. R. Benson playing Shakespearean heroines, the major part of her work was in current popular commercial successes, e.g. *The New Magdalen* and *The Corsican Brothers*. As it was impossible to survive as an actress playing only in Ibsen or for enlightened private societies, she was forced to play in the commercial theatres, even after her success as Nora. Of her performance in *The Cotton King* at the Adelphi in April 1894, the *Era* reviewer wrote: 'Miss Achurch has shown amazing adaptability in the way in which she has turned her hand to melodrama'.[48] Such roles, however, were not particularly attractive to her, nor ideally suited to her style of playing. As W. Davenport Adams pointed out: 'It is in roles out of the common rut and susceptible of unconventional treatment that Miss Achurch is likely to succeed in future'.[49] The most successful part of her career was Nora; but her performance as Rita Allmers in *Little Eyolf* (1896) also brought much critical acclaim, and inspired a revealing comment from Shaw: 'With all her cleverness as a realistic actress she must be classed technically as a heroic actress'.[50]

Elizabeth Robins began her career in her native America playing with the Boston Stock Company, and toured with Edwin Booth in Shakespeare and romantic drama. Her first performance in Britain was in *Little Lord Fauntleroy*, starring Vera Beringer, in 1889; and this led to her playing her first Ibsen part, Martha Bernick in *Pillars of Society*, mounted later that year as a benefit matinée for the child actress who played Olaf. Elizabeth Robins played several parts at the Adelphi, where in the house of melodrama she showed herself capable of improving on current melodramatic acting. An article on her work in *The Theatre* (1 September 1891) admired her 'intensity and earnestness. They were more artistic, though not quite so dramatic as those of the usual Adelphi heroine'. Although she 'eschewed the ordinary melodramatic methods', her style pleased the Adelphi audiences. However, William Archer, her collaborator over many Ibsen ventures and her partner in the New Century Theatre, makes the same observation on her style as Davenport Adams did on that of Janet Achurch: 'In dealing with commonplace parts, she was apt to appear to less advantage than more commonplace actresses'.[51] The common factor between the styles the two actresses used in heroic drama and in their Ibsen roles appears to have been emotional intensity, but the Ibsen parts used this quality in more profound characters.

The background of Herbert Waring demonstrates again the importance of experience in both the heroic and the naturalistic. His career began in 1877 as a walking gentleman at the Adelphi, and continued in Edward Terry's company playing in *Caste*, *School*, *Ours* and *Society*. Later he worked for five years at the St. James's with Hare and Kendal, Robertson's legitimate successors. Lewis Waller abandoned temporarily the leading men in heroic drama to play opposite Elizabeth Robins in her series of Ibsen plays at the Opera Comique in 1893. These parts showed him in a new light: 'As Solness he looked beneath the surface of the part, abandoned the hero's claim to be heroic, and played not like a leading actor, but the unhinged architect of Ibsen's puzzling pages'.[52] Shaw refers to Leonard Outram's 'apprenticeship as a heroic rhetorical actor';[53] and W. L. Abingdon, the villain of many Adelphi melodramas also turned to Ibsen, playing Dr Rank to Rose Norreys' Nora in 1891 and Hjalmar in the Independent Theatre Society's *The Wild Duck* in 1894. Athol Forde and Frances Ivor both had experience in Wilson Barrett's company before playing their Ibsen parts.[54] Provided he had not become steeped in artificial conventions, the Ibsen actor could exercise his intelligence in adapting what he had learned in the schools of the naturalistic and romantic theatre and thus give his performance both psychological and physical truthfulness in addition to powerful emotional intensity.

In an interview in *The Star* (6 June 1891), Ellen Terry gave as the reason why so many actors and actresses were anxious to tackle Ibsen's dramas that they were so easy to play. The dialogue was natural and easy to speak, much easier than poetic dialogue. While this statement can be taken as an example of an actress of 'the old school' failing to understand the intellectual and emotional complexities of Ibsen, it is also interesting that Ellen Terry as a player of experience recognized the quality of his writing. She was wrong, of course, in imagining that natural dialogue demanded less technical skill than a more stylized verse form. To appear to be talking naturally on stage is not, as many actors had to learn, to speak as one would in one's own drawing-room. Shaw saw the greatest technical demand on the performers as being the need for perfect diction – a valid point in plays in which character and meaning are exposed in discussion rather than in action. In a letter to Archer, after seeing the Achurch/Charrington production of *A Doll's House* in 1889, he wrote: 'I am alive to the necessity of perfect diction when an attempt is made at realism in the pitch of conversation'.[55] He found most of the performers difficult to hear even from the fourth row of the stalls, and he levelled a similar complaint against Elizabeth Robins'

Hedda Gabler; 'What is wanted is not loudness but a little more deliberate intention and distinctness'.[56] Henry James echoed Shaw's complaint of inaudibility in the case of Waring at the Opera Comique matinées: 'I thought Waring extremely good ... *but* distinctly not loud enough. You *were* – keep it up, up, up',[57] he wrote to Elizabeth Robins.

Less demanding critics apparently found the diction of the Ibsen performers perfectly satisfactory. *The Hawk* (13 June 1893) described Elizabeth Robins' Agnes in *Brand* as 'beyond all praise from the elocutionary point of view', and Bernard Gould as Brand 'spoke the lines admirably'.[58] The Hawk review of *The Master Builder* (28 February 1893) remarked that the players 'delivered their lines as though they were from a play by Shakespeare himself',[59] indicating a degree of stylization as well as a high standard of speech.

Janet Achurch had to face criticism of her delivery in both the 1889 and the 1892 performances of Nora. William Archer thought she was prevented from being the ideal Nora by 'her voice and tricks of utterance. At other times she goes in for motiveless fortes and pianos which mar the smoothness of it'.[60] Walkley in *The Star* (20 April 1892) found her voice 'not in perfect control', and Shaw complained of 'harslmess of tone'. These faults, however, seem to have been corrected by the time she revived the piece in March 1893:

> The exaggerations and the crudities which we had to deplore in the revival at the Avenue Theatre last April have disappeared, and the reading is once more artistic, harmonious and full of concentrated cleverness.[61]

Even Shaw, the perfectionist, found her 'very good vocally' in *Little Eyolf*.[62]

In 1929, J. T. Grein wrote that, 'Even our Ibsen performances in retrospect suffered from the artificial rhetorical style then prevailing on our stage'.[63] And one must assume he referred to all the 1890s Ibsen productions, not just to the Independent Theatre Society's presentations. In view of frequent comment by contemporary reviewers on 'naturalness', one can only assume Grein is speaking with hindsight viewing the productions twenty years later when the intervening work of Barker and others had made British acting more like it is today. With a few exceptions the style of delivery in Ibsen's plays seems to have reached a reasonable standard and to have been relatively 'naturalistic', at least in the context of contemporary fashion.

The translated dramas of Ibsen differed from regular theatrical fare, not only in their intellectual content, but also in the importance the dramatist gave to lesser roles, e.g. Engstrand in *Ghosts* or Ulrik Brendel in *Rosmer*sholm, so that a high standard of *ensemble* playing was demanded. When these parts were occasionally played as stereotyped stock characters (e.g. Charles Hudson's playing of Brendel as a conventional stage drunkard) the whole effect of the piece was weakened. But such lapses were rare. Elizabeth Robins, commenting on the first Achurch/Charrington production of *A Doll's House* wrote: 'Each person in the cast seemed the heaven appointed person for the part'.[64] The excellence of minor characterization was noticed in *Pillars of Society* in 1889; and even the conservative *Era* (23 April 1892) wrote of the production *A Doll's House* in that year:

If only for the sake of a tout ensemble not often to be found in these days of shifting casts and often altered companies. ... all admirers of fine and subtle acting should see *A Doll's House* at the Avenue Theatre.

That any degree of success in *ensemble* playing was achieved at first seems remarkable in view of the practical difficulties faced by the actors trying to mount Ibsen's plays. Almost all of them were presented on a limited budget, in theatres hired for a short period with a scratch company. Although a fairly large group of actors was interested in performing in Ibsen's plays, the productions happened so irregu-larly that their regular theatre commitments often made it impossible to take part. Elizabeth Robins sums up the difficulties in *Theatre and Friendship*:

> Each new production meant, not as in regular theatres the carrying on of a business of which the framework remains the same, the heads of Departments and most of all the company the same. Each new play given outside the London managements meant a new attack and a fresh campaign. It meant canvassing the field for a new theatre (the same one was seldom available), it meant the delicate vital business of choosing a new cast, it meant working in one's view of stage-management, often with a new stage manager. [65]

From time to time problems resulting from the lack of a permanent organiza-tion were not happily overcome. In a letter to Mrs Hugh Bell about a perfor-mance of *A Doll's House* in Brighton in October 1892, in which Janet Achurch played Nora and Elizabeth Robins Mrs Linden, Henry James wrote that the latter had 'no picture to fit into, no ensemble to compose with'.[66] This play and *Hedda Gabler* ran as matinées at the Theatre Royal in Brighton while Mrs Langtry and the Haymarket company presented *The Queen of Manoa* in the evening. Herbert Waring had been unable to recreate his old part of Helmer owing to a previous engagement at the Garrick. Constant changes of cast led understandably to irritation on the part of Janet Achurch. Ellen Terry's daughter, Edith Craig, played Mrs Linden on a tour in 1897; and Shaw wrote: 'Janet is so loathingly sick of rehearsing it with new Lindens that she wants Edy to get through in one rehearsal'.[67] By this time, Janet Achurch had played with five different Mrs Lindens and three different Helmers in five different theatres in London.

From the very beginning of her attempts to mount Ibsen, Elizabeth Robins had seen the importance of keeping together a permanent company of enthusiasts; and this was one of the motives behind her attempt to found a joint management with Marion Lea in 1891. The failure of this effort and subsequent unsuccesful attempts by Achurch and Charrington left the English attempts at Ibsen, at any rate for Shaw, inferior to the production of *Rosmersholm* by Lugné Poë's company, brought to London under the auspices of the Independent Theatre Society in 1895. Despite outstanding individual performances by Robins, Achurch and Mrs Patrick Campbell, Shaw felt the *Little Eyolf* company had not worked long enough together.

The *ad hoc* system, however, seemed to William Archer to have some advantages in the commitment and dedication it demanded of the performers. In his review in *The World* (21 June 1893) of Beerbohm Tree's *An Enemy of the People*, he described the performance as 'distinctly below the level of the so-called "scratch performances"'. These were more satisfactory 'because they have not been treated as mechanical matters of business and routine but studied and staged by artists with special intellectual and technical qualifications for their work'. The performance seemed to have suffered from all the faults the critics found in actor-managers' theatre. Tree as Stockmann, despite the fact that he was made up as Ibsen (rather a cheap idea) and had great difficulty remembering his lines, seems to have given a good performance; but little or no attention had been paid to the crowd, which Archer was quick to notice, and he describes their reactions to Stockmann's big speech as being 'monotonous and lacking in gradation'. Despite her awareness of the difficulties, Elizabeth Robins found that there were fewer actors 'playing the lone hand'[68] in her Ibsen companies than in the regular theatre. Talking of the production of *Hedda Gabler*, she writes of how much she enjoyed 'the rehearsals everybody keen, excited, pulling with us (few London plays have been rehearsed more carefully)'.[69] Her friend and colleague, Marion Lea, she found ideal in this respect: 'Perhaps more than anyone else I ever worked with, Marion Lea had the sense of playing with the whole orchestra'.[70]

Another problem mentioned by Elizabeth Robins was the lack of a director, although William Archer seems to have been extremely helpful with both the Robins and the Achurch/Charrington presentations. His advice seems to have gone further than merely advising on the Norwegian background and altering the dialogue of his translation where necessary. 'Nothing escaped him from the slightest inflection of voice up to the crescendo of a climax or the smallest altera-tion of text',[71] wrote Elizabeth Robins about his work on the production of *Little Eyolf* in 1896. In the first production of *A Doll's House*, Archer worked very closely with Charrington. In a letter to his brother, Charles, he described how Achurch initially played the last scene 'querulous, whimpering and wretched'.[72] Archer indicated his dislike of this interpretation to Charrington; and at the following rehearsal, she played it exactly as Archer had wanted.

Archer worked very closely on both the translations and the productions of most of the early Ibsen performances. His absence from the scene of the presentation of *The Lady from the Sea* (1891), translated by Mrs Aveling, may have been one of the reasons for the very harsh reviews received by the performers. They were described as incompetent, incapable and amateur. Leonard Outram and Edith Kenward, who had both appeared in *Ghosts* earlier in the same year, received some praise; but whether the reason for the almost unanimous condemnation of the production was on account of the miscasting of Rose Meller as Ellida, the fact that this particular play was too 'poetic' for English actors and and English audience to cope with, or that there was no direction either from Archer or from any of the actors, is uncertain. *The Lady from the Sea* is interesting in that it is the only play by Ibsen presented in London in the 1890s in which the acting is unanimously attacked by critics. Charles Charrington directed *The Wild Duck* as well as *A Doll's House* with intelligence and sensitivity; but, according to Shaw, he was very difficult to work with, and Elizabeth Robins and Florence Farr found him unsympathetic. For the most part, actors who presented Ibsen directed themselves, which, despite their sympathy with the plays and their understanding of what was required, was not a happy situation with such works. In discussing *The Master Builder* venture Elizabeth Robins writes:

Herbert Waring and I had not only ourselves to think about, we had everyone else's part and clothes to think about, the rightness of the scenery, the lighting, the advertisements, the seating – all the thousand things that make up the production as a whole.[73]

Apart from Charrington and Archer (who was after all a critic, not a full-time director), few stage-managers' were capable of tackling an Ibsen play even if they had been willing to do so. Elizabeth Robins was very scathing about current standards and found most stage-management in the commercial theatre restrictive of the actor's freedom. In view of subsequent events, Elizabeth Robins was proved right when she wrote: 'To a greater extent than I realised at the time we had unsettled the more intelligent and ambitious members of the regular companies'.[74] Although the actors who played in Ibsen were not widely known, nor particularly influential, nor able to command a large personal following, the artistic and intellectual challenge of the plays attracted some of the most capable of the younger members of the profession. Criticism of the period attacked the plays with an irrational ferocity resulting from prejudice; but the actors, in almost every production, received considerable praise.

Once one had played in Ibsen, it was difficult to return to what Elizabeth Robins and Marion Lea referred to as 'the hack-work of the stage. That was what we called playing even the best parts in plays selected by the actor-manager'.[75] The Ibsen actor would look around for similar parts and find them in the presentations of the Stage Society, and later of the Court Theatre under Vedrenne and Barker. From its beginnings in 1899, rising out of the ashes of the Independent Theatre Society, the Stage Society almost took over Ibsen productions in England with British premières of *The League of Youth* (1900), *When We Dead Awaken* (1903) and *Lady Inger of Ostrat* (1906). Janet Achurch and Charles Charrington were prominent in the Society's productions, while Florence Farr, Charles Fulton, Mrs Theodore Wright and Athol Forde were among the Ibsen actors who worked with Barker at the Court. What they had learned in playing in Ibsen's dramas was of great help to them in tackling the plays of Shaw, Barker and Galsworthy.

A good summing up of the style of acting in the first productions of Ibsen's plays in Britain comes from a comment by Herbert Waring on Charles Fulton's performance of Gregers Werle: 'Personality, technique, intellectual grasp, and a most discreet and judicious use of the trained actor's resources were allied in this instance with happiest results'.[76]

The opportunities which Ibsen gave to his actors, and even more particularly to his actresses, were fully met by most of them; and the style of playing these pioneers evolved has become a vital strain in the twentieth-century British acting tradition.

Notes

1. *Sporting and Dramatic News*, quoted in W. Archer, 'Ghosts and Gibberings', *Pall Mall Gazette* (8 April 1891). Reprinted in *Ibsen, the Critical Heritage*, edited by Michael Egan (London, 1972), p. 210.

2. Herbert Waring, 'Ibsen in London', *The Theatre* (1 October 1894).

3. *The Quintessence of Ibsenism* was originally written as one of a series of lectures, delivered to the Fabian Society in the summer of 1890, the overall title being *Socialism in Contemporary Literature*. The series, chaired by Annie Besant, included lectures on Zola, Russian fiction and the English novel. Shaw was, therefore, not attempting to give an allround critique of Ibsen's work but to deal with those aspects of it which fitted into the scheme of the lecture course. At the height of the controversy in 1891, Shaw published it, but a more revealing statement of Shaw's general view of Ibsen was his preface to *The Irrational Knot*, written in 1905, in which he describes taking part in a reading of *A Doll's House* in which Eleanor Marx played Nora '– its novelty as a morally original study of a marriage did not stagger me as it staggered Europe ... Indeed I concerned myself very little about Ibsen until, later on, William Archer translated *Peer Gynt* to me *vica voca*, when the magic of the great poet opened my eyes in a flash to the importance of the social philosopher'. *The Irrational Knot* (London, 1924), p. 19.

4. 'A confession of their crimes by Janet Achurch and Charles Charrington from the cell of inaction to which they were condemned in the latter half of the year of grace, 1893'. *The New Review* (April 1894).

5. Mrs Hugh Bell, *Landmarks* (London, 1929), p. 111.

6. Elizabeth Robins, *Ibsen and the Actress* (London, 1928), p. 31.

7. W. Archer, 'The Mausoleum of Ibsen', *Fortnightly Review* (July 1893).

8. *Ibsen and the Actress*, p. 55.

9. 'Ibsen in London', in Egan, *op. cit.*, p. 328.

10. Henry James 'Ibsen's new play', *Pall Mall Gazette* (17 February 1893), reprinted in *The Scenic Art*, edited by Allan Wade (New Brunswick, 1948), pp. 256-260 and in *Theatre and Friendship*, pp. 92-97.

11. The acting of these two productions I have already discussed in my article 'Continental Plays presented by the Independent Theatre Society, 1891-1898', *Theatre Research International* (October 1975).

12. *Ibsen and the Actress*, p. 15.

13. *Ibsen and the Actress*, p. 39.

14. 'Ibsen in London', in Egan, *op. cit.*, p. 330.

15. Elizabeth Robins, *Theatre and Friendship* (London, 1932), p. 189.

16. Letter from Henry James to Elizabeth Robins (25 November 1894), quoted in *Theatre and Friendship*, p. 162.

17. Large extracts from the Prospectus are quoted in *The Era* (20 February 1897); and A. B. Walkley's article on it for *The Times* is extensively reprinted in *Theatre and Friendship*, p. 193.

18. Letter from Shaw to Elizabeth Robins (1 December 1896) in Bernard Shaw, *Collected Letters, 1874-1897*, edited by Dan H. Laurence (London, 1965), Vol. I, p. 707.

19. *Black and White* (6 June 1891).

20. *Ibsen and the Actress*, p. 56.

21. *Ibsen and the Actress*, p. 52.

22. Egan, *op. cit.*, p. 270.

23. Letter from Henry James to Elizabeth Robins (21 February 1893), quoted in *Theatre and Friendship*, p. 102.

24. *The Star* (24 February 1891).

25. *The Speaker* (28 November 1896).

26. A. Sutro, *Celebrities and Simple Souls* (London, 1933), p. 70.

27. *Saturday Review* (8 May 1897).

28. G. B. Shaw, *The Quintessence of Ibsenism* (London, 1891), p. XX.

29. 'Ibsen in London', in Egan, *op. cit.*, p. 329.

30. *The Star* (21 April 1891).

31. Leon Edel, *Henry James: the Treacherous Years, 1895-1901* (New York, 1969), p. 31.

32. Charles Fulton played Krogstad in *A Doll's House* (1891), Knut Brovik in *The Master Builder* (1893), Gregers Werle in *The Wild Duck* (1894), and Kroll in *Rosmersholm* (1908).

33. G. B. Shaw, ' "Ghosts" at the Jubilee', *Saturday Review* (3 July 1897); in Egan, *op. cit.*, p. 382.

34. *Black and White* (28 February 1891).

35. *The Theatre* (1 April 1891).

36. *Referee* (17 May 1891); in Egan, *op. cit.*, pp. 250-1.

37. *The New Review* (July 1893).

38. M. A. Franc, *Ibsen in England* (Boston, 1919), p. 93.

39. W. Lewis Bettany, 'Four leading men', *The Theatre* (1 September 1892).

40. *The Theatre* (1 July 1889).

41. Published in Henry Arthur Jones, *The Renascence of the Drama* (London, 1895), p. 165.

42. Inadequate setting was the result of lack of money, although Shaw felt that rather than resort to shabby settings such as that used for *John Gabriel Borkman* (1897) it would have been better to have no setting at all. A review of the Australian tour by Achurch and Charrington where more resources were available compares their setting for *A Doll's House* to one by the Bancrofts: 'The scene was worthy of the best efforts ever made in this direction by the Bancrofts at the Haymarket'. Austin Brereton, 'The Theatre in Australia', *The Theatre* (1 January 1890).

43. *Ibsen and the Actress*, p. 11.

44. *The Theatre* (1 April 1893).

45. *Ibsen and the Actress*, p. 53.

46. Michael Orme, *J. T. Grein, The Story of a Pioneer: 1862-1935.* (London, 1936), p. 85.

47. *The Theatre* (1 July 1893).

48. *The Era* (14 April 1894).

49. W. Davenport Adams, 'Actors of the Age', *The Theatre* (1 August 1893).

50. *Saturday Review* (28 November 1896).

51. *The World* (3 March 1897).

52. *The Theatre* (1 July 1893).

53. '"Ghosts" at the Jubilee', in Egan, *op. cit.*, p. 383.

54. Athol Forde played Kroll in *Rosmersholm* (1891) and Knut Brovik in *The Master Builder* (1893). Frances Ivor played Madame Helseth in *Rosmersholm* (1893), Mrs. Solness in *The Master Builder* (1893) and the Gypsy in *Brand* Act IV (1893).

55. Letter from Shaw to William Archer (11 June 1889), in Dan H. Laurence, *op. cit.*, Vol. I, p. 214.

56. Letter from Shaw to Elizabeth Robins (April 1891), *ibid*, p. 292.

57. Letter from Henry James to Elizabeth Robins (21 February 1893), *Theatre and Friendship*, p. 102.

58. *The World* (7 June 1893).

59. Egan, *op. cit.*, p. 289.

60. C. Archer, *William Archer* (London, 1931), p. 181.

61. *The Era* (18 March 1893).

62. *Saturday Review* (28 November 1896).

63. *The Sketch* (18 December 1929).

64. *Ibsen and the Actress*, p. 13.

65. *Theatre and Friendship*, p. 189.

66. *Ibid*, p. 70.
67. Letter to Ellen Terry (20 July 1897), in Dan H. Laurence, *op. cit.*, Vol. I, p. 785.
68. *Ibsen and the Actress* p. 34.
69. *Ibid*, pp. 17-18.
70. *Ibid*, p. 34.
71. *Ibid*, p. 5I.
72. *William Archer*, p. 182.
73. *Ibsen and the Actress*, p. 44.
74. *Theatre and Friendship*, p. 201.
75. *Ibid*, p. 33.
76. 'Ibsen in London', in Egan, *op. cit.*, p. 330.

Originally published May 1976 (Vol. 15, No. 1).

Phases of Style and Language in the Works of Henrik Ibsen

Trygve Knudsen

1

Many Norwegian writers in the nineteenth century, including not a few of the most prominent of them, took an active part in the controversies that raged over the language question. Bjørnson worked for the cause of riksmål, for example, and Garborg for landsmål, and after them, right down to the present day, there have been other authors, among them Nils Kjær, Arnulf Øverland and Sigurd Hoel, who have also taken part in public debate on the language situation. Their commitment in this way is not surprising, for what is at stake is the language they themselves use, the very medium of their artistic expression.

As a partisan or propagandist in language matters, Ibsen will be rightly thought to be of limited interest. He was reluctant to engage in any activity that might have distracted him from his work of artistic creation. Generally speaking, allusions to the language situation in Norway are found only in works from the first twenty years of his literary career, and it is only in that period that Ibsen can be said to have taken any direct part in the language discussion.

Yet although Ibsen was thus for most of his career comparatively indifferent to the outward aspects of these controversial matters, he had nevertheless a most potent influence on the development of Norwegian literary language and style, achieved first and foremost through the impact of his realistic dramas. And from the point of view of stylistic history, his work is of particular interest because it mirrors, in a way at once more typical and more independent than that of any other author, the sequence of the various phases of style and linguistic expression in nineteenth-century Norwegian literature.

2

Sometime in the 1880s Ibsen was asked which dramatists he had known when he wrote *Catilina*. He answered: 'Only Holberg and Oehlenschläger'.[1] This reply has not altogether satisfied literary historians, who think that he certainly forgot to mention Schiller and Shakespeare (particularly his *Julius Caesar*) as influential, among others, in forming his dramatic technique and general attitude in that play. But, even so, concentrating as I wish to do on Ibsen's style and language, it seems essential to take his reply seriously and to give due weight to the influence exerted upon him by Oehlenschläger and by Danish literature in general. We find, in fact, that in his first works Ibsen fully adopts the traditional poetic style which had been pioneered by Johannes Ewald at the end of the eighteenth century and further developed by the later Danish Romantics. A principal characteristic of this style was that it aimed at creating a lofty poetical atmosphere, which could only be sustained by the exclusion of everyday modes of speech and colloquial idiom.

To produce such a lofty, dignified style two linguistic means were especially employed. On the one hand, the authors used archaic Danish forms and a word-order that was obsolete in the ordinary language; and on the other hand, they constantly introduced rhetorical questions and exclamatory phrases, both foreign to everyday speech. A characteristic of the style is the ejaculation *Ha!*, which Ewald had introduced and which had called forth Wessel's uncomplimentary adjective, *hastemt* (bombastic, highfalutin' superior).

These elements in the Danish style had been thoroughly assimilated by the young Ibsen, and he employed them consciously and assiduously in *Catilina*. The extant drafts of the play show us in detail how he worked. In most cases his corrections are designed to make his word-forms or word-order agree with those sanctioned by the Danish poetic tradition. *Ha!* is multiplied, and it is typical, for instance, that while *gaae* and *staae* are used in the stage directions the forms in the dramatic dialogue are the archaic *gange* and *stande*. Other forms are *vorde* for *blive*, *sjunge* for *synge*, *sjunke* for *synke*, *hvo* for *hvem*.

In 1875, 25 years after its first appearance, Ibsen published a revised edition of *Catilina*. Here we find striking evidence both of the development of Ibsen's own stylistic power and of the general advance in Norwegian literary taste in the intervening years. Without losing any of its poetic character, the dialogue has now been almost completely pruned of the traditional embellishments – the use of *ha!* is reduced to a minimum. Otherwise the most obvious general difference between the two is the far greater conciseness of expression in the later version.

Kjæmpehøien was Ibsen's first work to be performed on the stage, in Christiania in September 1850. It was mostly written while he was still in Grimstad but not finally finished until after his move to the capital. It is generally counted an Oehlenschläger pastiche, and although this description does not entirely fit the historical outlook revealed in the play, it certainly fits its motives and style. This play was radically revised for the Bergen theatre in 1853, and again in this new version we can find palpable evidence of the author's advance in dramatic ability, experience and self-confidence. The play has become, in short, more Ibsen and less Oehlenschläger. But all the same he is in general working in the same traditional mould as before. The words that are used to give the proper flavour to this play about Norse Vikings in Sicily belong to the vocabulary established by Oehlenschläger and other Danish authors of the 'Golden Age'. They are words like *Skjald* (scald, poet) and, very characteristically, *Ludurhorn* (horn, lur). *Ludur* is not Norwegian but an adaptation from Icelandic, commonly used by the Danish Romantics whose authority Ibsen is following. Even the Norwegian *Gut*, which replaced the *Dreng* of the first version, was not really contrary to the Danish tradition, since it had been adopted, almost as a favourite word, by Oehlenschläger and was also used by Grundtvig.

After his arrival in Christiania in the spring of 1850 Ibsen lived as a student and in a completely fresh milieu. National Romanticism was in full bloom in the capital city. The Norwegian variety of Romanticism had foundations of its own in the folk-tales, folk-legends and folk-music, all of which had been brought to light from their rural obscurity during the previous twenty years. In his first summer in Christiania Ibsen began *Rypen i Justedal*, subtitled, typically enough, *A National Play*. He did not finish it, but later he completely re-made it as *Olaf Liljekrans*. Critics have pointed out resemblances between the motives and character groupings of *Rypen i Justedal* and those found in certain works by Danish authors, who may have influenced him, particularly Henrik Hertz. But the most striking feature in this fragmentary work lies in the marked echoes we hear from Welhaven, who in his lyrical poetry was the most prominent representative of the new National Romanticism. It must be observed, too, that Ibsen's immediate source for the play was a collection of Norwegian popular legends. There are many words in the play that belong naturally to the atmosphere of National Romanticism – a few, among scores, are: *sæter* and *sel* (chalet, pasture shed), *li* (mountain slope), *granli* (slope covered with spruce), *granholt* (spruce wood), *aare* (hearth), *jente* (girl). Words like these are purely Norwegian, not Danish, and some of them even appear in forms that would not normally be counted proper in the literary language – *Haugafolket* (fairy folk), for example, and *Huldra* (with the definite article, more commonly *Huldren*, forest fairy). The Icelandic form *Ludur*, used in *Kjæmpehøien* on Oehlenschläger's authority, is always replaced in *Rypen i Justedal* by the Norwegian equivalent, *Luur*, definite form, *Luren*.

From a literary point of view *Rypen i Justedal* is no more than a piece of prentice-work and it has not unnaturally sunk into oblivion. But it has its significance: it marks one of the stages Ibsen passed on his way to complete mastery over his chosen instrument and it shows us how he enriched his language with new elements.

3

The works mentioned so far belong to the first half of what we may call Ibsen's apprenticeship. The second half of this period consisted of the six years he spent in Bergen (1851-7). He went there to take up the post of so-called 'theatre poet' at Den Nationale Scene, the theatre founded by the famous violinist Ole Bull for the encouragement of Norwegian drama. Ibsen's chief duty was to write a new play for performance on 2 January each year, the anniversary of the theatre's foundation.

Contemporary Danish literature continued to influence him in this period, more or less strongly. But no single dominant influence can be detected – his different works show influence from different Danish writers and the styles are variegated.

His first play in the Bergen series was *Sancthansnatten*, a sort of modern prose play in spite of his description of it as 'a fairy comedy'. Its roots lie on the one side in Shakespeare's *Midsummer Night's Dream*, and on the other side in the work of the great Danish author and critic, J. L. Heiberg. Heiberg's favourite form was prose dialogue interspersed with lyrics and precisely the same form is found in *Sancthansnatten*.

Although this first Bergen play was a decided failure on the stage, it still offers various points of interest. It is by no means unimportant from a literary point of view, for example, to realise that the hero, the student Julian Paulsen, is the prototype of Peer Gynt and Hjalmar Ekdal. And stylistically the play marks another and very important step towards Ibsen's final emancipation from Oehlenschläger. On the model of Heiberg's work, and because the characters are supposed to live in modern times, Ibsen used prose for the dialogue, a prose which is not without its realistic touches even though it does not achieve the truly conversational modern style he was to perfect later. A final point of interest offered by *Sancthansnatten* is that it shows us something of Ibsen's attitude to the language situation in Norway at the time. Julian, the hero, is a caricature of national enthusiasm – his nationalism is false, setting its standards only by superficial outward forms, devoid of inner truth. Ibsen sneers at the idea of restoring the ancient Norse language on the basis of the most archaic dialects still alive in the country. Ibsen, it is true, favoured the aim of creating a national Norwegian literature, but in reviews written in these years he maintained that this could only be achieved by authors capable of penetrating nationalism's façade and giving their work a true national tone.

Ibsen's own dramatic output in the Bergen years constitutes by itself an important contribution towards the achievement of a national literature with authentic inner qualities. Without exception these plays are set in the Norwegian past, with subjects derived from medieval ballads, from sagas or remote historical times. Such themes made various stylistic demands, but in essence the problems can be reduced to one: the problem of pastiche. How far and in what way should a modern play make use of imitation or an adapted language in order to give an atmosphere in keeping with the remote age in which the events are set?

Both the Danish and the Norwegian authors who attempted a poetic revivification of the past were faced with this question, and in general their answers were the same. Theoretical aspects of the problem of pastiche had been discussed most thoroughly in Denmark, and practical solutions had also been more numerous there, where the literary soil was more fertile than in Norway. Danish literary influence in these matters was strongly felt by Ibsen, as by others, but even so his works clearly reveal a certain special Norwegian colouring. This is partly due to the subject matter and partly due to the fact that he worked in an atmosphere alive with patriotic enthusiasm and he was himself conscious of his task as a national poet.

Ibsen's first Bergen play on a historical theme was *Fru Inger til Østeraad*. It is set in sixteenth-century Norway, so that the problem of stylistic imitation is less urgent there than in his later Bergen plays. In tracing Ibsen's artistic and stylistic development, however, this play is of great significance.

Until the production of *Fru Inger*, Oehlenschläger had been the great and uncontested authority. His position was virtually unchallenged, even though some writers, Danish and Norwegian, had moved towards emancipation in minor matters – in the abandonment of iambic verse, for example, in some parts of their plays. The novel – indeed, revolutionary – thing about *Fru Inger* is that it is all in prose. As has been said: 'This play inaugurates a new dramatic trend, with aims quite different from the old Romantic ones'.[2]

The style of *Fru Inger* holds some echoes of the Sagas of the Kings, the only sagas Ibsen knew at this time, through the medium of Jacob Aall's translation. The saga-style is reflected especially in an elaborate prose rhythm, with the use, for example, of word-doublets, sometimes reinforced by alliteration and assonance: *Mod og Mandskraft*; *uden Ly og Leie*. But the echoes are not sufficient to justify any description of the style as pastiche.

Another source of the style and language of *Fru Inger* must also be considered. A recent study[3] has demonstrated the striking resemblances that exist between this play and the play *Svend Dyrings Hus* by Henrik Hertz, published in 1837. The resemblances are so close that in many cases we could exchange lines of dialogue between the two plays without altering the stylistic impression at all. As we know, Ibsen indignantly denied that his next play, *Gildet paa Solhaug*, was influenced in any way by Hertz, and he would doubtless have raised an equally vehement protest against the findings of the above-mentioned study of *Fru Inger*. And, to my mind, Ibsen's protests would, at any rate to some extent, be justified. We should remember that Hertz and Ibsen had made independent studies of the old Norse prose style, as far as that was possible through the translations at their disposal, and both of them were attracted by its clearcut and unornamented features. And finally there remains an essential difference between *Svend Dyrings Hus* and *Fru Inger*: Hertz's play is written largely in verse, with prose used only in minor and less important scenes, while Ibsen's play is in prose throughout, irrespective of whether the thoughts and sentiments to be expressed are lofty or trivial.

Another point to Ibsen's credit is his attempt – deliberate enough, as it seems – to characterize his people by their style of language. This is most conspicuous in Fru Inger and in Eline. The former's speeches have an unsentimental quality, even a hard, cynical ring, but Eline, except when she is talking to her mother, is emotional and lyrical in her expression, especially in the comparisons she introduces, although she is never allowed to relapse into the long rhetorical and exclamatory speeches so dear to the heroes and heroines of Oehlenschläger. There are also some scenes in the play, especially where servants are talking together, in which the conversation has a real colloquial flavour.

In his next play, *Gildet paa Solhaug*, Ibsen was brought face to face with the problem of imitating or adapting a style suitable for a setting in the remote past. Some twenty years later, when his publisher suggested a revised edition of the play, Ibsen referred to it, depreciatingly, as a 'study'. This description of his must apply first and foremost to the style of the play. The scene is laid in Norway in the fourteenth century, the age of the ballads, and Ibsen coloured his dialogue by imitation, often close, of the popular ballad style. Sometimes he used direct quotation from ballads. It is obvious, however, that this style in the drama serves very limited dramatic purposes; only the three leading characters use it, and then only when moved by passionate feelings over great issues. Otherwise the dialogue is in prose. In trying out this method Ibsen had a two-fold aim. On the one hand, he provided a colouring suitable to the time and place of the events; and on the other hand, the stylistic differentiation also marks a dramatic differentiation between the matter which is central and important and that which is peripheral and less important.

Ibsen's imitation of ballad style depended on his own thorough knowledge of Landstad's great collection of ballads, published in 1853, and this was his main inspiration for the play. The language of Landstad's collection is, however, the dialect of West Telemark, and this could not be directly adapted for use within the framework of the common literary language. Ibsen solved this problem by clothing the Norwegian ballad material in the linguistic forms authorized by the Danish 'Golden Age' poets in their own adaptations from Danish ballads. (We cannot presume that Ibsen at this stage had any first-hand knowledge of Danish medieval ballads. Contemporary critics maintained that Hertz was again his model, but Hertz was certainly not the only Danish writer known to Ibsen who had made such use of Danish ballads.) A prominent feature in this adapted ballad style is inevitably the use of poetic archaisms – *vorde min viv*, for example, instead of *bli min hustru*. But Ibsen also introduced a good many forms and words which are purely Norwegian, e.g. *foss, li, ur, fedle, ek* (Danish *Eg*), *berg* (Danish *Bjerg*).

The problem of pastiche became still more urgent in *Hærmændene paa Helgeland*. As I mentioned above, the aesthetic problems connected with pastiche had received fuller discussion in Denmark than in Norway. The leading Danish authority in the field was Carsten Hauch, who maintained that modern playwrights and novelists dealing with saga-themes should strive to render the tone of the sagas as faithfully as possible in their style, in order to produce an atmosphere proper to the milieu. This view was fully accepted by Ibsen, who just at this time (around 1855) was widening his knowledge of the sagas by reading the *Völsunga saga* and the Icelandic family sagas in the Danish translations of C. C. Rafn and N. M. Petersen respectively. It was Ibsen's opinion that Petersen had eminently succeeded in reproducing the tone of the sagas, and his own saga-style in *Hærmændene paa Helgeland* was formed on the pattern of Petersen's. Perhaps the most dominant feature in this imitation is to be found in the word-order, above all in the use of inversion, when sentences are given an emphatic beginning by a word or phrase shifted from its normal position: *Dyrt skal du bøde for de ord* (*Du skal bøde dyrt for de ord*); *Vidt for jeg i viking* (*jeg før vidt i viking*); sometimes the shift is combined with ponderous alliteration: *Mangt værk mægter mands vilje at fremme*.

The copious use of this construction, suggestive as it is of gravity and gloomy fate, most strikingly affects the rhythm of the whole play. Other words that evoke the desired atmosphere have an antique technical sense: *herse*; (*jeg byder dig*) *selvdømme*; *eftermaalsmand*; or they are lifted straight from the sagas: *æt, idrætsmand*. Most such words had already been used in Danish translations and poetry, but some specifically Norwegian forms also occur, *sørpaa* for Danish *sydpaa*, for example.

For decades it was the general opinion that *Hærmændene paa Helgeland* represented the perfect re-creation of genuine saga-style. But voices were also raised in protest, and the loudest among them was Bjørnson's. Ibsen, he thought, had indeed reached a pitch of perfection in the style of *Hærmændene* – but it was the perfection of imitation, just such as he had achieved on a different model in *Gildet paa Solhaug*. To Bjørnson both plays were achievements of sterile virtuosity, they were coldly artificial, their characters lacked inner warmth and truth. As he looked upon it, Ibsen in his imitative saga-style had been misled by one of the delusions of Romanticism. To Bjørnson it was essential that a modern author must take his starting point in the language of his own day and age, not in the style of some remote period. He adds that Ibsen's *Hærmændene* urged him more than anything else to publish as soon as possible his own drama of the thirteenth century, *Halte-Hulda*. Altogether he found the virtuosity of Ibsen's imitation of saga-style in that play both distasteful and frightening.[4]

Kongsemnerne, Ibsen's next historical play, did not appear until 1863, and it admirably illustrates the development in his views on style after the production of *Hærmændene*. In this new play there is a striking change of front. He now makes no attempt to offer a detailed imitation of saga-style. When the emphatic inverted word-order, which was so distinctive of *Hærmændene*, now appears, it is not as an ubiquitous mechanical device but as a rare and effective means of achieving stress at special moments. *Kongsemnerne* is not, in fact, the earliest evidence we have that Ibsen was abandoning his pastiche saga-style. His altered views can be clearly seen, for example, in his review[5] of Bjørnson's *Sigurd Slembe*, where he pointed out that the tone of the language in this saga-play was not that of the sagas, and added 'nor should it be', when the author's aim was to represent through his characters universal human conflicts independent of time and distinct historical periods. There can be no doubt but that in this Ibsen was deeply influenced by Bjørnson, whose views he ended by adopting: living individuals should speak a living language, whether the play is a saga-play or not.

4

Bjørnson was not however the sole influence. Ibsen returned to Christiania in 1857 to take up the post of 'artistic director' of The National Theatre. The main aim of this theatre was to promote a Norwegian scenic art emancipated from the overwhelming traditional Danish influence. This policy was put into practice first by encouraging Norwegian actors and actresses in order to end the virtual monopoly held by Danish players, and second by authorizing a stage pronunciation founded on a Norwegian base to replace the traditional Danish stage speech, which even native Norwegian players had been forced to adopt. The most prominent figure in the execution of this policy was Knud Knudsen, the theatre's language adviser and an ardent language reformer. In contrast to Ivar Aasen, who had established his landsmål on the basis of rural dialects and thus completely divorced it from the existing literary language, Knud Knudsen wished to accept this same traditional literary language and freely 'norwegianize' it, in spelling, vocabulary and pronunciation. Ibsen shared Knudsen's views to the full – I mentioned above the ridicule he poured on ideas of a complete restoration of the language on the basis of old Norse in *Sancthansnatten*. Contact with Knudsen over several years called forth in him a more conscious feeling of the need to make the existing literary language a truly Norwegian vehicle. We consequently find that from 1857, his first year in Christiania, and down till about 1870, he took a more active part in the debates on the language situation. From our present point of view, we may regard these same years as forming Ibsen's second period as a creative writer. The impulse that sprang from Knud Knudsen was acknowledged by Ibsen himself in a greeting he sent on Knudsen's eightieth birthday.[6] There he thanks him for 'den sproglige Vækkelse' for which he is indebted to him.

Ibsen's new active interest was evinced first in newspaper articles and even in poems[7] on the subject of the language situation. In terms that sometimes strike a note of passion he described the way in which a truly national linguistic and literary development in Norway was retarded by the immense weight of the authority and prestige accorded to the Danish literary tradition and the Danish language. This is the only period in his life when Ibsen publicly advocated definite viewpoints in the language controversies. Indeed, in the late 1860s, we witness a unique spectacle: Ibsen actually joins a committee for the promotion of a practical end. As one of the Norwegian representatives he attended the Scandinavian congress in Stockholm in 1869, a congress which met to draft proposals for a unification, or at least a mutual rapprochement, in matters concerning the orthography of written Danish, Norwegian and Swedish. Knud Knudsen also supported this move, and saw no inconsistency between it and his own efforts to norwegianize the Dano-Norwegian literary language of his own country. The draft of rules which was the outcome of the congress was never officially ratified, but Ibsen himself adopted the rules at once and used them faithfully in all his works from 1869 onwards. On his authority, some other Norwegians practised this spelling, Hans E. Kinck for instance, in the first decades of his literary career.

It is also characteristic of this second period in Ibsen's life as a writer that his original works contain frequent allusions to the language disputes. In *Kjærlighedens Komedie*, for example, he mentions 'Knudsen's Grammar', and particularly his advocacy of replacing Danish intervocalic and final *b* and *g* in spelling by *p* and *k*. Vinje, the most prominent landsmål author of the 1860s, is referred to twice. He first appears as 'Dølen' in *Kjærlighedens Komedie*: 'Ej Hver, som ynder at haandtere Sølen, maa derfor tro sig Ligemand med "Dølen".' (This allusion is so strictly local that it has been veiled in the English translations I have seen.) The second and the most notorious allusion to Vinje comes in Act 4 of *Peer Gynt*, where Ibsen decides linguistic self-sufficiency and cultural isolationism in his presentation of Huhu. This picks up the earlier ridicule expressed in *Sancthansnatten*. Ibsen wished to preserve the well-established literary language, Danish-based though it was, and to make it into something truly Norwegian.

Finally, in considering Ibsen's more positive approach to the language question in this his second period, we should consider his own practice in his original works. Here we find, right from the outset of this period in 1857, a markedly new departure. Of great significance in this connection are his rhymes. In his works up to then he had often been content with eye-rhymes, mechanically following Danish habits and presupposing a non-Norwegian pronunciation (rhymes like *ryggen* : *lykken*, for example). Now he shows himself careful to base his rhymes on the standard pronunciation of his own language, something which is especially evident in *Kjærlighedens Komedie* and *Peer Gynt*. It has been truly said that this new procedure may in itself be counted a further step on Ibsen's road towards linguistic realism. But it accords most significantly with the demands of Knud Knudsen, who steadily emphasized the importance of following educated standard speech in the efforts to be made to norwegianize the literary language.

It is natural then that Ibsen's sympathy for Knudsen's aims should be reflected in the linguistic forms he himself used in his plays from this period. Of great interest in this respect is the fragmentary draft of a romantic opera, *Fjeldfuglen*, which he began in 1859 as an adaptation of *Rypen i Justedal* and *Olaf Liljekrans*. We should remember that the theatre with which both Ibsen and Knudsen were connected was a militant institution, founded in opposition to the older Christiania theatre, which was run on traditional lines and chiefly staffed by Danish players. The opera text from 1859 shows Ibsen fully adopting the norwegianizing policy of Knudsen and the theatre for which he worked. In this text specifically Norwegian words and forms – belonging to the Norwegian scenery and the rural setting – are far more numerous than in any of his earlier works. And as well as this and of still greater significance, we find that he norwegianizes words that belong to ordinary everyday speech, using *graate* for *græde*, for example, and still more radically, *lauv* for *løv*. All such 'national' forms had been given warm public recommendation by Knud Knudsen. The opera fragment may thus be said to mark a summit on Ibsen's road to the norwegianizing of the literary language. Ibsen himself felt later that he had gone too far, especially in forms like the *graate* and *lauv* just mentioned. But if we disregard these extreme forms, we are fully justified in saying that the language of *Fjeldfuglen* , insignificant as the piece is from a literary point of view, points forward directly to the language of *Peer Gynt*.

Kjærlighedens Komedie, written in 1862, is one of the more important pieces in the period before the composition of *Peer Gynt*, and it offers much of interest for a student of Ibsen's language and style. The first draft of the play was in prose, but it found its final form in verse, a verse so unconstrained and flexible that it allowed free play to the author's abundant fancy. No inconsistency is felt between the fluent conversational rhymes and the realistic modern setting – Fru Halm's garden on the outskirts of Christiania, a microcosm indeed of the capital city itself. And the text is full of allusions to facts, circumstances and people in the town. In spite of the verse form, the upper-class conversation of Christiania is audible through the metre, and from speech of this nature quite a number of special Norwegian forms found their way into the drama, in defiance of the rules of the traditional Danish-based literary language.

Students of Ibsen commonly point to *Kjærlighedens Komedie* as the first decisive evidence of his shift from the romantic to the realistic and, in style and language, from largely archaic models to those of contemporary living speech. This opinion may be counted valid, though with some reservations. As I pointed out above, Ibsen's new attitude is discernible before 1862, as part of his response to 'den sproglige Vækkelse' he owed to Knudsen. It is indeed right, however, to regard the norwegianizing of the literary language, in the ways advocated by Knudsen, as in itself an important step towards realism. The truly significant point about *Kjærlighedens Komedie* is that it shows us Ibsen for the first time committed to realism on a broader scale, to realism as an inner principle of phrasing and linguistic

form, harmonizing with the intention of the whole play. We may contrast it with *Fjeldfuglen*, where we often have the impression that the many novelties in word-forms, some of them very radical, are there only as part of a norwegianizing programme and do not meet any true artistic requirements.

After *Kjærlighedens Komedie* it is not surprising that Ibsen's next play, *Kongsemnerne*, saga-play though it is, should not appear in the saga-style he had affected in *Hærmændene paa Helgeland*. In the following verse-plays, *Brand* and *Peer Gynt*, we find the range and power of his dramatic verse-making vastly increased. In *Brand* there are the grave hammer-strokes of regular trochaic and iambic verse, and in *Peer Gynt* a variety of playful rhythms, often in the free style of the folk-song. Both plays have many specifically Norwegian elements in their vocabulary, more so in *Peer Gynt*, where especially in Acts 1-3 and 5 they occur in great abundance. Inspired by the work of Asbjørnsen and Moe, Ibsen made bold use of such native elements, but always with unerring taste and in such a way that they add greatly to the charm and vividness of the diction.

5

Ibsen called both *Brand* and *Peer Gynt* 'dramatic poems'. As we know, they were the last plays to be written in verse. The long series of prose dramas, on which his worldwide fame is chiefly founded, was inaugurated by *De unges Forbund*, produced in 1869. This and all the succeeding plays, with one exception, have modern settings and discuss modern problems. The exception is *Kejser og Galilæer* (1873), which goes back to the 1860s in origin and which, in spite of being a historical play, is concerned with a conflict of ideals that has universal application. At any rate, the prose style of this trilogy bears no obviously archaic stamp, even though the sublime subjects discussed in the dialogue often require a lofty or pathetic mode of expression. Similar modes are otherwise found, and then sporadically, only in Ibsen's symbolic dramas from the late 1880s and 1890s. A noteworthy feature in the language of *Kejser og Galilæer* is the relatively high frequency of Germanisms, which is of course related to the fact that the trilogy shows definite influences from German philosophy and intellectual trends.

Leaving aside this historical trilogy, we may return to *De unges Forbund*, which introduces Ibsen's third period as a creative writer. He was himself aware that this play marked a turning-point and that in this kind of work new stylistic demands were being made of him. In letters from this time he describes the play as 'completely realistic', and says at the same time that artistically and stylistically it was the most elaborate work he had so far composed. We know from his statements that in the earlier periods of his career he had felt most at ease with verse, and his virtuosity as a verse-maker is fully demonstrated by *Kjærlighedens Komedie*, *Brand*, and *Peer Gynt*. Now his task is to create a prose style for which the only touchstone is to be the touchstone of truth in the presentation of a contemporary milieu and everyday life. Verse cannot be used, and all poetical ornament is banned – banned too are the special stylistic features of the historical plays where vocabulary and word-order had been used to produce a remote archaic atmosphere.

At this point it is not out of place to recall that in his early years Ibsen had produced a sort of modern prose play, *Sancthansnatten*. It is especially instructive to compare it with *De unges Forbund* and to observe what an enormous distance lies between the two in style and in the author's attitude towards the stylistic problem. It would be hard to maintain that he was much bothered by the problem of style at all when he wrote the earlier play – it belongs to his prentice period and is formally modelled on Danish work, particularly that of Heiberg. The situation is quite different in *De unges Forbund* and in the other plays that followed it. Ibsen was no longer a groping beginner but an author who had arrived at clearcut views of his own. Realism had become his guiding principle, and the translation of this principle into a practical style for use in dramas with a modern setting meant complete adherence to truth in the presentation of his characters' conversation. The basis of his stage language must be the actual speech of living people, or more particularly – given the settings of his plays – the speech of Norwegian townspeople of the upper and middle classes.

Naturally, this practice inevitably involved, at least to some extent, the norwegianizing of the language, a further development away from the Danish-based literary idiom. As we saw above, Ibsen was strongly influenced by Knud Knudsen and he had consciously norwegianized from the late 1850s onwards. In his modern conversation dramas he followed that same principle, but there is still an important distinction to be made between the old and the new in this respect. It is striking and significant, for example, that special Norwegian elements are incomparably more numerous in *Peer Gynt* than in *De unges Forbund*. In part this is due to the diversity of milieu in the two plays, but a much more important factor is that in the younger prose play Ibsen was striving to give the illusion of contemporary reality through the speech of his characters and had to concentrate on the genuineness and spontaneity of the whole conversational stream, regardless of the norwegianizing of isolated elements in the vocabulary. Indeed, from the late 1860s onwards, we can see that Ibsen was reluctant to use specifically Norwegian forms too freely – partly of course because he did not wish to repel his many Danish (and Swedish) readers.

But Ibsen was not now tied to a particular linguistic programme. If special Norwegian words were needed to maintain the natural tone of a dialogue, he had no hesitation in using them. Novel Norwegian elements, not previously at home in the traditional literary language, are in fact by no means uncommon in these later works. But what had special importance for him was the idiomatic authenticity of the whole movement of the speech of his characters. In other words, the syntax had to ring true.

The most characteristic syntactical feature in Ibsen's realistic prose plays is his use of the suffixed article. In certain cases the suffixed article is used in Norwegian in a manner different from Danish and consequently different from the traditional literary language of nineteenth-century Norway also. A particularly distinctive usage is found in phrases of the type, *det lyse solskinnet*, where the noun has the suffixed article as well as being constructed with the prepositive article before the adjective. It is especially in works from the late 1870s and 1880s that Ibsen made comparatively frequent use of this construction, which so readily gives the impression of easy, unaffected Norwegian speech. In *Rosmersholm*, for example, the idiom is heard even from Rosmer and Rebekka: *de hvide hestene*; *alle de nye tankerne*; *alle de gamle fordommene*.

As well as being of intrinsic interest, this detail can also have dramatic point, for the use of such a linguistic habit may help to define the social and cultural background of an individual character. To look at *Rosmersholm* again, for example, we find that Rector Kroll, the advocate of traditional correctness and old-fashioned views, never uses the suffixed article in this way, in contrast to Rosmer and Rebekka, who both represent a more emancipated attitude towards life and its problems. The idiom is by no means all-pervading, however, in the speech of Rosmer and Rebekka, but its use is strictly limited by stylistic considerations. It is not found when the subject of the dialogue is serious, elevated or pathetic. When, towards the end of Act 3, Rosmer says, 'Men så var der jo denne skumle, uoverstigelige mur imellem dig og den hele, fulde frigørelse' – then the writing of 'mur*en*', 'frigørelse*n*', with the suffixed article, would have been felt as an unpleasant lapse of taste in any kind of educated riksmål. On the other hand, Madame Helseth, the old maidservant, invariably uses the construction with both prepositive and suffixed article and this accords with the everyday character of her outlook.

Ibsen's most careful and detailed rendering of illiterate and vulgar speech is to be found in plays from the 1880s, especially *Vildanden* and *Gengangere*. The two most striking examples are Engstrand the carpenter in *Gengangere* and Gina Ekdal in *Vildanden*, memorable not only because of the sheer power of Ibsen's inventiveness in characterizing them linguistically but also because of the subtlety of the distinctions he is able to draw in rendering their speech. Engstrand's language contains typical non-standard vulgar forms of common words, e.g. present participles in *-s* (*berusendes* for *berusende*, *vejfarendes* for *vejfarende*), and forms like *sjømænder* for *sjømænd* and *gælen* for *gal*. At the same time, he has an evident hypocritical predilection for elements that reflect the typical style of the clergy. Gina Ekdal has some vulgarisms in common with Engstrand – *altingen* for *alting* is one – but what truly distinguishes her speech is her extravagant use of loanwords that are not proper to her real background. Ibsen lets her corrupt such words in a most genuine and vivid way. A few examples among many are *retusere* (for *retouschere*), *ha noget at dividere sig med* (*dividere* for *divertere*), and perhaps the crowning example, *fysiske raptuser*, doubtless for *psykiske raptuser*, since she is here referring to the late Fru Werle. Gina has picked up all these words in the years she has spent in the house of Werle the wholesaler, as housemaid and as his mistress. Ibsen has contrived in a wholly convincing way to mirror her antecedents in her language – and, as we know, those antecedents are of prime importance in the central issue of the play.

Another noteworthy example of characterization through language is Burgomaster Stockmann in *En Folkefiende*. His vocabulary and syntax are utterly formal, the language of official documents, completely untouched by the colloquial levels of speech from which the conversation of the other characters in the play is derived.

The source of Ibsen's language in the so-called 'symbolic' dramas of the 1890s is fundamentally the same as that found in the more pronouncedly realistic plays of the two preceding decades. In these later works, for example, the typical everyday use of prepositive and suffixed article occurs entirely naturally in plain conversation, and characters may show the same individual variations in its usage as before. In *Bygmester Solness* we find that Hilde, the representative of youth, uses the construction more frequently than any of the other characters.

On the other hand, the subject-matter and atmosphere of these later plays are to some extent more elevated, less ordinary, than those of his earlier works. The visions and exclamations of Johan Gabriel Borkman, for example, could hardly be adequately conveyed in the tone of trivial everyday conversation. In such a case the language becomes lofty and pathetic, closer in manner to Ibsen's early plays than to his plain realistic style of the 1870S and 1880s.

In spite of this, it is still possible to maintain that the basis of Ibsen's dramatic language remains fundamentally unaltered throughout these later periods. His ear was still attuned to the spoken Norwegian of the upper and middle classes. I do not of course mean that he presents, as it were, a tape-recording of everyday urban speech with all its trifling and incidental elements. He starts from that everyday language and sharpens and refines it, organizing and manipulating subject-matter and dialogue in accordance with his firm artistic aims. He succeeds throughout in creating an effective and realistic linguistic medium by leavening the literary language with certain typical and significant elements from the spoken idiom, adapting everyday modes of expression for use in the standard written language. I have already demonstrated his special use of the typical colloquial construction with the suffixed definite article. Further examples of the way in which he makes his stage Norwegian truly alive are to be found, for example, in certain peculiarities of word-order: *Var der tårn pa det huset også?*; in the use of repeated unstressed pronouns: Hilde: *Jeg synes det er så ligetil, jeg. Det er snilt af Dem det!*; in the summing-up, using pronominal terms, of complex, emphatic parts of a sentence: Hilde: *Alle mulig småting, så husker han dem på flækken*; in the introduction of interjections and unstressed modifiers in which Norwegian speech is so rich: Hilde: *Isch, nejda*; *da* is very common and very typical in functions like the following: *Nej, det har jeg da ikke. Hvorfor ikke det da?* In the vocabulary we find that words belonging to upper and middle class urban diction are introduced into plain conversational dialogue. Such terms are in contrast to the specifically Norwegian vocabulary introduced in works of the National Romantic period. In them the settings and themes were predominantly rural whereas the Norwegian elements in the diction were chiefly drawn from country speech.

(It is a sad fact that practically all of the characteristic linguistic features mentioned above defy translation. The special atmosphere they evoke simply cannot be attained in another language, unless perhaps it could be done by abandoning direct translation and attempting some process of re-creation.)

As we have seen, there is nothing haphazard about Ibsen's use of distinctive linguistic elements. He employs them in a completely purposeful way towards the realization of his characters, ranging freely from the formal official language of the first half of the nineteenth century to the authentic vulgar idiom of the 1880s. The urban speech which lies behind his language is that of Christiania (Oslo) and other towns of south-east Norway. Ibsen came from Skien, and the key to the secret of his linguistic mastery is no doubt the complete familiarity his birth and upbringing gave him with urban speech in all its varieties. His own native linguistic experience was the inexhaustible storehouse on which he could draw.

In some cases East Norwegian characteristics are especially striking in the speech of Ibsen's characters – never more so, to my ear, than in the speech of Gina Ekdal. Ibsen meant us to think of her, I believe, as a Christiania woman, and it seems to me that her lines, and especially her corruptions of literary loan-words, only sound really authentic in the characteristic word-melody of the capital and of eastern Norway. Behind forms like *retusere* and *dividere*, quoted above, can be unmistakably heard the ordinary East Norwegian pronunciation, *rétusere*, *dívidere* (with stress on the first syllable and Double Tone). In Bergen and western Norway the common pronunciation in *dividére* coincides with the standard, and from Gina this would sound distinctly peculiar – or it would at any rate to me, an East Norwegian!

It is appropriate to consider for a moment the revolutionary changes that took place in the stage-pronunciation in Norway during Ibsen's career and in the light of his own development. Up to the 1860s the Norwegian theatres employed Danish players almost exclusively, and the few Norwegians who acted were under a traditional obligation to adopt a Danish pronunciation. It was partly in reaction against this monopoly that Ole Bull's theatre in Bergen and the National Theatre in Christiania were founded. Then, slowly, during the 1860s and 1870s, the situation began to alter, although without leading automatically to the full and free use of Norwegian speech on the stage. In this transitional period, the old Danish norm for the stage was supplanted by another one, in some respects almost as arbitrary. Now, according to authoritative literary opinion, the only sounds fit to be heard from the stage were those of educated Bergen speech, while the speech of eastern Norway remained offensive to the cultured ear. Eminent scholars supported this dictum with the heavy artillery of their learning. P. A. Munch, for example, the undisputed authority in historical and linguistic matters, maintained that the public were fully justified in preferring the Bergen pronunciation and rejecting that of eastern Norway on the grounds that Bergen was surrounded by country districts in which the most pure and perfect Norwegian dialects were to be found, dialects that still bore the true stamp of the Old Norse language, while in East Norwegian speech this venerable heritage had been corrupted beyond all recognition.

This barring of East Norwegian speech from the stage, though an accepted fact for some time, never became fully established as a principle and during the 1890s it was silently abandoned. Ibsen's direct share in producing this result through his work with the pioneering theatres in Bergen and Christiania cannot be counted great. But it is equally undeniable that his modern plays had a profound influence on the development of Norwegian stage pronunciation. Their conversational style made the employment of Norwegian casts essential and was entirely incompatible with the exclusion of an East Norwegian pronunciation from the stage.

Not all of Ibsen's plays of course are set in Christiania and the south-east. *Samfundets støtter*, for example, is apparently set in a small town on the south coast, where shipbuilding is a major occupation. Ibsen had spent six years of his youth in that part of the country, in Grimstad, and some reminiscences of Grimstad speech are to be found in his writings from all periods. A conspicuous one is *stakker* for East Norwegian *stakkar*, with the corresponding adjective *stakkers* for *stakkars*. Ibsen picked up a few nautical terms in Grimstad, too – not many, it seems, and he does not always use them accurately, but he turns his little knowledge to skilful account in *Terje Vigen*, for example, and in Act 5 of *Peer Gynt.*

6

This survey of the phases of Ibsen's style and language may be concluded by a brief mention of the part played by foreign languages in his work and of the style of his private correspondence.

Swedish and German are the most influential foreign languages, and Ibsen usually borrows words and phrases from them in an intentionally playful way. This is especially evident in the many Swedish terms which he introduces into *Peer Gynt* and the so-called 'Balloon Letter' to a Swedish lady. Some of his Germanisms, however, appear to be quite unconscious mannerisms, as in the case of certain interjections used in the plays of the 1870s and 1880s: *ah* (*ach!*), *ah hvad* (*ach was!*), *ej hvad* (*ei was!*). Some French words are found in *Gengangere*, but only in the speech of Osvald and Regine, where they serve obvious purposes of characterization. Osvald's *vermoulu* directly echoes the word used by his French physician, and Regine's French phrases occur exclusively in her conversation with Engstrand, to whom they are unintelligible, and they serve to mark her feeling of distance from him and the distaste he inspires in her. English elements are extremely rare, and Ibsen's knowledge of English was very poor. *Master* Cotton in *Peer Gynt* offers a well-known example, and we may note how Ibsen first spelt in manuscript the Englishman's opening words: 'Werry well' !

We have many of Ibsen's private letters and they adequately reveal his personal written language. In general their style is colourless, impersonal, official. He clearly stuck to the stylistic patterns he had been taught during his schooling in the late 1830s and early 1840s. The innovations found in the different phases of his literary output leave almost no traces at all in his letters – there is none of the romantic vocabulary of his early plays and none of the colloquialisms of the realistic dialogue of his modern plays. Throughout his life his style of letter-writing resembles most closely the speech of Burgomaster Stockmann in *En folkefiende* or Rector Kroll in *Rosmersholm*. These resemblances exist, but otherwise there was no exchange across the barrier he erected between the style of the works he created as a dramatic artist and the style of the letters he wrote as a private citizen.

But it is Ibsen's plays that have been influential, not his letters, and it is thanks not least to the plays that the style of Burgomaster Stockmann has since disappeared almost entirely from Norwegian literature. Ibsen's modern plays have had in this respect a deep and widespread influence, far more than have the plays and novels of his great contemporary Bjørnson, for example. The reasons for this are complex; I shall point simply to two vital factors. In the first place, we must recognize that Ibsen had complete control over his linguistic medium and that his taste was wise and sure (the same cannot always be said of Bjørnson). And in the second place, we must emphasize the importance of the fact that Ibsen's linguistic background was the speech of Christiania and south-east Norway. Already before Ibsen's mature periods, starting in the latter half of the eighteenth century and given new impetus by the Asbjørnsen and Moe folk-tale editions of the mid-nineteenth century, there was a natural and general trend which gave the language of this part of the country a dominant position in the development of Norwegian riksmål. And, however little Ibsen contributed as a propagandist in matters affecting the language situation, this trend was inevitably continued and reinforced by the immense influence of his superb art.

References

Joh. Storm, 'Ibsen og det norske Sprog'; in *Henrik Ibsen. Festskrift i Anledning af hans 70de Fødselsdag*, edited by *Samtiden*, 1898, 172-205.

D. A. Seip, 'Henrik Ibsen og språket', in *Studier i norsk språkhistorie* (1934), 228-238.

D. A. Seip, 'Henrik Ibsen og K. Knudsen. Det sproglige gjennembrud hos Ibsen', *Edda*, I, 145-63.

D. A. Seip, 'Ibsens rettskrivning og sprogform', in *Samlede verker, Hundreårsutgave* (1928), I, 16-24.

Ragnvald Iversen, 'Rim og uttale hos Henrik Ibsen', *Acta Philologica Scandinavica*, III, 136-71.

Ragnvald Iversen, 'Henrik Ibsen som purist i "Catilina" 1875', *Edda*, XXX, 96-100.

Leif Mæhle: *Ibsens rimteknikk*. Oslo 1955.

Notes

1. Henrik Jæger: *Henrik Ibsen 1828-88. Et literært livsbillede*, Copenhagen, 1888, p. 45.
2. Olav Dalgard: 'Studiar over *Fru Inger til Østeraad*', *Edda*, XXX (1-47), p. 8.
3. Olav Vindenes: 'Sproget i *Fru Inger til Østeraad*', *Acta Philologica Scandinavica*, XI, 201-51, especially pp. 242-43.
4. Bjørnson's views are expressed in a letter to the Danish critic Clemens Petersen; see *Gro-tid* I, pp. 52-55.
5. Henrik Ibsen, *Samlede verker, Hundreårsutgave* (1930) XV, pp. 330, 331.
6. Henrik Ibsen, *Samlede verker, Hundreårsutgave* (1949) XVIII, p. 306.
7. Highly significant is 'Maageskrig', *Samlede verker, Hundreårsutgave* (1937), XIV, pp. 227-9.

Originally published May 1963 (Vol. 2, No. 1).

Ibsen's Use of the Pronouns of Address in Some of His Prose Plays

Robert Ola de la Maire Amundsen

In modern English usage the availability of only one pronoun of address, the universally used *you*, precludes the utilization in literature of the sociological and psychological implications of the contrasts and polarities that are inherent in two separate pronouns of address, such as the Norwegian *du* and *De*. Their usage is very similar to that encountered in the other Scandinavian countries and also Germany, with its *Du* and *Sie*, or France, with its *tu* and *vous*.[1]

Precisely because the pronouns of address tend to be taken for granted as a normal and inevitable part of the syntax their function as a dramatic tool can easily be underestimated. But as Francis Berry notes: 'When a dramatist has two words to imply contrasting ways of regarding a person then he has (at least) a powerful psychological advantage at his disposal in the creation and ordering of his drama'.[2]

In Ibsen's drama the way characters express and define their social and personal relationships and attitudes by the way they address each other will often yield valuable insights into wider issues and themes of the plays. In the case of the pronouns of address it is useful to distinguish between their normal 'non-intentional' use and their specific 'intentional' use by the author. In the latter case their usage is such that they function as explicit verbal features whereby the author or playwright can draw attention to areas of implicit meaning. In the compressed syntax of Ibsen's stage dialogue where language is often reduced to metaphoric brevity, the way people elect to address each other in itself assumes the status of metaphor. In a paper entitled 'The Pronouns of Power and Solidarity', Brown and Gilman provide an elaboration of what an author's deliberate use of the pronoun of address might involve:

> Sometimes the choice of a pronoun clearly violates a group norm and perhaps also the customary practice of the speaker. Then the meaning of the act will be sought in some attitude or emotion of the speaker. It is as if the interpreter reasoned that variations of address between the same two persons must be caused by variations in their attitudes towards one another.[3]

Brown's and Gilman's comments are very much in accord with Ibsen's intentional use of the pronouns of address, as will be seen from those examples that have been selected from *A Doll's House*, *Ghosts*, *The Wild Duck*, *Rosmersholm*, *The Lady from the Sea* and *Hedda Gabler*. It could be argued that in *Hedda Gabler* the pronouns of address are one of the key dramatic devices in the play because they contribute to the human and hence dramatic dimension of Hedda herself. The loss of at least part of this dimension is to the detriment of English translations of the play.

In the final version of *A Doll's House* Helmer's explicit reference to the use of *du* by Krogstad sums up his attitude to the latter when he tells Nora that a working relationship with Krogstad in the bank would be impossible because:

> Det er et af disse overilede bekendtskaber, som man saa mangen gang senere hen i livet generes af. Ja, jeg kan gerne sige dig det lige ud: vi er dus. Og dette taktløse menneske lægger slet ikke skjul paa det naar andre er tilstede. Tvertimod, – han tror, at det berettiger ham til en familiær tone imod mig; og saa trumfer han hvert øjeblik ud med sit: du; du Helmer. Jeg forsikrer dig, det virker højst pinligt paa mig. Han vilde gøre mig min stilling i banken utaalelig.[4]

> (It is one of those acquaintanceships one enters into rashly and which frequently prove so embarrassing later on in life. Well, I may as well tell you frankly; we call each other *du*. And this tactless fellow makes no effort at all to conceal the fact when other people are present. On the contrary, he thinks it entitles him to use a familiar tone towards me, and he constantly keeps blurting out: '*du*, *du* Helmer.' I assure you, he would make my position in the bank intolerable to me.)

Rolf Fjelde, in common with most other translators of this play, appears to overcome the difficulty of the pronoun *du* by rendering that particular part of the above passage thus:

> ...we're on a first-name basis, ... and so every other second he comes booming out with his 'Yes, Torvald' and 'Sure thing, Torvald!'[5]

In a sense, translating the relevant passages this way conveys the issue, i.e. Helmer's bourgeois sensitivity to his social position and reputation, and hence his need to dissociate himself from a man with a dubious reputation. But the real distinction, the use of *du*, is a finer one and English translations can only provide a partial solution because Ibsen tells us that they were *not* on Christian name terms. Hedda, for instance, who observes the social conventions no less fastidiously than Helmer, abhors and rejects the way Løvborg uses *du* when he addresses her. On the other hand, on no occasion does she object to Løvborg's using her Christian name as long as he always employs the formal pronoun. Helmer resents Krogstad's use of *du* because it implies a level of intimacy which exceeds the use of the first name virtually without exception.

In the same play both Mrs Linde and Krogstad not only address each other by their surnames but they also use *De*. From their conversation at the beginning of Act III, however, it emerges that at one time they had been more or less engaged and it is therefore probable that at that time they would have used both *du* and each other's Christian names. Amongst other things, their use of the formal *De* reveals a certain degree of vulnerability since at this stage in their relationship there is a sense of mutual uncertainty, embarrassment perhaps, which requires the psychological protection afforded by *De*. However, as soon as Mrs Linde has intimated to Krogstad that she would like to take up again a relationship that never quite got off the ground, the pressure of Krogstad's emotion bursts to the surface when he exclaims 'Kristine!'. And whereas Krogstad continues to address Mrs Linde by her Christian name after this point in their dialogue he nonetheless continues to use *De* rather than *du*. By this highly economic means at his disposal the playwright has been able to indicate that the ice has been broken between the two of them, but their relationship has not yet reached a sufficient degree of rapport for the use of the familiar pronoun.

In *A Doll's House* the use Ibsen made of the distinction between the two pronouns for deliberate dramatic purposes was limited to the telling manner in which Helmer's social and personal prejudices are contained in his pithy 'vi er dus'. This isolated instance of the usage of *du* in *A Doll's House* is worth recording because this is the play where Ibsen seems to have first discovered its usefulness as an effective and highly economic dramatic device. Interestingly, Helmer's remark that he and Krogstad used *du* to each other was added in the final version of the play as part of the revisions Ibsen made which served to clarify and condense the issues of the play. In later plays Ibsen was to draw on the dramatic potential inherent in the real-life usage of *du*, *De* and other forms of address so that in *Hedda Gabler*, for example, Hedda deliberately exploits the conventions underlying this usage as a psychological tool to manipulate relationships. And in the plays following *A Doll's House* the *du*/*De* distinction increasingly occurs as an integral part of language, as can be seen from the draft versions.

Though Hedda's consciousness of language is not matched by Mrs Alving, the way people address each other at crucial moments in *Ghosts* is an example of the careful craftsmanship that went into the verbal texture of that play. Towards the close of Act I, after Manders has delivered himself of a homiletic harangue designed to open Mrs Alving's eyes to *his* version of the truth, there is a pause before Mrs Alving summons the courage to speak *her* version of it. Since past and present interact closely in every character in *Ghosts* Mrs Alving's reminder to Manders of their former relationship and of his subsequent 'betrayal' triggers off strong emotions in Manders. The past and present react together in the mind, as it were, in one of a series of staccato responses to Mrs Alving's peeling away of successive layers of the past, and he asks her:

Helene – skal dette være en bebrejdelse, saa vil jeg be Dem overveje – [6]

(Helene – if this is intended as a reproach, I must ask you to consider –)

Manders' muted reply is somehow an outward projection of past and present, in his inadvertent use of the name he called her in the past, with the formal *Dem* of the present. The coupling of the Christian name and the formal pronoun achieves a subtle incongruity in Manders' juxtaposition of emotion with formality, as happened in the scene between Krogstad and Mrs Linde in *A Doll's House*. Even when his clerical poise has been briefly upset and he forgets to address Mrs Alving by her surname, his use of *De* can also be interpreted as a kind of self-protection.

It is a vivid moment of truth for Mrs Alving when Osvald and Regine reanimate the past by re-enacting a scene that she recalls only too well from her married days. As Osvald makes advances to Regine in the dining room, she exclaims:

Osvald da! Er du gal? Slip mig.[7]

(Oh Osvald! Are you mad? Let go of me!)

Only a few minutes previously Regine had observed the norm of conventional address when she asked him whether he wanted red or white port, by using his surname and the formal pronoun. Now, through the half-open door of the dining room this becomes 'Osvald' coupled with the familiar *du*. The public and the private worlds of the Alving estate are fleetingly revealed in Regine's double standards in addressing Osvald; in a sense, illusion and truth are contained in the formal and informal pronouns of address respectively. Also, Regine's use of *du* and 'Osvald' in Act I prefigures that crucial moment in Act III when he openly asks her to address him in this way. In Act II Regine maintains a polite distance to Osvald in Mrs Alving's presence while Osvald persists in his use of *du* towards Regine, thereby giving further emphasis to his confession that he sees salvation for himself in Regine's 'joy of life' (*livsglæde*).

However, the gravity of Osvald's plight comes fully to light when it appears that his real salvation lies not so much in sharing Regine's *livsglæde* as in enlisting her support so that she can give him 'a helping hand', as he euphemistically puts it. Thus the play provides Osvald with the strongest possible motive for establishing a very close relationship with Regine, particularly at the point in Act III when he has perceived the inevitability of his destiny.

Osvald's final request of Regine is made under the pressure of strong emotion:

Hvorfor kan du ikke sige du til mig, Regine? Hvorfor kalder du mig ikke Osvald?[8]

(Why don't you say *du* to me, Regine? Why don't you call me Osvald?)

In English translations Osvald can only ask Regine to call him by his Christian name, but in fact his request to Regine comes in *two* parts; the first part of his request is that she call him *du*, and then he asks her to use his Christian name. This order is deliberate since the use of the second person singular bespeaks greater intimacy. Mrs Manders confirms this indirectly by giving her consent to such a usage by telling Regine that she will shortly be allowed to go along with Osvald's explicit wish. The blood tie between Osvald and Regine is revealed, and hence the use of *du* can be justified from Mrs Alving's point of view. Her disclosure thwarts any designs Regine may have had on Osvald, and Regine's reaction to this disclosure is that for her the use of the familiar pronoun had signified something other than a brother-sister relationship:

– Ja, nu faar jeg vel sige Osvald da. Men det var rigtignok ikke paa *den* maaden, jeg havde ment det.[9]

(– Well I suppose I'd better say Osvald now. Though *that* wasn't quite the way I had intended to use it.)

In *Ghosts* the use of *du* first hints at, then *confirms*, the existence of relationships (i.e. Mrs Alving and Manders, Regine and Osvald) not apparent at the outset of the play.

Similarly, *Rosmersholm* makes use of the implications of *du* for dramatic effect. Initially, it is of some importance for Rosmer to allay any suspicions Kroll may have had regarding his and Rebecca's relationship; Rosmer already fears that his brother-in-law will easily draw the wrong conclusions if he is allowed to do so. In Act I this fear on Rosmer's part is subtly revealed in his slight slip of the tongue when he attempts to reassure Kroll that 'both Rebek – both Miss West and I know that we did everything in our power for the poor dear'. Of course, the use of *du* between Rebekka and Rosmer throughout the play betokens a close relationship between them, and in Act III one suspects that Rebekka deliberately gives this away by addressing Rosmer by the informal *du* when he enters to find Kroll and Rebekka together in the lounge:

> REBEKKA: Han vilde helst ikke ha mødt dig, Rosmer.
> KROLL: (*Uvilkaarligt*). Du!
> REBEKKA: Ja, herr rektor. Rosmer og jeg – vi siger du til hinanden. Forholdet imellem os har ført det med sig.[10]

> (REBEKKA: He would rather not have met you, Rosmer.
> KROLL: (*Involuntarily*). Du!
> REBEKKA: Yes, Mr Kroll. Rosmer and I say *du* to each other. Our relationship has led to that.)

As can be seen from the original Norwegian text, Rebekka uses the name 'Rosmer' all the time; she never uses his Christian name. English translations, on the other hand, in order to achieve the effect produced by the informal pronoun, employ the Christian name instead, as in Michael Meyer's translation. The substitution of the Christian name for *du* appears to be a minor issue, since translators often are called on to make heavier compromises than this one. Nonetheless, since Ibsen scarcely ever leaves the tiniest detail of language to chance something of relevance to the play can often be inferred from apparent textual minutiae, as for example that a wife should call her husband by his surname rather than his Christian name. So, in this connection, it may be worth recalling that in *The Wild Duck*, *The Lady from the Sea*, *Hedda Gabler* and *When We Dead Awaken*, Gina, Ellida, Hedda and Maja, while addressing their husbands by their surnames, nevertheless use the informal pronoun, just as Rebekka uses 'Rosmer' and not 'Johannes'. It should also be noted that while the informal pronoun of address was used between married couples at Ibsen's time, just as today, a wife's use of her husband's surname did sometimes occur. Sometimes it would betoken affection and respect and not infrequently it would signify the husband's superior social status. Gina's use of her husband's surname can be explained in this way. Ellida Wangel makes it clear towards the end of the play that she has never regarded her life with Wangel as a genuine marriage because of her 'pact' with the Stranger. It is possible to explain the use of her husband's surname as a symptom of the sense of alienation she feels towards him. While Ellida's situation with regard to Dr Wangel is not deliberately willed, since it is a necessary consequence of the influence she is under from the Stranger, it is quite clear that Hedda, the most self-aware of all Ibsen's heroines, consciously avoided addressing her husband as 'Jørgen' except when she uses it for a particular reason, such as at the very end of Act I when she looks at him in veiled contempt and lets him know that she has at least one source of amusement to fall back on, namely her pistols. This remark is clearly intended as a humiliating snub. The impact of the insult is intentionally exacerbated through her use of his Christian name since she is drawing his attention to her remark by addressing him in an unaccustomed way. A further example of this will be noted in the discussion of *Hedda Gabler* below.

In the case of Rosmersholm Rebekka's use of 'Rosmer', rather than 'Johannes', hints at several factors which stand between them in the play, e.g. Beata, the whole Rosmer tradition, as well as Rebekka's own paralysing awareness of the ambiguity in her relationship with Rosmer. Finally, it is significant that in *When We Dead Awaken* Maja, who feels that she and Rubek have never lived in a home together, only a house, and who agrees with her husband that they have never had anything to say to each other, should reveal this gulf between herself and her husband by using his surname. It is equally significant that Irene, Maja's 'anti-type', should use Rubek's Christian name.[11]

A brief look at *The Lady from the Sea* reveals a use of *du* and *De* which in important ways defines the respective attitudes of the Stranger and Ellida to each other. Northam has noted that 'the Stranger has come to take Ellida away in fulfilment of their earlier marriage – his outlandish appearance mirrors his lack of conventional scruples'.[12] And so, it should be added, does the directness and intimacy of his address in his use of her Christian name. It is not only the Stranger's use of the Christian name, but much more the use of the informal pronoun which contributes to her initial reaction which is a compound of surprise, anxiety and annoyance at the attitude of the intruder whom at first she does not recognize. It is instructive to observe the alternation in the use of the informal and formal pronouns of address by the Stranger and Ellida respectively in their jerky first exchanges where the *du* and the *De* mirror the battle between them as the two pronouns are exchanged in a flurry of stichomythic counterpoint:

> ELLIDA: Å kære, – kommer du da endelig!
> DEN FREMMEDE: Ja, endelig en gang.
> ELLIDA: Hvem er De? Søger De nogen her?
> DEN FREMMEDE: Det kan Du vel forstaa.
> ELLIDA: Hvad er det! Hvorledes tiltaler De mig! Hvem ser De efter?
> DEN FREMMEDE: Jeg ser vel efter dig.[13]

It may, or may not, be significant that the formal *De* outnumbers the occurrence of *du*, but it would seem to bear on Ellida's overtly defensive posture vis-à-vis the Stranger in the crucial scene where they first meet. She shelters behind the verbal screen of the formal pronoun, as it were, and her copious use of it in the above example and elsewhere during her first confrontation with the Stranger makes it clear that it functions as something more than mere formality. In the above example Ellida's line: 'Hvorledes tiltaler De mig!' (How is it you address me!) serves three purposes. Firstly, it indicates her immediate awareness that she is being addressed in an unacceptably intimate manner and that she regards the use of her Christian name and *du* as rudeness; secondly it is a rebuke to the Stranger; and, thirdly, it serves to remind the audience that the mode of the Stranger's address is an issue at this point in the play. It is also clear from the immediate context in which Ellida's exclamation occurs that her reaction is directly occasioned by the Stranger's use of *du*.

As the garden scene progresses the Stranger, apparently oblivious to Ellida's whole bearing, blithely persists in addressing her as *du*, even after Dr Wangel's arrival on the scene. As Ibsen had intended, there is something dream-like and unreal in the intruder's whole appearance in this scene and the calm, controlled rhythm of his speech remains strangely unaffected either by Ellida's nervous exclamations or her husband's stern rejoinders. The point of this is that the Stranger's use of the familiar pronoun of address embodies a projection of their past relationship into the present where, from his point of view, she still belongs to him by virtue of their symbolic 'wedding'. To the Stranger the past still lives on as a reality and he shows this through his consistent use of *du* during his and Ellida's first and last encounter, thereby demonstrating his claim upon her and his 'licence' to use the informal pronoun of address. Within the overall context of the world of this play the nature of the imagery, the deliberate ambivalence and ambiguity of the Stranger and his claim on Ellida symbolised by the linked rings, it is clear that her attraction to him has marked libidinal implications. The Stranger's use of *du* in this context further points in that direction.

During their second encounter Ellida's irrevocable decision to renounce her unbidden suitor's claim upon her produces an immediate reaction in the Stranger who surrenders his hold on her. The 'spell' has been broken – there is a sudden transmutation of 'Ellida' into the impersonal 'frue' and, no less significant, of *du* into *De* in the Stranger's parting line, delivered just as he has returned to the other side of the fence, the world outside Wangel's world:

> Farvel, frue! (*han svinger sig over havegærdet*) Fra nu af er De ikke andet – end et overstaaet skibbrud i mit liv.[14]

> (Farewell, madam. (*he vaults over the garden fence*) From now on you are nothing more to me than a shipwreck I happened to survive.)

The draft has:

> Farvel, Ellida!
> Fra nu af er du ikke andet end en halvglemt drøm (skibbrud) i mit liv.[15]

The fence on stage is the tangible physical correlative to the separation that arises between the Stranger and Ellida by virtue of her decision. Just as the garden fence, separating her world from his world, becomes a physical metaphor for what has happened, the instantaneous transition from the informal to the formal pronoun used to address Ellida becomes the verbal metaphor for the severing of the bond. In other words, there occurs a kind of interanimation here between language and its physical correlative. In the draft of the play, included above, the Stranger continues to address Ellida as he has throughout the play, i.e. by her first name and *du*. In the final version of the play Ibsen has introduced the significant change from the intimate to the formal mode of address, with the switch from 'Ellida' to 'frue' and from *du* to *De*, thus emphasising the change that has come over their relationship with the cancellation of their pact. If this final encounter between Ellida and the Stranger were to be described in more Freudian terms, it would seem that with the rupturing of the potential libidinal ties between them there is no longer any basis in reality for the Stranger's preferred *du*. In these terms the cancellation of their 'sexual contract' by the Stranger is signalled by his abrupt transmutation of the *du* into *De*. Silverberg has the following observation that may be marginally relevant to the type of distinction between the two pronouns of address that has been mentioned above:

> It is an interesting fact that a prostitute and her client usually address each other as 'Du' before and during intercourse, while she is offering and giving gratification of infantile libidinal drives, whereas after the act is completed it is not at all unusual for them to address each other as 'Sie'.[16]

Of all Ibsen's plays *Hedda Gabler* provides some of the best illustrations of how, for the requirements of the theatre, significant information and comment can be conveyed in ultra-economic fashion by the operation of these two pronouns. In his review of *The Oxford Ibsen*, Vol. VIII, John Northam makes an appropriate comment about Hedda and Solness that is also relevant to a consideration of the role of *du* and *De*:

> For Hedda and Solness do not exist in a vacuum; by their uniqueness they transform the relationships into which, as social beings, they must necessarily enter. ... Thus Hedda and Solness are not only unique personalities in themselves, but also stimuli for subtle, mobile relationships that are developed and explored throughout each play.[17]

A totally conscious and willed use of language is one of the means available to Hedda to transform the relationships into which she enters, and she exploits the resources of both names and personal pronouns in her interactions with her husband, his aunt, Mrs Elvsted and not least, Eilert Løvborg. Whereas the use of the pronouns of address by many of Ibsen's characters is only partly deliberate, often automatic and unreflected, Hedda's intelligent and conscious use of these pronouns provides her with access to and even control over other minds, other destinies. They are for her a subtle psychological tool which, in conjunction with a number of other strategies, enables her to gain temporary domination of, among others, Eilert Løvborg. In this context Northam sees her as 'a kind of poet of living who dare not live the poetry herself and who therefore must exert domination over Løvborg to do her living vicariously for her'.[18]

From Hedda's point of view, Mrs Elvsted must be wooed and charmed into submission as a necessary prelude to tackling Løvborg. Act I provides an excellent study in how the psychological distance between two human beings is substantially reduced when the substitution of an informal for a formal mode of address can help to break down human barriers and defences quickly.

Before examining this case with regard to Mrs Elvsted and Eilert Løvborg it is necessary to note how Hedda's attitude to Tesman's aunt is immediately signalled in the most economic and telling way possible when, on speaking her first words in the play, Hedda addresses her aunt as *Frøken* Tesman (*Miss* Tesman) in stark contrast to Miss Tesman's cordial tone towards Hedda, underscored by her use of Hedda's own name:

Godmorgen, kære Hedda! Hjertelig godmorgen![19]

(Good morning, Hedda dear! A very good morning to you!)

In the final version of the play the aunt's cordiality was intensified by the addition of '*hjertelig*'. Hedda's coolness towards the aunt is set off against the aunt's spontaneity and warmth. Two contrasting attitudes, two separate worlds have been presented, and the initial impression given by Hedda's reserve is soon confirmed when she asks Miss Tesman to sit down:

...vil De ikke ta plas, frøken Tesman?[20]

(Won't you take a seat, Miss Tesman?)

Incidentally, in the final version of the play *frøken Tesman* has been substituted for the draft version's *tante Jane*. Thus, in his revision of the play Ibsen has heightened the contrast in the respective attitudes of Hedda and Tesman's aunt towards each other.

Of course, a translation misses Hedda's further rebuff here since the use of the formal pronoun *De* would have been uncomfortably obvious to both Tesman and his aunt. Since Miss Tesman is Tesman's foster mother, as well as being his closest relative, it would have been natural for Hedda to use both 'Aunt Julle' and *du*, just as her husband does. Hedda denies intimacy by failing to adopt the mode of address expected of her. Her rebuff is unmistakable and it has obviously not been lost on the aunt who now begins to address Hedda more obliquely, for example in the third person singular, as 'den unge fruen' (the young mistress), or, 'lille fru Hedda' (little Mrs Hedda). This is clearly a mode of address that Hedda would instinctively dislike with its overt reference to her as a married woman and the unpleasant implications this has for her since the aunt makes it clear that she associates wifehood with motherhood. Thus the aunt signals both embarrassment and a withdrawal of at least some of her sympathy for Hedda by ceasing to use the Christian name only. The subtle shift in the aunt's attitude after Hedda's first snub can also be noticed from the fact that aunt Julle seems to avoid addressing Hedda directly by either of the two pronouns.

After the second snub administered by Hedda to the aunt, involving the aunt's hat, and after Tesman's reference to his wife's appearance, the aunt addresses Hedda as 'Hedda Tesman', a subtle and indirect way of returning Hedda's coldness. The aunt has thereby let Hedda know that she prefers to regard Hedda as Tesman's wife, as someone whose identity and social position derive from the Tesman, rather than from the Gabler, family. Tesman, not usually sensitive to such subtleties, has nevertheless noticed Hedda's use of the formal pronoun of address. After Aunt Julle has left he immediately asks Hedda to begin addressing the aunt differently:

Hvis du bare kunde overvinde dig til at sige du til hende. For min skyld, Hedda? Hvad?[21]

(If only you could induce yourself to call her *du*. For my sake, Hedda? What?)

Tesman is here indicating some awareness of the social and psychological role of language in asking Hedda to use *du* towards his aunt. His reminder implies that *du* and *De* not only express attitudes and relationships; these pronouns also redefine and modify relations; hence his request that she begin using the informal pronoun and thus express her acceptance of not only the aunt but thereby also *himself*. The beginning of Act IV once again amply confirms Hedda's reluctance to relate to the aunt, either personally or socially, in any other way than via the oblique formal pronoun. The aunt, on the other hand, has again reverted to using 'Hedda' and the intimate *du* which is the dramatist's shorthand way of pointing out that it is Hedda who has turned her back on the world of the Tesmans, and not vice versa. To the end the aunt remains 'Miss Tesman' in Hedda's vocabulary, just as Hedda's husband, with one or two exceptions, remains 'Tesman', not 'Jørgen'. Or, as Bjørn Hemmer puts it: 'She has isolated herself from the world of the Tesman's of her own free will and forfeited her opportunities there if, indeed, she ever had any there at all'.[22]

The cosy intimacy of the Tesman world with its ingenuousness and human warmth is manifested on the verbal level particularly in Act I, among other things, in the copious use of the intimate *du* in the conversation between Tesman and his aunt immediately following his first appearance on stage. In this scene between the aunt and the nephew there is a highly colloquial use of the pronoun in which it is not a necessary part of the syntax but an embellishment to the language affecting the tone and tenor of what is being said. For brevity's sake only two examples have been included here. Aunt Julle says to Jørgen:

Ja, du har nok ikke spildt din tid paa bryllupsrejsen, du, Jørgen.[23]

Jørgen says to his aunt:

Du tænker nu ogsaa paa alting, du, tante Julle.[24]

This scene abounds in similar examples in the dialogue between the aunt and her nephew, and the *effect* of this tautological use of the *du* is to call attention to the close ties that exist between aunt and nephew. The dialogue conveys the 'regressive' mode of the cosy chatter of parent and child and it is indicative of the kind of rapport that Jørgen tried to establish vis-à-vis his wife without success.

But Hedda does not always reject intimacy. It can also be willed into existence by the use of the informal pronoun, which is exactly what happens when she decides to worm her way into Mrs Elvsted's confidence and thus break 'Thea's hold over Løvborg and exert the influence herself'.[25] During the preliminary introductions that follow Mrs Elvsted's first appearance in Act I Hedda addresses her by her surname and the formal *De* in complete accordance with the conventional norm. Again, as in the scene where Hedda meets Miss Tesman for the first time, Hedda sets the tone of the conversation. Since she is Mrs Elvsted's social superior, in addition to her need to bully, quite a lot is made in this Act of Hedda's insistence that Mrs Elvsted must use the informal pronoun of address and call her by her Christian name. As reflected in the way she addresses Mrs Elvsted Hedda's whole attitude towards the latter is in significant contrast to her behaviour towards Miss Tesman. Hedda's pretext for this rapid rapprochement was that they used *du* to each other at school, as well as each other's Christian name. Mrs Elvsted denies that this was the case. Hedda's inability to recall Mrs Elvsted's Christian name correctly indicates that they were not very close in the past.

Hedda's switch from *De* to *du* is virtually thrust upon Mrs Elvsted and the latter's difficulty in adjusting to the use of *du* is seen in the play as based on a psychological difficulty in overcoming both her private and social inhibitions towards Hedda.[26]

That the convention of using *De* to persons outside the immediate family, and to individuals of higher social rank, was a deeply rooted practice, is subtly suggested by the way in which Mrs Elvsted twice forgets herself and reverts to the pronoun of formal address. The first time this happens Hedda reminds her of her lapse by a gentle slap across the hand, and when she forgets herself once again her final struggle to bring herself to use *du* is elegantly indicated by the following slip of the tongue:

> HEDDA: – Og din mand – ? Han er vel sagtens ofte ude paa rejser?
> MRS ELVSTED: Ja. De – du kan vide at som foged maa han tidt rejse omkring i distriktet.[27]

> (HEDDA: And your husband? I suppose he often has to travel about?
> MRS ELVSTED: Yes. You see, Mrs – er – you see, Hedda, as he is in the charge of the administration of the district he often has to be away a lot.)

Mrs Elvsted's reluctance to dispense with the *De* should also be seen as a shorthand way of illustrating the gradual abandoning of her defences against Hedda's attempts to gain her confidence. And once Mrs Elvsted is seen to use *du* comfortably Hedda steps up her efforts to extract all the information she can from her visitor regarding the precise nature of her relationship with Løvborg. Both Rolf Fjelde's and Michael Meyer's translations fail to render Mrs Elvsted's difficult transition from the formal to the informal pronoun. Meyer's translation attempts to solve the problem by making it difficult for Mrs Elvsted to use the name 'Hedda', rather than 'Mrs Tesman'. But in the original text Mrs Elvsted has no difficulty in using the name 'Hedda'. On the contrary, the play suggests that it is the personal pronoun *du* that requires the greater effort due to the greater social and personal intimacy it implies. Although the above is a minor textual detail it shows how even a tiny grammatical feature can act like a code which not only concentrates meaning but which can also uncover the ceaseless undercurrents that motivate the surface actions on stage.

As in the case of Ellida Wangel and the Stranger the distancing effect of *De* makes it act like a psychological buffer, protecting the individual against unwanted encroachment. Hedda, who has amply demonstrated her awareness of this aspect of the formal *De* in her relations with both Aunt Julle and Mrs Elvsted, applies this awareness of language most revealingly and effectively to regulate her relations with

Løvborg. Her strategy towards her old friend is to steer a precarious middle course between the extremes of formal detachment and personal intimacy. Or, as one critic puts it: 'Hedda bends Eilert Løvborg to her will as Omphale enslaved Hercules'.[28]

One of Hedda's main concerns in her past dealings with Løvborg had been to discourage him from relating to her on anything but the Platonic level, although she indirectly hints that it might well have been her cowardice (*feighed*) that precluded something more than friendship. In Act II, when Hedda and Løvborg find themselves alone in the room for a short time there is a sense in which the past is recalled and relived while they go through the pretence of looking at Hedda's picture album.[29] Løvborg reproaches Hedda for having married Tesman and exposes his highly emotional state when, for the first time during their conversation, he addresses Hedda as *du*. Hedda immediately rebukes him sharply, but at this point Tesman enters briefly and it is not until he has left the room that Løvborg (and the audience) is given the reason for Hedda's remonstrance. Because of its dramatic suddenness Løvborg's transition from the ,impersonal *De* to the personal *du* turns out to have provoked Hedda. Immediately after Tesman has left Løvborg repeats his question as to why she had gone ahead and married Tesman, to which Hedda retorts:

> Blir De ved et sige du til mig, saa vil jeg ikke tale med Dem.[30]
>
> If you keep on saying *du* to me I shan't speak to you.

Løvborg thereupon asks whether he may be allowed to use the intimate pronoun at least when they are alone. To this, Hedda replies:

> Nej. De kan faa lov til at tænke det. Men De maa ikke sige det.[31]
>
> No. You may think it, but you must not say it.

It is slightly incongruous, and it also leads to inconsistencies, when translations such as Meyer's, Arup's and Fjelde's make Hedda say that Løvborg may think her Christian name but not use it. In the Norwegian text, of course, Løvborg is permitted to use her first name whereas he may not use *du*. It is inconsistent when translations then continue to render the original text where Løvborg carries on addressing his friend by her Christian name immediately after she has forbidden its use, according to the translation. In the original text, Hedda's permission for the use of her Christian name is at the same time a clear hint to Løvborg that he may go so far, but no farther. That final degree of intimacy which the *du* would betoken is denied him whereas Hedda has explicitly encouraged its use in Mrs Elvsted since she obviously poses no immediate threat to Hedda and certainly not the kind of potential sexual threat that Løvborg represents.

When Løvborg for the last time reverts to the forbidden *du*, his use of this potent pronoun signals a crucial moment in his talk with Hedda as he reacts to what he believes, or hopes, to be a possible admission by Hedda of her love for him. Løvborg's suppressed emotion which has been felt in his language rises to the surface of the conversation and erupts into the terse: 'du og jeg' (you and I), a climactic compression of language to the point where, taken literally, it and the issue are identical. And this is the issue for Løvborg, no more, no less. The intensity and the directness of the expressed emotion, and the laying bare of the truth at this juncture, makes the use of *du* inevitable in this context. It is a fleeting, and final, stripping away of the surface of formality that protects Hedda against a reality she is unable to deal with. Hedda's ban on the use of the familiar pronoun also acts as an immediate curb to Løvborg's exclamation indicating that he has strayed dangerously close to the truth. Significantly, Hedda's objection to Løvborg's use of *du* is unavailable to an English translator, and so the sense one has in the original version of her precariously maintained defences being undermined by what is to her a highly subversive word whose use can only be allowed where it does not threaten her status or her schemes, must be lost.

Immediately after Hedda's and Løvborg's confrontation they are joined by Mrs Elvsted. The surface configuration of their relationship is indicated in the way these three people address each other, according to the rules laid down by Hedda. With Løvborg's reluctant use of the polite *De* he is denied the role of confidant, while Mrs Elvsted's status vis-à-vis Hedda, contrary to what would have been the norm, has now advanced to the level of the familiar pronoun. But as the play shows, neither Løvborg nor Mrs Elvsted feels entirely at ease with the pronouns of address assigned to them by Hedda, at least not initially. The modes of address, then, have become a token of the uneasy personal and social relations for those of the characters most immediately affected by Hedda's person. This general feeling of unease which pervades Hedda's relations with everyone, including Brack, is strikingly revealed in her refusal to use the familiar *du* to her husband's aunt, though the latter makes it clear that she wishes to be fully accepted both in social and personal terms by Hedda, in the way she address Hedda at the outset. Similarly, Løvborg's explicit attempt to induce Hedda to agree to the mutual use of *du* has failed, while Mrs Elvsted's use of that pronoun does not correspond to either her real social or personal situation relative to Hedda. Also, of course, there is something 'wrong' in Hedda's failure to reciprocate her husband's use of the Christian name.

At the beginning of the final Act, Hedda uses her husband's Christian name for the first time since Act I. Tesman erroneously construes this conspicuous change in Hedda's mode of address as both heightened affection on her part and, by inference, as an implied acceptance of the Tesman world, as witnessed by his delighted: 'Oh, Aunt Julle will be ever so pleased!'. Even Brack, though Hedda's social equal, is kept at arm's length by being addressed by his title and surname. Again, reciprocity of address is not observed since Brack's mode of address is considerably less formal; he only switches to her surname when others are present; otherwise he prefers to address her as 'Mrs Hedda' ('fru Hedda'). Immediately before Hedda shoots herself he even drops the 'fru' and simply calls her 'Hedda', thus revealing what had been hinted at in his exclusion of her married second name, namely that he sees her in terms of General Gabler's daughter, rather than Tesman's wife. Løvborg's avoidance of her married name similarly reflects his unwillingness to accept her new social identity as Tesman's wife.

Hedda's own distorting and blurring of relationships through her deliberate manipulation of the pronouns of address is consistent with her voluntary and involuntary blurring of the delicate dividing lines between illusion and reality. Thus, language provides Hedda with access to reality and, concurrently, with protection and retreat from it. This dual tendency in Hedda's own nature is acutely focused in the person of Eilert Løvborg. Only through Løvborg was she, as she puts it, able to 'peep into a world – which one is not allowed to know anything about'. Typically, Hedda remains at one or two removes from the realities of life and her language enables her to sustain this distance. Her image of the vine-leaves is a conspicuous example of reality hidden behind Hedda's projected life-lie, an extravagant poetic gesture which Løvborg immediately recognizes for what it is, and which is finally identified by Hedda herself as a fiction. There are also other examples in the play when Hedda poeticizes life, but such moments are recognizable symptoms of illusion-making. On the other hand, the pronouns of address are less conspicuous and more subversive in their effect on Hedda's immediate environment than language which proclaims its function more colourfully.

In more than one of Ibsen's plays the modes of address form patterns that correspond to patterns of subjugation and submission. For example, Hedda's refusal to allow Løvborg to conquer her through the use of the intimate *du* is in one respect similar in motive to Ellida Wangel's consistent use of the formal *De* to the Stranger. Both Løvborg and the Stranger confront the women on whom they have designs, not with claims of the ideal, but with more earthly claims. From the women's point of view both men pose a sexual threat to the women they insist on addressing as *du*, and in both of these cases the women in question, the potential 'victims', persevere in the use of the formal pronoun. This can be thought of as a case of semantic conflict which mirrors a sexual conflict. Silverberg has pointed out that 'the taboo against the use of *Du* corresponds quite exactly to the taboo against revealing one's own name'. Silverberg is here referring to the convention regulating the usage of the formal and informal pronoun of address in Germany, which is similar to Norwegian usage. He goes on to a more detailed discussion of the psychological and psychonalytical implications of *du*, and quotes Sir James Frazer's *Golden Bough*:

> In fact, primitive man regards his name as a vital portion of himself and takes care of it accordingly. Thus, for example, the North American Indian 'regards his name, not as a mere label, but as a distinct part of his personality, just as much as are his eyes or his teeth, and believes that injury will result as surely from the malicious handling of his name as from a wound inflicted on any part of his physical organism'.[32]

Silverberg's paper, written in the heyday of Freudian psychology, inevitably sees the habits underlying the use of the German *Du* and *Sie* as being sexually motivated. Despite the limitations of this approach, the case Silverberg makes for the origin of the pronouns of address should not be ignored.

In the case of Hedda and Ellida it tends to confirm the impression created by these two women that they feel exposed to a sexual threat, in a very wide sense. Silverberg speculates that:

> the personal pronouns first came into use as a result of this name-taboo. If people were afraid to reveal their names to enemies and strangers, it would be impossible for them to address each other on any business whatsoever, unless one invented some more oblique

way of addressing a person than the blunt use of his name as the subject of a sentence. In such a manner the term *Du* or its equivalent may have developed among the Indo-Germanic races. Then it was felt, for the reasons given above, that this term was also too close to the nucleus of the personality, and strangers were addressed in the plural instead of the more direct singular.[33]

Silverberg's hypothesis is appropriate in the case of Hedda because her fear of personal intimacy, just as her abhorrence of any reference to pregnancy or death, was Ibsen's perceptive way of portraying her excessive vulnerability. Indeed, the pronoun *du* is so menacing for Hedda in many situations because it penetrates through her defences to the nucleus of her personality. In the case of Eilert Løvborg she had to deny him a continuation of even the platonic friendship he reminds her they once shared because in the past it had threatened to develop into something more intimate. As Hedda explains it, she had to terminate their relationship

...da der var overhængende fare for at der vilde komme virkelighed ind i forholdet.[34]

(...when there was an imminent risk of reality entering into our relationship.)

Unfortunately, Meyer's and Fjelde's translations have neglected to render 'virkelighed', an absolutely key word in this passage. Ibsen added it in the final version of the play. In the early draft, *Hedda*, it appears that Hedda broke with Løvborg because of her fear of scandal, and she does not use the word 'virkelighed'. Her use of the word 'virkelighed' shows great insight on Hedda's part and it is perhaps the most explicit of her self-revelations in the play. Løvborg is dangerous to Hedda because through his past role of confidant he has come closer to the real Hedda than anyone else, and also because of his attempt to re-establish their formal rapport, for example through the *du* which she makes taboo. To paraphrase Frazer, Hedda regards *du* not as a mode of address, a label, but as a real part of her selfhood. Her tragedy is that she is obliged to expend so much effort and energy protecting that very part of her personality, her sexual identity, which the repressive bourgeois morality of her father, an archetypal representative of society, had crippled. It appears that it was Løvborg who provided Hedda with the only glimpse she ever had of those biological and physical realities of human existence which, in the play, she takes such pains to suppress.

Since the English language has ceased to ascribe two pronouns of address to the public and private spheres respectively, the English pronoun *you* could not in an English version of the play fill a woman like Hedda with this kind of fear. Since the pronoun *you* does not carry within it any differentiation between the private and public spheres of a person's role, it obviously cannot serve the same functions as the separate *du* and *De*. In *Hedda Gabler* the tragic dimension is in part generated by the disjunction between her private and public self, where the latter seems always to have taken precedence over the former. Her extreme awareness of the discriminate function of the pronouns of address can therefore be best explained in terms of the divisions within her own identity which seem to find their correlative in the clear social and psychological divisions inherent in the familiar *du* and the formal *De*. It is interesting in this context to find Silverberg making a clear distinction between the private and the public aspects of personality, which he terms the 'Du-personality' and the 'Sie-personality':

> A child in Germany today begins life as 'Du' and is called 'Du' by everyone until he reaches a school grade roughly corresponding in age to early adolescence when he begins to be called 'Sie'. All his infantile tendencies would therefore tend to be associated with his Du-personality, and his acquired, more social traits with his Sie-personality. These latter are the result of the child's contact with the culture that surrounds it.[35]

Even if such anthropological and psychoanalytic accounts of the origins and the functions of the pronouns of address as those provided by Silverberg and Frazer may be only partially helpful in accounting for their dramatic function within *Hedda Gabler*, for instance, it is nonetheless necessary to interpret Hedda's sensitivity to these pronouns as something more than a mere perfunctory adherence to social conventions for their own sake. To adapt Silverberg's designation, if Hedda's 'Sie-personality' is a product of the society that surrounds her this would account for her difficulty in reconciling herself to her private identity, her 'Du-personality'. In a more general sense, her tendency to dominate others (she is not a general's daughter for nothing), for example Mrs Elvsted, Løvborg and the Tesmans, of which her need to dictate and define the modes of address is but one example, helps her avoid domination by others. Consequently, her private self is less likely to be exposed and challenged.

In this connection it is rather more than a coincidence that the shaping, paternal influence in Hedda's life, the general, was as magisterial and authoritative a figure as any Ibsen could have chosen to represent the archetypal ruling father figure. The symbolic portrait, constantly gazing out at Hedda from the wall of the inner room, is the unremitting reminder that she has her origins in a public figure. The suggestiveness of the portrait is clear; Hedda has her origins in an 'institutional' public figure and in the play no other determining factors are visible to suggest alternative influences in her personal and social make-up. Since her background and upbringing appear to have resulted in an inadequate development of her '*du*-personality' there are few viable options to her other than to perpetuate and sustain her public identity through a rigid clinging to the codes and conventions of her class. As the play demonstrates, her conscious manipulation of the conventions of personal address becomes an essential means towards this end, and the two pronouns of address become key metaphors for this process.

Notes

1. Although the formal pronoun of address, *De*, is fading from everyday use in Norway, W. V. Silverberg's account of the familiar pronoun *Du* in Germany before World War II could also serve as a description for the corresponding norm in Ibsen's day:

   'Anyone who has lived in Germany and is on speaking terms with its language has sensed the feeling of taboo that surrounds the use of the term *Du* in addressing others. It may be used freely in addressing children (approximately under high school age), members of one's family and intimate friends. It may not be used in addressing strangers, servants and tradespeople, or individuals with whom one is not on very intimate terms. One may have been acquainted with an individual for years, seeing him every day (as in the case of business or professional associates) and yet, unless the requisite degree of intimacy exists, one would not dream of addressing him with the familiar *Du*. This would represent an unpardonable liberty and, in many cases, would be felt as an insult. Even foreigners who trespass unwittingly into this field of taboo (the Americans and the English are the most frequent offenders) are regarded somewhat askance and are forgiven wholeheartedly only by those who understand that the distinction does not exist in the offender's native language.' (W.V. Silverberg, 'On the Psychological Significance of Du and Sie', in *The Psychoanalytic Quarterly*, Vol. 9, 1940, p.512.)

Brown and Gilman also provide an account of the distinctions between the formal and informal pronouns of address in several European languages, as well as a few examples of the way Elizabethan and Jacobean dramatists employed thou and you for dramatic purposes, in a paper entitled 'The Pronouns of Power and Solidarity'. The paper has been reprinted in: *Communication in Face-to-Face Interaction*, ed. John Laver and Sandy Hutcheson (Penguin Education, 1972). Page references are from this edition.

2. Berry, Francis: *Poet's Grammar* (London, Routledge and Kegan Paul), p.92. Berry also discusses the thou/you distinction in Shakespeare's Sonnets.
3. Brown and Gilman, *op.cit.*, pp. 123-24.
4. Quotations in Norwegian from Ibsen's work have been taken from the Centenary Edition, *Hundreaårsutgaven, Henrik Ibsens Samlede Verker,* 21 vols, ed. Francis Bull, Halvdan Koht, Didrik Arup Seip (Oslo 1928-57).
   The English translations of these quotations from Ibsen are my own adaptations of various translations. These adaptations are not meant to be proper translations in their own right since their main purpose is to illustrate where and how the pronouns of address occur and function in the language.
   S.V. IX, 80 (The Centenary Edition is referred to as S.V.)
5. Fjelde, Rolf: *Ibsen, Four Major Plays*. Signet Classics, p.78.
6. S.V. IX, 80.
7. S.V. IX, 85.
8. S.V. IX, 121. This line also occurs in the early draft of the play.
9. S.V. IX, 123. The draft contains this line.
10. S.V. X, 415. The draft contains this line. In Michael Meyer's translation Rebekka uses Rosmer's Christian name; and in McFarlane's version she is made to call him 'my dear'. Both these translations are an attempt to convey the intimacy of *du*.
11. It seems to be more than mere chance that in the vast majority of plays where a married couple has children, the wife calls her husband by his Christian name. For instance, this is true of Mrs Bernick, Nora, Mrs Stockmann, Mrs Solness and Rita Allmers.
12. Northam, John: *Ibsen's Dramatic Method*, (New ed. Oslo, 1971).
13. S.V. XI, p.104.
14. S.V. XI, p.154.
15. S.V. XI, p.242.
16. Silverberg, *op. cit.*, p.51 1.
17. *Forum for Modem Language Studies*, 4/1968, pp.217-22.
18. Northam, *op. cit.*, p.222.
19. S.V. XI, p.304.
20. S.V. XI, p.308.

21. S.V. XI, p.308.
22. Hemmer, Bjøm: *Ibsen og Bjørnson: Essays og Analyser* (Oslo, 1978), p.252.
23. S.V. XI, p.299.
24. S.V. XI, p.299.
25. McFarlane, *The Oxford Ibsen* Vol. VII, p.14.
26. Addressing Hedda, Mrs Elvsted in the same scene notes that: 'Vore kredse var jo saa rent forskellige' (We moved in such completely different circles.) In the draft version of the play, too, Hedda persuades Mrs Elvsted to use *du* to her, in preference to the formal pronoun. Mrs Elvsted's difficulty in remembering to use *du* towards Hedda also occurred in the draft.
27. S.V. XI, p.317.
28. Holtan, Orley I.: *Mythic Patterns in Ibsen's Last Plays* (University of Minnesota Press, 1970), p.82.
29. Before Hedda married she and Løvborg had pretended to be reading a magazine when they were sitting in the same room as General Gabler.
30. S.V. XI, p.346.
31. S.V. XI, p.346.
32. Silverberg, *op. cit.*, p.513.
33. Silverberg, *op. cit.*, p.514.
34. S.V. XI, p.348.
35. Silverberg, *op. cit.*, p.511.

Originally published May 1981 (Vol. 20, No. 1).

Apostasy in Prose[1]

James McFarlaine

> The principle division in the history of Western literature occurs between the early 1870s and the turn of the century ... Compared to this division all preceding historical and stylistic rubrics or movements – Hellenism, the medieval, the Baroque, Neo-classicism, Romanticism – are only subgroups or variants.
>
> (George Steiner, *After Babel*, London 1975, p.176.)

The title of this Symposium is a long one: 'Preludes to Modernism: literature, art, music and thought in the period 1870 to 1914'. Almost, indeed, an Opening Statement in itself.

Nevertheless, it was thought it might be helpful if I were briefly to sketch out some rough kind of framework within which, as we listen to the individual papers, the separate contributions might be placed. As I do this, I shall not – deliberately not – attempt to say anything new. The greater part of what I shall have to say in the next fifteen to twenty minutes will consist of references to or quotations from the work of others who have given their scholarly attention to the period to which this Symposium is addressing itself. I shall also beg leave to plagiarise myself here and there where it seemed to me that things I have said on other occasions might usefully be recalled in this present context.

[The speaker then went on to give a brief outline of the nature of the period, to indicate some of the more fundamental changes that had taken place in thought and in attitudes, and to catalogue some of the more significant names and achievements attaching to these years. He examined the widely held view that this period of change was qualitatively and quantitatively different from other periods of cultural change in the history of mankind.]

Within this period of profound change, drama was of course not exempt; and the chasm which separates contemporary drama from the drama of the first half of the nineteenth century – from Schiller and Kleist, from Hugo and de Musset, from Grillparzer and Hebbel – is huge. That proposition which – explicitly or implicitly – serves as the starting point for a great many histories of modem drama is also one which focuses the attention very much on the period between 1870 and the end of the century. It is a proposition which was given its most succinct formulation by Kenneth Muir:

> The most important event in the history of modem drama was Ibsen's abandonment of verse after *Peer Gynt* in order to write prose plays about contemporary problems.[2]

The restless exploration of the resources of prose as a dramatic medium, the extension of the concept of 'poetry' to embrace much linguistic territory that was previously neglected or even despised are things seen as having their origins in this decision of Ibsen. It is an idea more often asserted than examined; and for an event of such acknowledged magnitude it has (I suggest) had less attention from commentators than it deserves. It is recognised as having been a very deliberate decision, born of a deeply held conviction; and Ibsen's revealing letter to Lucie Wolf some years after the event is regularly quoted in evidence. I remind you that in May 1883 Lucie Wolf, an actress at the Christiania Theatre, wrote to Ibsen asking if he would compose a Prologue to be declaimed at a forthcoming festival occasion in her honour. Let us remind ourselves of the precise terms of Ibsen's reply. No, he said:

> I wish I could comply with your request. Nothing would please me more than to be able to do it. But I cannot; my convictions and my artistic principles forbid me. Prologues, epilogues, and everything of the kind ought to be banished from the stage. The stage is for dramatic art alone; and declamation is not a dramatic art.
>
> The prologue would of course have to be in verse, since that is the established custom. But I will take no part in perpetuating this custom. Verse has been most injurious to the art of the drama. A true artist of the stage, whose repertoire is the contemporary drama, should not be willing to let a single line of verse cross his or her lips. It is improbable that verse will be employed to any extent worth mentioning in the drama of the future since the aims of future dramatists are almost certain to be incompatible with it. Consequently it is doomed. For art forms become extinct, just as the preposterous animal forms of prehistoric times became extinct when their day was done.
>
> A tragedy in iambic pentameters is already as rare a phenomenon as the dodo ... During the last seven or eight years, I have hardly written a single line of verse, devoting myself exclusively to the very much more difficult art of writing the straightforward, plain language spoken in real life.

> Gid jeg så sandt kunde efterkomme Deres anmodning. Intet skulde været mig kærere. Men jeg kan det ikke; jeg kan det ikke for min overbevisnings og for min kunstbetragtnings skyld. Prologer, epiloger og alt sligt noget burde ubetinget forvises fra scenen. *Der* hører kun den dramatiske kunst hjemme; og deklamation er ikke dramatisk kunst.
>
> Prologen skulde naturligvis være pa vers; thi så er jo skik og brug. Men jeg kan ikke være med på at holde denne skik og brug i live. Verseformen har tilføjet skuespilkunsten overmåde megen skade. En scenisk kunstner, der har sit repertoire i samtidens skuespildigtning, burde ikke gerne tage et vers i sin mund. Den versificerede form vil neppe finde nogen nævneværdig anvendelse i den nærmeste fremtids drama; thi fremtidens digteriske intentioner vil sikkert ikke kunne forliges med den. Den vil derfor gå til grunde. Kunstformerne dør jo ut lige så vel som urtidens urimelige dyreformer døde ut, da deres tid var omme ...
>
> En femdoblet jambe-tragedie er jo allerede nutildags en ligeså sjelden forekomst som den fugl dodo ... Jeg selv har i de sidste 7-8 år neppe skrevet et eneste vers, men udelukkende dyrket den ulige vanskligere kunst at digte i jævnt sandfærdigt virkelighedssprog. (HU, XVII, p.510 f.2)

But this was not the simple, almost casual switch from one medium to another which many commentaries seem to imply. I shall want to try to show that the factors which were at work in Ibsen's mind at the time he took this decision, the way in which he then found himself – sometimes deliberately, sometimes involuntarily – modifying his dramatic policies and methods in the light of practice and experience, and the residue which these shifts and re-orientations left in his work are elements in an extremely complex act of intellectual and cultural apostasy. I see them as things worth tracing in some of their finer details not only for the light they shed on the new direction taken by his own drama but also for the impact they had on European drama in general in these years and for long years to come.

The first question to clarify is therefore: which were these years of decision? *Peer Gynt* appeared in 1867, one year after the publication of *Brand*; the first of his prose 'dramas of contemporary life', *Pillars of Society* (*Samfundets Støtter*) appeared in 1877. Ten years of prime life, from the author's fortieth to his fiftieth year. A decade of greatly varied endeavour, in the course of which he published three works of vastly different quality: a roistering comedy called *The League of Youth* (*De unges Forbund*) in 1869, a volume of his collected *Poems* (*Digte*) in 1871, and his vast 'world-historic' drama, *Emperor and Galilean* (*Kejser og Galilær*) in 1873.

Arithmetic alone, if nothing else, indicates how central this last work, *Emperor and Galilean*, is to our present purposes. Completed when the author was 45, it comes almost exactly midway in the period we have selected as crucial: that decade between Ibsen's abandonment of verse after *Peer Gynt* and the start of the cycle of prose plays about contemporary problems. It also, significantly, comes very nearly at the mid-point of Ibsen's creative career as a whole, extending as it does from his first drama *Catilina* in 1850 to his last, *When We Dead Awaken* (*Når vi døde vågner*), in 1899. Moreover, the occasion of the publication of *Emperor and Galilean* was the very first time that Ibsen, openly and unambiguously, declared himself on the side of a realistic prose dialogue as the preferred medium of drama and expressed his hostility to what he referred to as 'the language of the gods'. It came in an exchange of letters in 1874 with Edmund Gosse. Gosse had sent Ibsen a review of *Emperor and Galilean* which he had published in *The Spectator*, and in which he had been incautious enough to remark that he thought the play would have been better for being written in verse. Not so, said Ibsen:

> I am greatly obliged to you for your kind review of my new play. There is only one remark in it about which I must say a word or two. You say that the drama ought to have been written in verse and that it would have gained by this. Here I must differ from you. As you must have observed, the play is conceived in the most realistic style. The illusion I wished to produce was that of reality. I wished to produce the impression on the reader [sic] that what he was reading was something that had actually happened. If I had employed verse, I would have counteracted my own intention and defeated my purpose ... Speaking generally, the dialogue must conform to the degree of idealisation which pervades the work as a whole. My new drama is no tragedy in the ancient sense. What I sought to depict were human beings, and therefore I would not let them talk the 'language of the gods'.

> For Deres velvillige anmeldelse af mit nye drama er jeg Dem særdeles forbunden.
>
> Der er kun et punkt deri, som jeg med et par ord vil omtale. De mener at mit skuespil burde være skrevet pa vers og at det vilde have vundet derved. Heri må jeg modsige Dem;

thi stykket er, som De vil have bemærket, anlagt i den mest realistiske form; den illusion, jeg vilde frembringe, var virkelighedens; jeg vilde på læseren frembringe det indtryck at det, han læste, var noget virkelig passeret. Skulde jeg have brugt verset, så havde jeg derved modarbejdet min egen hensigt og den opgave jeg havde stillet mig ... I det hele taget må den sproglige form rette sig efter den grad af idealitet, som er udbredt over fremstillingen. Mit nye skuespil er ingen tragedie i den ældre tids betydning; hvad jeg har villet skildre er mennesker og just derfor har jeg ikke villet lade dem tale 'gudernes tungemål'. (HU, XVII, pp.121ff.)

Emperor and Galilean was planned as a trilogy – three dramas of 3 acts, 3 acts and 5 acts respectively; but at a comparatively late stage in its composition it was re-modelled as two inter-related five-act dramas – an uneasy structure, which immediately betrays something of the severely intractable nature of the material, but also at a deeper level endorses by its form something of the unfinalised, unresolved nature of its message.

Taken together, the ten Acts of *Emperor and Galilean* follow the career of Julian the Apostate, his rise to imperial power and his attempts to reintroduce the old paganism into the Christianised Roman Empire of the 4th century AD. The action of the first half, entitled *Caesar's Apostasy*, moves from Constantinople to Athens and to Ephesus, and eventually to Lutetia and Vienne in Gaul, covering the ten years between AD351 and AD361, by which time the hero has become Julianus Apostate and has ritually broken with the Christian faith. The second drama, entitled *Emperor Julian*, follows the events of the years from AD361 to AD363, tracing the decline of the emperor hero against a Christianity powerfully reasserting itself, moving from Constantinople to Antioch and then to the Eastern territories of the Empire and to the plains beyond the Tigris where Julian finally meets his death at the hands of one of his own soldiers.

After the completion of the work, Ibsen steadfastly and repeatedly insisted on three things about it: that it was highly subjective; that, despite the remoteness in time of its subject matter, its relevance to the contemporary world was both deliberate and of the greatest importance; and that for those who cared to look, his (Ibsen's) own philosophy of life and art was clearly visible there for anybody who could read the signs. To the end of his life, he also liked to suggest that of all his work this was his supreme masterpiece.[4]

Ibsen made a number of separate but abortive approach runs to his material before he finally began writing the version as we now know it. One of the projects which we know he had carried with him when he left Norway in 1864 for what was destined to be a 27 year self-imposed exile was a plan for a tragedy to be called 'Julianus Apostata'.

Between that first unformed plan and the completed drama nine years later lies a period of great turmoil for Ibsen, in which artistic as well as material success was mixed with protracted soul-searching and anguished enquiry and in the course of which his 'world view' – if I may use that term to mean his *Weltanschauung* – and his artistic credo underwent fundamental change.

I want to suggest that one might identify here three main phases, which I will call (a) the ethical apostasy; (b) the aesthetic apostasy; and (c) the new vision. I must needs speak of them as though they were consecutive, though in reality they were closely intermeshed, with shifts in anyone area inevitably having repercussions in the others.

The vehemence of Ibsen's repudiation of his tribal ethic – by which I mean that body of beliefs and values distinctive of Norwegian culture and society at the time – is an indication of why he should have found the theme of Julian's apostasy so apposite to his dramatic intentions. On 16 September 1864 he wrote to Bjørnson:

> Here in Rome there is a blessed peace in which to write; at present I am working on a longish poem and I have in preparation a tragedy 'Julianus Apostata', a work which I embrace with unrestrained joy and which I am sure will go well for me. I hope to have both these things ready by the spring, or at least by next summer.

> Her i Rom er der en velsignet Fred til at skrive i; fortiden arbejder jeg paa et større Digt og har i Forberedelse en Tragedie 'Julianus Apostata', et Arbejde, som jeg omfatter med en ubændig Glæde og somjeg vist tror skal lykkes mig; till Vaaren eller ialfald udpaa Sommeren haaber jeg at have begge Dele færdige. (HU, XVI, p.102)

The following spring, his plan for a Julian drama was still alive and active. When he applied back to the authorities in Norway for a grant to enable him to extend his time in Rome, he wrote that he would shortly be preparing a substantial drama on a theme taken from Roman history. In the event, however, it was not Julian who first served as the bearer of his new convictions, but Brand: most conspicuously in the poetic drama of which he is the eponymous hero, but perhaps even more eloquently in the opening section of the long but unfinished narrative poem which is generally known as 'the epic Brand'.

It was this poem which, in the most forthright and uncompromising way, announced that its author was breaking with his own past, turning away from the earlier sentimentalities of Norwegian national romanticism, in order to dedicate himself to communicating the truth about present concerns. The poem stood both as a condemnation and as a manifesto, and is probably one of the most important programmatic statements about his work and beliefs that Ibsen ever made.

In effect, the poem was a call to Ibsen's fellow countrymen to repudiate the lying pretence that had been infecting all levels of public and private life. The past, he insisted, was dead; the Viking spirit upon which the people so pathetically prided themselves was no longer a living thing but a rouged and embalmed corpse, pestilential. The ancient grandeur had vanished, and the modern generation was too puny even to attempt to wear the trappings of those earlier heroic ages, too feeble to be worthy of its inheritance. Therefore, the poem declares, he has turned his eyes and mind away from the soul-dead tales of the past, away from the lying dreams of the future, in order to enter the misty, rain-swept world of the present.

So that when Ibsen turned from his narrative poem to begin work on *Brand* as we now know it, it was inevitable that the new work should be above all else an act of repudiation and disavowal, a passionate denial of earlier assumptions and beliefs, a vehement apostasy. Compounded of distate, guilt, contempt and frustration, it represented a breakaway from what Ibsen now recognised as a whole world of false values and spurious ideals. It cut free from the past, from an existence of inauthentic living and writing. He wrote as one possessed; and in less than four months the new work – a huge and powerful dramatic statement – was complete.

He was drawn to scrutinise whole areas of his earlier life and career: his own childhood and his relations with his parents, brothers and sister; his earlier authorship, its aims, its purposes, and its disappointing achievements; his earlier unthinking acceptance of a whole range of conventional beliefs and current ideas; the frustrations and humiliations of his professional life in the theatre – 'a daily repeated abortion', he was later moved to call it. He found himself with a new awareness of standards and values fundamentally different from those that continued to serve his contemporaries and countrymen back home. He was moved to contrast the realities of his Italian experience with the defensive fictions of the Norwegian Myth as he had experienced it, notions to which he had himself shamefully given currency by his pen, the lies that told of the decay and effeteness of Mediterranean culture as compared to the gale-swept, invigorating strength of the North.

He began to recognise the crippling provincialism of that way of life which had been his lot for half a lifetime and which he now recognised as hollow and empty and based on cruel self-deception. He squirmed as he recalled the active part he had played as a writer in promoting these delusions, in promulgating these lies. He raged at the realisation that chauvinistic social and cultural forces had somehow manipulated him, had exploited his talents in the interests of a spurious and lying idea.[5]

These passions were however important less for their own sake than as a kind of fuse that set off a veritable explosion of thought and feeling in his own inner life. Things he had suffered and proved on his own nerves, things he had 'lived through' – a phrase Ibsen gave high value to as meaning something different from his merely having witnessed, or experienced from the outside – now combined to impose upon him a fundamental reappraisal: the social pressures, the cultural impositions, the received ideas, the wishful thinking, the public hypocrisy, the individual self-deception, the false assumptions, the spiritual chauvinism, the empty big-mouthed phrases which he now heard as though across the entire length of Europe, were now all distanced and seen for what they really were.

The second stage of his apostasy – what I have called his aesthetic apostasy – was less explosive, more protracted, more diffuse. Ibsen was not unaware that these more obvious changes in values and attitudes would have repercussions elsewhere in his artistic beliefs; and one letter which he wrote from Rome to Bjørnson back in Norway spoke of how he had purged himself of 'aestheticism' – 'det Æsthetiske' – a highly complex concept in Scandinavian thought in this Kierkegaardian era. This, he realised, was something which had up to then exerted a powerful influence over him: now, however, he had come to see that 'aestheticism of this kind ... (is) as great a curse to poetry as theology is to religion' (Æsthetik i denne Forstand forekommer mig nu at være en ligesaa stor Forbandelse for Poesien, som Theologien er det for Religionen. HU, XVI, p.111).

In all this matrix of ideas, however, there was one belief where Ibsen's views had conspicuously not yet changed: his view of the role of verse in drama, at least in his own drama. Very shortly after completing *Brand*, Ibsen wrote (on 4 December

1865) to Clemens Petersen, one of Denmark's leading critics, to reassert his own belief that verse was for him the natural dramatic medium:

> You once wrote about me that verse form with symbolic overtones was my natural bent. I have often thought about this. I believe the same myself; and it is in accord with this view that my work (*Brand*) has taken shape.

> De har engang skrevet om mig at den versificerede Form med det Symbolske bagved var min naturligste Retning. Jeg har ofte tænkt derover, jeg tror selv det samme og i Overensstemmelse hermed har Digtet formet sig. (HU, XVI, p.122)

There seems little doubt that if Ibsen had persisted at this stage with *Emperor and Galilean*, it would have been in verse. As it happens, in the summer of the following year (1866) he still had Julian in his sights, and his correspondence has several references to the possibility of his 'starting in earnest' on Julian. But again another project displaced it – this time the writing of *Peer Gynt*. He started work on this shortly after New Year 1867 and it was complete some nine months later.

Perhaps even at the time – certainly later – Ibsen began to worry a little about the sheer speed and facility with which he had been able to complete these verse dramas: *Brand* in four months; *Peer Gynt*, which, according to its author, 'followed of its own accord', in nine: and both of them unusually long and complex works.

These were years when argument about the concept of 'poetry' and the meaning of 'beauty' led to much earnest and often cloudy public debate in Scandinavia; and from many remarks scattered about his correspondence of this time it is evident that Ibsen brooded much on these and related matters, and especially on how current interpretations of these terms might bear upon his own methods and practices.

In the middle of his work on *Peer Gynt* there appeared in the Danish press a review of *Brand* by Georg Brandes, the young Danish iconoclast whom Ibsen had not yet met but whose views were in time to have a profound influence on Ibsen, on Scandinavian drama in general, and on the spread of literary realism throughout the whole of Europe.

This review, though generally appreciative, must have given Ibsen occasion to pause and ponder. In it, Brandes warmly approves of the passionate intensity of Ibsen's message, the strength of his moral indignation, his hatred of falsehood and deceit. But when it came to the *poetry* in the work, he declared that in comparison with the rich poetry of Ibsen's earlier (prose) work *The Pretenders*, *Brand* represented a retrograde step. Brandes urged Ibsen to abandon the direction he had taken with the earlier (verse) *Love's Comedy* and *Brand* and return to the path of true poetry.

Ibsen must have found himself wondering whether the bleak honesty of his new vision was best matched by what he was later to call 'the language of the gods', i.e. verse; and he had to face to question squarely whether the relationship between 'truth' as he now envisaged it and 'beauty' as it was conventionally taken to be was any longer valid.

After the completion of *Peer Gynt*, he awaited the reviews in the Scandinavian press – and especially the judgement of the influential Clemens Petersen – with more than usual apprehension. When it came, it was altogether worse than he had expected. Not because it was generally hostile and dismissive, but because it was compounded of the kind of literary and aesthetic judgements he was most concerned to repudiate. The fury with which Ibsen received this review, and the vehemence of his response, justifies me at quoting at some length from the Petersen review, which began ominously by bluntly asking: Was this poetry?

> All poetry is the transmutation of reality into art. Even the most fleeting impressions of beauty in everyday life are precisely this. The view over the harbour when the rain eases and all the boats hoist their sails in the sunlight; the sight of a group of animals, who have stopped motionless in the forest as though Pan were playing for them and who then suddenly, released from their enchantment, go chasing off across the plain; the sight of a man straining with every fibre of his being in quiet self-satisfaction but who nevertheless finds inexpressible joy in it because he is sacrificing himself for something he loves; whenever one encounters something of this kind in real life which leaves on one an impression of beauty and which rouses feelings of poetry, this is due solely to the fact that reality, at such a moment, presents itself to one as art ... But if this transmutation into reality is to be successful, so that the raw material of reality is absorbed by art's form and thereby wholly becomes poetry, then art makes its distinct demands, just as reality makes its, and if both demands are not completely met, then the transmutation fails and poetry remains absent, even though there may otherwise be sufficient both of art and reality in the work. But this is precisely how things are in Herr Ibsen's last two works: they might rather be said to have come to terms with these demands than fully satisfying them. Neither *Brand* nor *Peer Gynt* are properly poetry, however great or interesting their immediate effect may be.

> Al Poesi er en Omsætning af Virkeligheden i Konst. Selv Hverdagslivets flygtigste Skjønhedsindtryk er ikke Andet. Naar Udsigten over Sundet, idet Regnbygen letter, og alle Skibene heise Seil i Solskinnet; naar Synet af en Rudel Dyr, der midt i Skoven staae forstenede i Lytten, som om Pan spillede for dem, og saa pludselig, løste af Fortryllelsen, jage afsted over Sletten; naar Betragtningen af et Menneske, der slider lige til den sidste Trevl sit Liv op i stille Opoffrelse, men netop deri har en usigelig fyldig Glæde, fordi han opoffrer sig for Noget, han elsker; naar saaledes Et eller Andet af det, der omgiver En i Virkeligheden, gjør et Skjønhedsintryk paa En og vækker Følelsen af Poesi, saa beroer dette ene og alene paa, at Virkeligheden i et saadant Øieblik kommer til at vise sig for En som Konst ... Men skal denne Omsætning af Virkeligheden i Konst fuldelig lykkes, saa at Virkelighedens Stof ganske gaar op i Konstens Form og derved helt bliver til Poesi, saa stiller Konsten sin bestemte Fordring, ligesom Virkeligheden stiller sin, og tilfredstilles ikke begge Fordringer fuldt ud, saa mislykkes Omsætningen, og Poesien udebliver, skjønt der maaskee ellers er Nok i Værket baade af Konst og Virkelighed. Men nu forholder det sig netop saaledes med Hr. Ibsens to sidste Arbeider, at de snarere kunne siges at have affundet sig med Fordringerne end opfylt dem. Hverken 'Brand' eller 'Peer Gynt' er egentlig Poesi, hvor stor og hvor interessant saa end deres øieblikkelige Virkning er.[6]

Ibsen's fury at this reception was matched only by his dismay – dismay, because what was being urged on him by these other commentators was precisely what he had after so much soul-searching repudiated: the romanticisation of life, the idealised view, the cosily sentimental. He was in despair that there should be so little understanding of his real purposes, and found it equally offensive to be praised for the so-called 'romantic beauty' of certain selected scenes as he was by the alleged uglinesses of others. There seemed to be a kind of smothering, all-enveloping, Boyg-like invulnerability about these critical judgements, deploying as they did their precious notions of 'beauty', 'truth' and 'poetry', which left Ibsen despairing of ever finding any rational way to refute them. He erupted in a long letter (9/10 December 1867, HU, XVI, pp.197ff.) to Bjørnson – probably the longest letter he ever wrote in his life – which is deeply eloquent of the depths to which he had been stirred by the article. Defiantly – and prophetically – he declared that *Peer Gynt was* poetry, and would be recognised as such, if not today then tomorrow: 'The concept of poetry in our country, in Norway, will come to conform to the work' (Min Bog *er* Poesie; og er den det ikke, saa skal den blive det. Begrebet Poesi skal i vort Land, i Norge, komme og bøje sig efter Bogen.)

Ibsen had as little satisfaction from Brandes's review, which also regretted the lack of 'beauty' in the piece:

> If the fine old rule of the French Romantics – 'The ugly is the beautiful' – is really valid, then *Peer Gynt* would be a work of beauty; but if there is any hint of doubt about this rule, then Ibsen's new work has failed totally. That it has failed *totally* does not of course mean that it is unsuccessful in all or indeed in most details. It is in no way denied that *Peer Gynt* in part contains great beauties, and in parts informs us – Norwegians and everybody – of a number of great truths; but beauties and truths are worth a good deal less than beauty and truth in the singular; and Ibsen's work is neither beautiful nor true.

> Hvis den franske Romantiks gamle, smukke Regel: 'Det Hæslige er det Skjønne' virkeligholdt Stik, da vilde 'Peer Gynt' være Skjønhedsværk, men hvis denne Regel er en Smule tvivlsom, saa er Ibsens nye Arbeide totalt forfeilet. At der er *totalt* forfeilet vil naturligviis ikke sige, at det er mislykket i alle eller endog i de fleste Enkeltheder; hermed skal paa ingen Maade være benægtet, at 'Peer Gynt' deels indeholder store Skjønheder, deels siger os Alle og Normændene især nogle store Sandheder; men Skjønheder og Sandheder ere langt mindre værd end Skjønhed og Sandhed i Enkelttal, og Ibsens Digt er hverken skjønt eller sandt...[7]

Later, when his immediate anger had subsided, Ibsen tried in a few lines in a letter to Brandes (15 July 1869, HU, XVI, pp.251ff.) to give a more sober account of his own views on 'truth' and 'beauty':

> Concerning those particular parts of *Peer Gynt*, I cannot agree with you. Naturally I bow to the laws of beauty, but I don't worry about the rules. You mention Michelangelo; in my opinion, nobody has sinned more against the rules of beauty than he; but everything he has created is nevertheless beautiful; for it is characterful. Raphael's art has never actually fired me; his figures have their home before the Fall; and in any case, Mediterranean man has different aesthetic values from us. He wants formal beauty; for us, even the formally un-beautiful can be beautiful by virtue of its inherent truth.

> Angaaende de visse Partier af 'Peer Gynt' kan jeg ikke være enig med Dem; jeg bøjer mig naturligvis for Skjønhedens Love; men dens Vedtægter bryder jeg mig ikke om. De nævner Michel Angelo; efter min Mening har ingen syndet mere mod Skjønheds-Vedtægterne end netopp han; men alt, hvad han har skabt, er skjønt aligevel; thi det er

> karakterfuldt. Rafaels Kunst har egentlig aldrig varmet mig; hans Skikkelse hører hjemme før Syndefaldet; og overhovedet, Sydboen har en anden Æstetik end vi; han vil det formelt skjønne; for os kan selv det formelt uskjønne være skjønt i Kraft af den iboende Sandhed.

The longer term consequences of these upsets were more profound. All this nugatory abstract argument about truth and beauty had nevertheless begun to face him with what was a very real and personal problem: whether the relationship between *what* he felt he now had to say and the medium he had chosen to say it in was the right one. He began to wonder whether the sheer facility with which the verse had come to him did not represent a danger signal, and may even have been detrimental to his achievement. Three short years after it appeared, he was calling *Peer Gynt* 'reckless'; and on 30 April 1892, writing to Edmund Gosse, he repeated the term: 'How far you will find pleasure in it (*Peer Gynt*), I don't know. It is wild and formless, recklessly written in a way that I could only dare to write while far from home' (Hvorvidt De vil finde behag i den, ved jeg ikke. Den er vild og formløs, hensynsløst skrevet, således, som jeg kun turde vove at skrive langt borte fra hjemmet. HU, XVII, pp.41f.).

Much later in life, in conversation with William Archer, Ibsen recalled the circumstances of those days:

> He wrote *Brand* and *Peer Gynt* (which appeared with only a year's interval between them) at very high pressure, amounting to nervous overstrain. He would go on writing verses all the time, even when asleep or half awake. He thought them capital for the moment; but they were the veriest nonsense. Once or twice he was so impressed with their merit that he rose in his night-shirt to write them down; but they were never of the slightest use... 'It is much easier', he (Ibsen) said, 'to write a piece like *Brand* or *Peer Gynt* than to carry through a severely logical (*konsekvent*) scheme, like that of John Gabriel Borkman, for example.'

Although his letters from these years make it clear that he had by no means abandoned his Julian project, Ibsen nevertheless found himself side-tracked in the winter of 1868-69 into writing *The League of Youth*, a polemical drama *à la Scribe* aimed directly at those of his contemporaries back in Scandinavia who had infuriated him by their mindless condemnation of *Peer Gynt*. Thereafter, he began assiduously to augment his collection of historical material; and during the summer months of 1869 he gave himself energetically to this task. But once again distractions obtruded. First he began making notes for a 'drama of contemporary life', which if it had materialised would probably have been something not unlike the later *Pillars of Society*; then he spent a number of anguished months selecting from his existing lyric and narrative poems – a task which he described as 'a cursed piece of work'.

The publication of his *Poems* in 1871 can now be seen also as a symbolic act. He had spent several strenuous and draining months preparing the manuscript, selecting and amending and arranging works written at many different periods and times over the previous twenty or more years. Having to re-live all those earlier attitudes and states of mind, most of which he had now completely outgrown and even wholly repudiated, had given him much mental torment. The task had exacerbated his current mood of anguished self-examination and analysis; and it also, fatefully as it happened, forged an inseparable connection in his mind between those earlier discarded values and beliefs and the medium of verse. It was now as though he was anxious to draw a line under this phase of his career and put it behind him. Apart from one or two additional poems which were then later incorporated into the second edition of 1874, Ibsen virtually wrote no more verse for the rest of his life.

Even more significant, however, is the fact that this revisionary self-examination coincided with a new and heightened awareness on his part of impending change of the most fundamental kind. The idea had taken firm root in his mind that some profound shift in the whole course of human destiny was imminent; that the moment was one of those rare transitional periods in history when the world was about to change direction, was ready to repudiate its past and embark on the exploration and the revaluation of its established values, to adopt new systems, new concepts, new modes of thought.

From 1870 onwards, Ibsen's letters, – especially those to Georg Brandes – began to carry phrases of enormous portentousness. Again and again in his correspondence he returned to this sense of present crisis. Sweepingly, he asserted his belief that the whole human race was on the wrong track, and that the existing state of affairs was untenable. He asserted the relativity of all received truths, the impermanence of all religious, moral and artistic values, and the need to give new meaning to old concepts. He anticipated the early collapse of many existing institutions and the abolition of statehood as consequences of the mortal combat which he saw taking place between two epochs, between – as he put it – yesterday and today. Nothing – not even the most immutable seeming of truths – could be exempt from scrutiny: 'Who will vouch for it that two and two do not make five up on Jupiter?' The situation required nothing less than what he called – in a letter to Brandes of 20 December 1870 – 'a revolution of the human spirit':

> World events occupy a large part of my thoughts. The old illusory France is now smashed; as soon as the new *de facto* Prussia is also smashed, we shall have arrived with a single leap in a new and emergent age! And how the old ideas will come crashing down about us! And not before time! ... The old concepts need a new content and new significance ... This is what the politicians will not recognise, and that is why I hate them. They only want specialist revolutions, superficial revolutions, in politics and the like. But that is only tinkering. What is needed is a revolution of the human spirit...

> Verdensbegivenhederne optager for øvrigt en stor del af mine tanker. Det gamle illusoriske Frankrig er slået istykker; når nu også det nye faktiske Preussen er slået istykker, så er vi med et spring inde i en vordende tidsalder. Hej, hvor indeerne da vil ramle rundt omkring os! Og det kan sandelig også være på tiden ... Begreberne trænger til et nyt indhold og en ny forklaring ... Dette er det, som politikerne ikke vil forstå, og derfor hader jeg dem. De mennesker vil kun specialrevolutioner, revolutioner i det ydre, i det politiske o. s. v. Men alt sligt er pilleri. Hvad det gjælder er menneskeandens revoltering... (HU, XVI, p.327)

This was the moment, it seems, when *Emperor and Galilean* began to take on a new and augmented significance for him. Previously one can well believe that it was the figure of the Apostate which had exerted the most immediate appeal to one who was himself engaged on a difficult and misunderstood apostasy; now, however, it was the historical circumstances of the age of Julian which began to preoccupy him. He came to see in those events of the 4th century AD a crisis of destiny in human affairs such as he was convinced mankind had reached in his own day. And the more he studied the signs in the contemporary scene, and the deeper he pushed into his dramatic material, the closer the relevance between the two epochs seemed to him to be. In October 1872, when he was halfway through the composition of *Emperor and Galilean*, he wrote to Edmund Gosse that the historical subject he had chosen had a much closer connection with the movements of the contemporary age than one might at first imagine; a year later and he went so far as to say that the course of recent events in Europe had made his drama even more timely than he himself had thought possible.

Many years later, in an after-dinner speech at a banquet in Stockholm on 24 September 1887, Ibsen returned to this whole question; he declared his continuing belief that the contemporary age marked an ending, and that something new was about to be born from it:

> I believe that the time is not far off when political and social conceptions will cease to exist in their present forms, and that from both of them there will arise a unity, which for a while will contain within itself the conditions for the happiness of mankind.
>
> I believe that poetry, philosophy and religion will be merged in a new category and become a new vital force, of which we who are living now can have no clear conception.
>
> ... Specifically and more particularly, I believe that the ideals of our time, whilst disintegrating, are tending towards what in my play *Emperor and Galilean* I designated 'the third empire'.

> Jeg tror at det nu ret snart forestår en tid, da det politiske begrep og det sociale begrep vil ophøre at existere i de nuværende former og at der ud af dem begge vil vokse sammen en enhed, som foreløpig bærer betingelserne for menneskehedens lykke i sig.
>
> Jeg tror at poesi, filosofi og religion vil smelte sammen til en ny kategori og til en ny livsmagt, som vi nu levende for øvrigt ikke kan have nogen klarere forestilling om...
>
> Navnlig og nærmere bestemt tror jeg at vor tids idealer, i det de går til grunde, tenderer imod det, jeg i mit drama 'Kejser og Galilæer' har antydet ved betegnelsen 'det tredje riget'. (HU, XV, pp.410ff.)

And there, at last, we have it: that evocative and latterly doom-laden phrase – in Norwegian 'det tredje riget', in English 'the third empire/realm', in German 'das dritte Reich' – a concept which, despite the semantic pollution it suffered in the third decade of this twentieth century, has a long and significant history. In Ibsen's drama it is made a central theme, with a total freight of encoded significance which takes one very near the threshold of tolerance.

When the concept of 'the third empire' first enters the play – in Act III – it is interpreted by the mystic Maximos in terms which are almost pure Joachism as we know it from history. It will be remembered that the 12th century Abbot Joachim of

Fiore identified three realms: the first being that of God the Father and the Old Testament, covering the period from Adam to Christ; the second being that of Christ and the New Testament, and destined to end as the first realm had done and be superceded by the third, that of the Holy Ghost. And Joachim's calculations had told him that this third realm was imminent. In the play, Julian finds that neither the degenerate Hellenism of the pagan community nor the degenerate Christianity of the court at Constantinople hold out any promise of fulfilment, so he seeks guidance about his true mission from Maximos the mystic. Thereupon, at a seance, a Voice tells him – with traditional oracular ambiguity – that his task is to 'establish the empire' (Du skal grundfæste riget).

The gloss which Maximos then puts on it in this imagined 4th century situation seems a clear invocation of the 12th century Joachim:

> There are three empires ... First, that empire which was founded on the tree of knowledge; then that empire which was founded on the tree of the cross ... The third is the empire of the great mystery, the empire which shall be founded on the tree of knowledge and the tree of the cross together, because it hates and loves them both, and because it has its living springs under Adam's grove and Golgotha.

> Der er tre riger ... Først er hint rige, som grundlagdes pa kundskabens træ; så hint rige, der grundlagdes pa korsets træ ... Det tredje er den store hemmeligheds rige, som skal grundlægges på kundskabens og på korsets træ tilsammen, fordi det hader og elsker dem begge, og fordi det har sine levende kilder under Adams lund og under Golgotha.

Maximos is thus made to serve as the spokesman for a recognisably orthodox trinitarian doctrine of history, based on the identification of three realms, in the third of which lies the promise of fruition. What Ibsen has in common with the historical Joachim is a disinclination or inability to define very precisely the specific nature ofthe future ideal era, and leaves its general nature to be vaguely divined by reference to the two empires which it supercedes. Where Ibsen differs from Joachim, however, is that in his account the two first realms – which alone can determine what the third realm is to be – undergo significant changes of identity as the action of the play progresses. Specifically, for the early Julian the first two empires are clearly identified as those of Dionysos and Christ; for the later Julian, the two empires take on the identity of the temporal power of the Roman Empire and the spiritual force of the Christian church. Sometimes other – more abstract – dualities seem to represent the two opposing worlds, conceived not as successive entities but as elements unendingly co-existent in time, from the interaction of which an as yet undefined 'third empire' is to emerge: freewill and necessity; the spirit and the flesh; the imperatives of duty and the pursuit of happiness. With so many legitimate pretenders in the course of the play to the first and second realms, the third realm inevitably becomes in this play something dauntingly polymorphous. This proliferation of reference has also, as a by-product, resulted in the recruitment by criticism (with varying degrees of success) of almost any thinker from the past whose patterns of thought were in any degree triadic as a mediator here in the search for meaning in the play: Lessing, for example, and Schiller and Hegel and Kierkegaard.

It is neither fitting nor feasible that I should attempt here any wider examination of its multiple functions within the play, its many manifestations, different semantic levels and planes of meaning. Instead I limit myself to isolating for brief comment one particular aspect of its multi-faceted life: that aspect which most nearly concerns the chosen theme of this paper.

Let us take the first three acts. In Act I Julian finds the atmosphere of the Christian court at Constantinople unwholesome and unacceptable; he experiences the hypocrisies and indeed cruelties of a Christianity becoming ever more degenerate; so that when a vision seems to command him to leave the city and do intellectual battle in the stronghold of the heathen, he departs gratefully. In the Athens of Act II, the corruption which has infected those who adhere to the older paganism is no less dispiriting; Julian seeks to live the joyous Dionysian life, but is sickened by the contrast between what he feels was the ancient beauty of pagan sin and the merely sordid practices of the present So that when he moves in Act III to seek wisdom in a life outside these confines, in some new revelation, the drama is seen as having prepared us for a 'third empire' which will supercede the realms of both Christ and Dionysos, and will transcend both hellenic sensuality and Galilean asceticism.

But when the moment arrives for Julian to articulate the lessons he has derived from his experiences in Constantinople and Athens, the terminology he adopts is arresting. As the supremely defining attribute of hellenic paganism, Julian selects 'beauty':

> Tell me, Basilios, why was pagan sin so beautiful? ... Wasn't Alcibiades beautiful when, aglow with wine, he stormed like a young god through the streets of Athens by night? Wasn't he beautiful in his defiance when he jeered at Hermes and hammered on people's doors? ... Wasn't Socrates beautiful in the symposium? And Plato and all the joyous revellers?...

> Sig mig, Basilios, hvor var den hedenske synd så skøn ... Var ikke Alkibiades skøn når han, hed af vin, som en ung gud stormed gennem Athens gader ved nattetid? Var han ikke skøn i sin trods, når han håned Hermes og hamred på borgernes døre ... Var ikke Sokrates skøn i symposiet? Og Platon og alle de glade svælgende brødre...

'Beauty' becomes a kind of single code-word, subsuming all the characteristic features of paganism in a single counter. The equivalent code-word in his vocabulary for Christianity is 'truth'. To the world he announces that his mission in leaving Constantinople was 'to uphold the truth of Christianity against the pagan lie' (...for at kæmpe imod den falske visdom – for at hævde den kristne sandhed imod hedenskabets løgn). It is therefore natural that his growing spiritual bewilderment presents itself to him in the form of a simple specific question: 'I often wonder whether truth is the enemy of beauty' (...så tænker jeg tidt på, om sandheden skulde være skønhedens fiende). And when, tersely, he sums up the reasons for his despair, his desperate need for some new revelation, he reaches out for his two code-words.

> The old beauty is no longer beautiful, and the new truth is no longer true.

> Den gamle skønhed er ikke længer skøn, og den nye sandhed ikke længer sand.

And at once those who can read the signs are aware that behind and beyond the more immediate ideological conflicts that beset Julian in his 4th century world there is another dialogue in progress. Ibsen here puts into the mouth of Julian a formulation which at once transposes a distant 4th century recognition into a contribution to mid-19th century aesthetic polemics. Julian's words silently reverberate with the hurt Ibsen felt at the insensitive Petersen review of *Peer Gynt* and Brandes's dismissal of the work as 'neither beautiful nor true'. No longer is he limited to the halting phrases of his letter to Brandes about the 'laws' and the 'rules' of beauty, in the course of which he found himself saying things like: '... The formally unbeautiful can be beautiful by virtue of its inherent truth'. Ibsen now enters the current debate in the one way he really felt competent to contribute: in the dramatic mode.

I have plucked out this one single strand from the enormously complicated weave of *Emperor and Galilean* to give some sort of indication of the obliquity of utterance to be found there. On the one hand we need to take seriously Ibsen's repeated assurance that there was in Julian's career much that echoed Ibsen's own inner anguish of these years; and equally, that the events of those remote 4th century days resonated strongly with what was happening in the late 19th century in Europe.

Emperor and Galilean is then seen to be an encoded declaration of the author's belief in the imminence of incommensurable change. As major components of this change, he identified fundamental shifts in one's understanding of what constituted 'truth' and 'beauty' and also consequently 'poetry', and in the prevailing ways of communicating them. By thus linking the quest for a new kind of truth and a new understanding of beauty with the leading concept of 'the third empire', Ibsen declared his belief that an essential constituent in the new age he so confidently predicted would be a new view of 'poetry', which for him meant above all dramatic poetry. The occasion for him was not one of merely negative apostasy; there was much more to it than the simple repudiation of the past, the de-idealisation of content and the de-ornamentation of dramatic language, so that – as he implies elsewhere in his letter to Lucie Wolf – the artist could not then dishonestly 'creep into the nooks and crannies of rhymed verse'. It was something much more positive, much more audacious, yet not easily defined except obliquely through the idiom of drama which was his natural mode of expression.

In both of his prognostications, Ibsen seems to have been proved right by events. Perhaps one would not wish to go with him to the extreme of pronouncing dramatic verse 'extinct' but – as Kenneth Muir points out – the best plays of the present century have been, and continue to be, written in prose, thus seeming to confirm Ibsen's prophecy that prose would be the principal dramatic medium of the future. Much more to the point, however, is that the new dramatic prose beginning with Ibsen is – if I may recall the phrases I used earlier from C. S. Lewis – prose of a new kind, almost in a new dimension, a prose dialogue which has led more than one Ibsen commentator to speak of the new creation as 'poetic drama in prose'.

As for the second: when Geoffrey Barraclough,[8] having identified what he calls the 'great divide' between the contemporary age and that long period of history running from the Renaissance to the age of Bismarck, examined the literature of the period, he found it remarkable that there were people at the time who seemed to be aware of the way things were moving, who sensed the unsettling impact of new forces, and whose perception that the world was moving into a new epoch was not simply an illusion. *Emperor and Galilean* was born of just such an apocalyptic vision; it was Ibsen's attempt to give expression to *his* sense of the 'great divide' as he felt it on his nerves, to embody it in a historical analogue. Disappointingly, it did not – some would say still *does* not – succeed in communicating its deeper meanings in the way Ibsen had intended. But it lies in his achievement to have detected this thing, to have responded to it, drawn attention to it, and by his own later practice, to have made a unique contribution towards its realisation.

Notes

1. This paper, together with an Opening Statement (here given only in paraphrase), was presented to the Seventh Burdick-Vary Symposium, held at the University of Wisconsin-Madison, 30-31 March 1984, on the theme of 'Preludes to Modernism: literature, art; music and thought in the period 1870 to 1914'.
2. 'Verse and prose', in *Contemporary Theatre*, Stratford upon Avon Studies, no.4, London, 1962, p.97.
3. References to Ibsen's works are to the *Hundreårsutgave*, ed. Bull, Koht and Seip (Oslo, 1928-1957), 22 vols.
4. See, for example, HU, XVI, p.371; XVII, p.66 and 73; XIX, p.229.
5. I consider these matters in rather more detail in the Introduction to *The Oxford Ibsen*, Vol.III (London, 1971).
6. Reprinted in Otto Hageberg (ed.), *Omkring 'Peer Gynt'* (Oslo, 1967), pp.40ff.
7. *Ibid.*, pp.50ff.
8. *An Introduction to Contemporary History* (London, 1964), p.17.

Originally published November 1984 (Vol. 23, No. 2).

Studies of Individual Plays

Love's Comedy

John Northam

A sentence or two in the *Oxford Ibsen*'s introduction to Volume II raises an interesting, perhaps fundamental, issue. On page 17, towards the end of his discussion of *Love's Comedy*, the editor writes:

> Thus, as Guldstad had forecast, three lives seem to be saved for happiness. Amid the laughter and cheers and singing at the end of the play, <u>the reason why the spectator is uneasy is that he knows from Ibsen's later plays</u> of the terror that lies in marriage between a Swanhild and a Guldstad ... <u>one recalls the terrible revenge Ibsen took in his later works</u> not merely on possessive, 'dolls house' marriages (such as that to Falk would probably have been), but also on loveless marriages; one thinks of the hollowness of all the other calculated, politic, socially arranged and financially inspired marriages, of the careers of Bernick and Mrs. Alving and Hedda Gabler and Borkman. <u>Only then does something of the true savagery of the irony in *Love's Comedy* become apparent</u>, making it impossible to share the view, often expressed, that Guldstad had somehow been given his author's endorsement.

The obvious qualifications that spring at once to mind (Haakon? Boletta?) are not the purpose of this essay. The fundamental issue is contained in the words which I have underlined in the quotation: how far can a critical method be justified which cannot find within the limits of the work under discussion the material for reaching a judgement about that particular work – not about its place in Ibsen's developing thought or technique, but about *Love's Comedy* itself? How reasonable is it to suggest that no spectator or reader in 1863 could hope to understand the true drift of the play because Ibsen had not yet written the plays from *Pillars of Society* onwards? The method implied by the quotation seems to suggest that a critic is entitled to bring to the consideration of a play (or of any form of literature – the issue is a general one) a set of pre-conceptions based upon material that exists outside the work itself; and that this material may be used, not to corroborate a judgement already firmly established by close analysis of the work in question, but as an essential prerequisite to any proper understanding at all. Mr McFarlane's admirable clarity of expression allows no doubt about his procedure: 'Only then (sc. after one has recalled the later plays) does something of the true savagery of the irony become apparent'.

This procedure seems to me so unpalatable that I have attempted an alternative: in this tentative essay I propose to limit my attention to the structure of the play itself.

The curtain rises on a charming set – cheerful but significantly divided:

> *... A beautiful garden, irregularly but tastefully laid out; the fjord and the outlying islands can be seen in the background. To the left of the spectator is the main building, with a*

> *veranda and above it an open window; to the right, in the foreground, an open*
> *summerhouse with benches and a table. The scene is bathed in the vivid light of late*
> *afternoon. It is early summer; the fruit trees are in blossom.*

To the left, appropriately on the veranda of the house, sit a group of ladies sedately occupied; to the right, in the less formal setting of the summerhouse, a group of men drink and sing in a Gather ye Rosebuds vein; Svanhild sits pointedly alone in the background between these two groups. Domesticity, masculine freedom, and a remote individuality poised between the two – this much is suggested by the set.

It soon appears that for most of the men masculine freedom is an illusion. Falk, the singer of the song, is the only one of genuine independence. Styver, once a poet, is poet no longer; is no longer even a lover, since he has become officially engaged. Guldstad has enjoyed the song, but being older condemns the moral. Lind seems to sympathize with Falk, but only as a follower.

The difference between Falk and the women shows clearly enough; they side with prudence and domesticity, and are on the whole uneasy at Falk's doctrine. The difference of outlook between the women and Falk has generated little heat so far; things warm up, however, when he moves away from his group and goes over to speak, like the aggressor that he is, directly against the women – he leans on the veranda rails and asks them for a potentially tragic boon. To inspire his poetry truly, he asks to be granted a great sorrow:

> Give me – if only for a month on loan –
> a harrowing, overwhelming, crushing sorrow,
> and all my poems would palpitate with joy.
> Or best of all, let me but fmd a bride,
> to be my all, my light, my sun, my God! ...
> You mustn't think that my intention was
> to take her to the funfair on my arm;
> [no, in midst of happiness's wild pursuit of joy,
> depart she must to eternity's primeval home.][1]
> I need a course of spiritual gymnastics,
> and perhaps that would be the way to get it.

The seriousness is, of course, offset by the levity of that ending, but the episode does set up a tragic resonance which is not allowed to die away unnoticed. Svanhild preserves and indeed amplifies it by challenging Falk's prayer; she wishes him exactly the sorrow for which he has just asked. Then she joins the ladies, having apparently taken sides in the conflict, yet in fact managing to preserve her unexplained aloofness in their midst by remaining 'cold and mute' to her mother's reproof. Something in her may fight against Falk, but something responds to his spiritual aloofness. Falk retreats back into the garden, away from the house – Ibsen is beginning to use the stage set to help characterize the values to which the characters incline.

The distinction between conventional, domestic comfort and the poetic ecstasy ofFalk begins to take on a more sombre significance when the talk turns to a spectacular example of domestic degradation – Pastor Strawman. His saga serves as a chilly warning to young lovers, and lowers the temperature of the play. We realize from this that Falk has indeed some grounds for serious discontent with the life that surrounds him – his revolt is not flippant merely or wanton. The depth of his discontent is revealed in his interview with Svanhild, which also reveals that for all her earlier impatience with him, she shares his feelings.

Falk asks Svanhild to change her name, because it is 'much too great, and strong, and stern, these days'. Svanhild's reply speaks for both of them:

> Yes, now we have a different set of virtues.
> Who is prepared to fight for truth these days?
> Who is content to stand or fall alone?
> Where are the knights of old?[2]

Their sentiments are generous and noble, but it is noticeable that they remain sentiments only. For all his talk, Falk has yet to .demonstrate his heroism in action. Something holds him back and prompts Svanhild to see him as 'like two different people that can't agree'. Indeed his only drastic action turns out to be unheroic, brutal and shocking: in a fit of poetical egotism, he kills Svanhild's favourite songbird as a petulant retaliation for the death of his own 'young, confident faith', killed in him by what he supposes to be Svanhild's engagement to Lind – it is, of course, her sister Anna who is so engaged. Whatever the provocation, Falk's action is unforgivable, and remains in the memory to cloud our attitude towards his exigent idealism.

This scene, then, which has revealed the common discontent of Falk and Svanhild as a yearning for the heroic in modern life, has deepened the tone of the play very considerably. Ibsen provides an accompanying touch of sombreness by darkening the set – it is now twilight for the revelation of domestic degradation in its full horror. Styver's obsession with money is presented more brutally now, and Pastor Strawman's arrival on stage (even with only eight of his twelve daughters in tow) makes a greater impact than did the mere narration of his story; the conventional hubbub over Lind's engagement to Anna seems to degrade the occasion – all these implied impediments to great action drive Falk into deeper isolation: he is left alone, appropriately, in a garden that has grown '*quite dark*', excluded from the lighted domesticity of the house. He speaks now with genuine and justified bitterness:

> All, all burnt out and dead... unrelieved squalor... !
> This is the way we go through life; in couples,
> [they huddle together like black tree-trunks
> left by a forest fire on the desolate plain...][3]
> nothing but ashes as far as eye can see...
> oh, is there no green life left anywhere!

(Svanhild comes out on to the veranda with a flowering rose tree.)

The symbolism attaching to Svanhild's entry is, of course, manifest; but it should not be passed over too quickly. We should notice that Svanhild is symbolized by a potplant and not by any wild bloom; and this fits in well enough with her persistent association with the house. For all her aloofness and all her sympathy with Falk, she is none the less involved in a way that he is not with the facts of domesticity. She shares Falk's horror of the degradation they see all about them, but she recognizes, from her own experience, how difficult it is to break away and become a rebel.

Falk assails her passionately and proposes highly undomestic love to her, love on very temporary terms. He accepts that his love must die; he makes no pretence of lifelong devotion. He claims the intensity of the moment for his own ends, to become thereby a poet. The egotism is attractive, but ruthless; and by reviving the imagery of the songbird in his speech Ibsen makes sure that we condemn the ruthlessness.

Svanhild rejects not the ruthlessness in him but the weakness.[4] If he indeed depends upon her love for inspiration, then he is less a falcon than a pitifully tethered paper kite. She urges him to action:

> let this day be for you a new beginning;
> go onwards by the strength of your own wings,
> let them sustain you, or else let you down.
> Writing a poem down on paper is
> something belonging within study walls,
> while only living deeds belong to life,
> and only they bear upwards to the heights;

They are still separated in this: Falk believes in the idea; Svanhild, reluctantly but firmly, in the fact. Svanhild retires once more towards the house, Falk remains in the garden while the song that opened the Act is sung offstage. Ibsen is repeating the terms of the dilemma, the facts of life versus idealism; but by now he has implied an interim judgement. Svanhild has been so much the more mature of the two; it is the immaturity of Falk that Ibsen leaves us with to end the Act. Stung by Svanhild's contempt, Falk determines to act; but there is something comically inadequate in his request to Guldstad to 'point out a goal for me – a mighty goal'; and something genuinely corrective in the answer: 'have a go at living'. This Falk agrees to do. From tomorrow he will create his poetry out of deeds. His final decision is to commit himself, to conform after all to the conventional usages he has so long long despised, so that he can fight society on its own terms:

> tomorrow, Svanhild, we shall be engaged.

Falk is not capitulating – the song of freedom reminds us of his ideals. Coming as it does from the fjord, it also reminds us that Falk, for all his talk, has performed within the safe and limited territory of a suburban garden. He has not ventured far. As the curtain falls, we feel that his search for freedom, for all his confident talk, has barely begun.

Falk's decision to move into society is reflected in the set of Act II; the scene is crowded with visitors, all the visual interest is focused in the veranda and the house, the song of freedom that ended Act I is counterbalanced by a song in a very different mode:

Welcome into our happy band
    now that your troth is plighted!

The social pressures are much heavier. We see them at work on Lind and Anna now that they have become officially engaged. Falk, more lonely than ever through the loss of his old companion, looks on this vulgar celebration as the murder of love, yet, for all that, the scene is cheerful enough – it is still a fine summer afternoon.[5]

Not that the implications of the set are enough to belie Falk. He is quite right to be indignant; social pressure is no joke. Lind and Anna are soon bludgeoned by it into renouncing his proposed career as a missionary, and already Lind's fine ecstasy of love is clouding over with thoughts of the future. Falk is witnessing, at close quarters, the effects of society upon a love so like his own in inception.

Falk symbolically renounces isolation by destroying the hideout he has shared with Lind (another purely destructive gesture, we note), and at last carries out in deed his promise to fight society on its own ground. He does so from the physical midst of society, for Ibsen places him on the veranda, amongst the gossiping guests, to deliver his attack.

Marriage, he says, is like cheap tea – a cause remnant of something that was originally delicate and fine. But he soon drops the graceful conceit, and attacks marriage directly as mere loveless habit. He exploits Strawman's unfortunate distinction between children of love[6] and children of marriage, and finally so upsets the gathering that he is asked to leave the house.

Supported by Svanhild, Falk decides to go further than denunciation. He proposes to act by living according to his own standards still, but in the midst of ordinary people in society:

right in the middle of life's tumult stands
the great church, where the truth shall ring out clear...
that little private pact between myself
and heaven is broken off; I'll not write poetry
within four walls; I'll live it in the open,
and fight my battle in the light of day...
my future lies along the beaten track
of customary usage, bound about
by every sort of prejudice and convention;
there like the others, I'll take my abode,
and place my ring on my beloved's fmger!
...Yes, and we'll show the world
that love has not yet lost its power, that love
can face the dull and grinding weekday round
and still remain stainless and undismayed...

Falk, we note, has changed; he now sees love, not as something momentary, solitary, outside society, but as something more durable even than social institutions, as something, in fact, that is immutable. Svanhild accepts his new offer of this new love. But the very immutability, in a play permeated with the seasonal imagery of nature, fills us with suspicion. Svanhild herself revives the imagery:

> Take me then as I am, I'm yours! The trees
> are putting out their leaves, and Spring is here!

With '*gay confidence*' she throws herself into his arms; but we are left wondering how their love is to enjoy a permanence denied to the rest of nature. Are they yet facing the facts?

The set of Act III differs markedly from all previous sets:

> *Evening and clear moonlight. Coloured lamps decorate the trees. In the background are tables laid with bottles of wine, glasses, cakes, etc. All the windows of the house are lit up, and from the inside are heard piano-playing and song during the scene that follows. Svanhild is standing by the veranda. Falk enters jom the right with some books and a portfolio under his arm. A servant follows him with a trunk and a portmanteau.*

The initial distinction is still implied, between the freedom of the garden and the domesticity of the house – Svanhild and Falk seem very isolated out there; but it is to be noticed that the garden itself has become, as it were, domesticated. It is hung with coloured lights; it has become part of the gregarious party spirit that dominates the scene. If there remains an element of genuine and now much more austere aloofness, it is provided by the clear moonlight that shines over all.

It is not essentially at variance with his intention to live a life of freedom within the ambit of society that Falk is about to leave this house and this garden – if we consider the situation realistically, he is merely going to find new digs; but it is disturbing to hear him, with this ambition in his heart, talking in imagery of complete isolation. Falk talks of himself as a solitary wanderer across the desert. His basic attitude towards life does not seem, after all, to have changed. There is, too, something chilling, in view of the shocking petulance of Act I when he killed the bird, in his reference to Svanhild as 'my songbird, sent by God to me alone!' It is his old ruthless egotism and not his new decision to live in society that is being emphasized here. And it finds an answering voice in Svanhild, who harbours a similar sense of loneliness:

> I was a stranger in my mother's house,
> I was alone, imprisoned in myself...

There is more than a touch of self-consciousness in her pity for Anna, 'child of the gay world' – to be pitied, not because of the dull prudentiality that seelp.s likely to control all her action in married life, but because she will have so many friends with whom to share her soul, instead of being able, like Svanhild, to pledge it all to one alone. This uneasy note of self-pride (or is it self-pity?) is summed up by Falk:

> Yes, it is you and I, the friendless ones,
> who possess happiness, life's richest treasure.
> We who stand outside in the silent night
> watching the gaiety through the window panes.

Cemented together by these common feelings,

> We'll be together and our life shall be
> a hymn to celebrate love's victory.

It comes as a sub-comic shock – though not as a complete surprise – to find, after these large affirmations, that Falk jibs at Svanhild's suggestion that they should start meeting society on its own ground by announcing their engagement; another sign of their real unwillingness to face society that they should scuttle away like guilty children when Svanhild's mother appears on the scene.

This skirmishing cannot be allowed to go on. will Falk do as he says and outface society? If so, how? Or will he continue to shun it? Since Svanhild is involved in his decision, her fate, too, demands to be clarified. Ibsen forces Falk to face society for the final showdown. He faces Strawman first.

It is a damaging attack that Strawman makes, for all his manifest absurdities. He ceases to be a clerical clown and becomes an eloquent preacher when he talks about home.

> ... My home –
> Mr. Falk! do you know what that word means?
> FALK: (*shortly*) I never had a home.

Home life, even Strawman's home life, is described by Ibsen in a spirit far removed from simple contempt:

> For every dream that perished in the strife,
> for every feather that broke in the storm,
> a little miracle was brought to life,
> and I returned thanks and praise to the Lord.

Beneath the social scarecrow there is some genuine feeling about family life.

The second confrontation is with Styver. We are by now so familiar with his prudential worries about money that we are surprised and impressed by his estimate of the purpose of his existence. He remains ridiculous and contemptible, of course; he merits Falk's confident lecture:

> I know that two can live their life together
> and still keep their enthusiasm fresh,
> their faith unsullied. Yours is the paltry dogma
> of a mean age: that the ideal comes second!

But Styver has a reply:

> No, it comes first; for its brief span is over
> like apple blossom's... once the fruit has set!

– and then, following up the implications of the imagery, he tries, in a moving fashion, to define the growth and development of love as he sees it:

> And when at last our love comes to an end,
> and dies away, to be reborn as friendship,
> that song will still bring back those former days.
> And though my back should grow bent at the desk,
> and though my toil should scarce suffice our needs,
> yet I'll return cheerfully to a home
> where music keeps alive fond memories.

> If there's an evening hour when we can share
> our peace... I'll never wish for any more!

This is sad, this is inadequate, but it is not contemptible. Falk seems to be unmoved, but Svanhild is not; she is '*pale and agitated*' though, it seems, merely by the deadliness of conventional ideas about marriage that she has just heard expressed.

Falk's comment on the episodes is not fair:

> Look at the priest,
> his wife, Lind, Styver – painted mummers all,
> truth in their mouths and lies within their hearts...
> and yet they're all of them quite decent people!
> They lie both to themselves and to each other,
> they're down and out, yet everyone imagines
> himself a Croesus, happy as a god:

This, we know, is simply not true. These people may normally play ignoble parts in the social comedy, but we have just had the privilege of hearing them speak without script; they do not imagine themselves Croesuses. Falk is trying to make out marriage to be more of a lie than it is.

Svanhild agrees with Falk, though now '*half afraid*'. We notice that she, too, in spite of her urging Falk to face society in action, now uses imagery of isolation:

> Oh, nothing is so easy as to follow
> the Bible's bidding, forsake hearth and home,
> and seek the love that leads forward to God.

At the same time she uses natural imagery that makes us question the possibility of the kind of durability that these two youngsters still hope to extort from their passion:

> How wonderful that a loving hand has guided
> my steps to our encounter in the spring

– an encounter which she believes is the prelude to a never-fading-love. But Falk himself, through the nature imagery again, reminds us of mutability:

> Then welcome, winter winds and bitter weather!

On what terms are these two to keep their private spring unchanged while the rest of nature changes all about them? They do not seem to see the difficulty fully, yet; but Ibsen has made sure that we do.

Falk's third confrontation is with Guldstad. Although he approaches from the house, with all the appearance of a man happily and fully domesticated in society, Guldstad confirms the impression made up from a number of trivial tokens of amicability that he is no clear-cut enemy of Falk's. His own youthful enthusiasms have not quite died. But his most startling contribution to the argument of the play is his suggestion that one antithesis (between poetry and life) has been false all along. Guldstad accepts the distinction between himself standing for 'sound, practical common sense' and Falk for 'youth and hope, and poetry', but he insists that his own plan is a form of poetry, too, in its own right – a poem in action, a factual poem.[7] His plan is to marry Svanhild himself.

As Guldstad speaks he demonstrates the basic decency, the maturity, by which he lives or plans to live. To begin with, his love for the girl is not a sudden infatuation:

> I've watched you grow, I've seen your spirit unfolding;
> everything I esteem in womankind
> I've found again in you.

In fact, he mistrusts love as the sole foundation for marriage. Love, he suggests, is a less reliable guide than marriage and betrothal:

> But love is blind; love chooses not a wife
> but a woman; and if she wasn't made
> to be a wife for you... Then you're done for.
> For a happy engagement is a matter
> not just of love, but of much else besides;
> of getting on well with the family,
> of sharing the same attitudes and tastes.
> And marriage? That's a veritable ocean
> of obligations and demands and claims
> that haven't very much to do with love...

The trouble with the Strawmans and the Styvers is not that their lives have been deficient in love, but that they have relied upon it too exclusively in their choice of mates. Marriage for love alone leads to bankruptcy. What Guldstad offers is more substantial:

> It is the quiet and warm-hearted flow
> of tender care, that can exalt its object
> as certainly as fevered adulation.
> It is a sense of happiness in duty,
> of fond solicitude, and domestic peace,
> of wills that each bow to the other's will,
> of watchfulness, that she may never hurt
> her foot against a stone, where she may go.
> It is a gentle hand to heal all wounds,
> a manly strength that bears with willing back,
> the even temper that outlasts the years,
> the arm that gives safety and firm support,
> All these things, Svanhild, I can offer you
> to build upon...

The *Oxford Ibsen* says that it is impossible to share the view that Guldstad has somehow been given his author's endorsement. If we confine our attention to what the play itself offers at this point, I doubt if we can resist the conclusion that Ibsen is presenting Guldstad's vision for, so far as it goes, approval. To that extent, Ibsen does endorse these views; but, as the play goes on to show, there are other views to be approved of simultaneously.

Having made his offer, Guldstad could not behave more honourably. He divests himself of all advantage. He leaves the way clear for Falk to make his own counter-proposal:

> I'm going in; let the game have an end.
> If you can swear, in honesty and faith,
> that you can offer her such true devotion,
> such firm support, such comfort in distress,
> as I can give her... well, so let it be;
> cancel the memory of what I said.
> I'll win a quiet victory all the same,
> for you will have won happiness, and that
> was what I wanted.

And then, to make the equality absolute and to silence a sneer from Falk, he proclaims his readiness to make over to them his fortune.

This offer, couched in terms as generous morally as financially, cannot be laughed off. Guldstad's intervention, as they both recognize, has dealt them the hardest blow. Life in marriage may be, for many, a sordid and degraded affair; but Guldstad has shown that it need not be so; at its best, it can offer fine things. It can, indeed, be poetry in action.

Falk's first response (its '*wild vehemence*' betrays his uneasiness) is to deny that what Guldstad has said can be true for them. But Svanhild begins to revert to her earlier sense of fact. She urges Falk not to deceive himself. She asks:

> And can you swear, solemnly, before God,
> that it (sc. your love) will never lose its fragrance and
> hang on like a withered flower? That it will last a lifetime?

This Falk cannot bring himself to swear. He knows, and she knows, that his love will not last as long as Guldstad's affection. They are faced with an alternative which they can no longer despise.

If the play ended here, Ibsen would be endorsing Guldstad's views in a very simple manner. Love would be discredited in comparison with affection based upon social loyalty. But Ibsen wants to endorse love, too.

The young couple accept Guldstad's definition of what he offers – there is no charge of duplicity or cynicism. But they suddenly perceive that, even though they cannot hope to live out an eternity of love, they can none the less win an eternity for their special, ecstatic love by breaking it off now. Svanhild announces firmly that she is not fit to be Falk's wife, but she has the vision to see that the deathless memory of their perfect love, whose great renunciation she has forced him to accept, has turned him into a genuine poet:

> My duty's done!
> I've filled your soul with light and poetry!
> Fly up! I've kindled you to victory.

What she had prayed for in Act I has come to pass: Falk has won himself a bride only to lose her for ever.[8] He has had his spiritual gymnastics. Their love can do less, but also more, than affection can ever generate.

It is, of course, a moment of achievement and sacrifice at once, of joy and grief:

Fly up ! I've kindled you to victory...
and my swan song is sung!

(*She takes off the ring and puts it to her lips.*)

And you, my dream,
dive down among the reeds of the salt sea
for ever! ... I'll sacrifice you instead.
...Now, Falk, I have renounced you for this life...
but I have won you for eternity!

At long last, these young people have come to recognize the truth of what Guldstad had tried to tell them, that there is more than one kind of poetry. Svanhild has always insisted upon poetry in action; now Falk himself declares that action itself, even in society, can become poetry:

every man's a poet
Whether in government, or school, or church,
whether his calling's glorious or lowly,
who in his work expresses the ideal.
Yes, I go upwards; the winged steed is saddled;
I know you have ennobled my whole life.

Ibsen is not endorsing either type of poetry to the exclusion of the other, he is endorsing both; the sorrow of the play resides in the impossibility of enjoying both together; the comedy in the fact that everybody enjoys something.

Appropriately enough, since Ibsen has so endorsed both of these antithetical values, the picture of social life that we are left with by the last scene of the play is above all cheerful; when the ordinary folk throng back on to the stage, they are themselves gleeful youngsters full of the carnival spirit. And, of course, the reader of the play has to remember that the set is still the cheerfully lighted garden and the illuminated house. The *Oxford Ibsen* is surely mistaken in suggesting that it is the depressed and degraded domesticateds who dominate the stage at this point; the visitors are specifically designated as '*the younger guests*' who come out '*amidst laughter and gaiety*' to dance 'a dance of fresh spring flowers, sweetly blowing' out there in the colourful garden. Ibsen refuses to leave us with a gloomy picture of life in society.

It is true that what we have seen persuades us that for many this youthful ecstasy must be shortlived, and that for many the outcome will be just that degradation that Strawman and company remind us of when they return to the stage to crow over the defeat, as they see it, of their dangerous enemy; but Guldstad remains to persuade us that theirs is not an essential compromise – something finer can come out of ordinary life and ordinary relationships:

Something has surely died within her soul;
but what still lives, I shall restore and heal.

At this point, Svanhild calmly, though sadly, accepts him, making this condition only, that they should remove from the neighbourhood.

Now that the issues have become dearly recognized as the choice between two different kinds of poetry, the denouement can be dear-cut and decisive. Once Falk recognizes that his particular kind of poetic idealism can never accommodate itself to permanent relationships, he abandons his attempt to reconcile it with life in society, and for the first time moves out of the cramping confines of the now domesticated garden into the dear moonlight and into the greater freedom of the fjords. It is no easy decision; he smiles and weeps together, so that Lind can say:

> You seem to have two different faces

He will be a singer of mingled joy and sorrow now; his gain will be his loss, but his loss, gain. Ibsen endorses the need for his sacrifice, the need for strenuous, uncompromising idealism even though it makes impossible the normal satisfactions oflife.

In spite of his mixed feelings, Falk is predominantly relieved to see his way dear; Guldstad is quietly happy; only in Svanhild is there genuine sorrow. She at last accepts the inevitable and uses the imagery of nature to express her condition:

> Now I must put my outdoor life aside;[9]
> the leaves are falling; let the world receive me.

She has been offered a choice between an ecstasy that cannot endure, and an affection that can. She would have both, but has chosen affection. Her choice has been free, and it was her own; her sadness comes from the impossibility of having both together.

This incompatibility is what Ibsen reinforces at the fmal curtain by making the music of the house party dash with the defiant song of the departing students and Falk.

If the spectator feels, as the *Oxford Ibsen* suggests, uneasy at the end of the play, it should not be because he feels that he has been called upon (ironically) by Ibsen to subscribe to sentiments which he cannot, on reflection, stomach – to side with Guldstad, or to agree that three lives have been saved for happiness. The spectator should feel the uneasiness appropriate to his sense of being presented, scrupulously, with two equally valid points of view, with two sets of values at once equally essential to the good life, yet incompatible. The play insists that we appreciate the value of Falk's passionate idealism, but also of those basic social virtues which idealism necessarily infringes but without which life is unlivable. The correct uneasiness is a response to Ibsen's own uneasiness as he contemplated the human situation of his time. He cannot see in *Love's Comedy*, he cannot see in his later plays, how to reconcile these conflicting claims, but neither can he see how he can renounce either one firmly in favour of the other. This is the problem that obsesses him throughout his working life; a problem that he never presumes to solve, merely to understand and illuminate. It is indicative that Ibsen covers the same ground in his maturity in *Lady from the Sea* still with the same scrupulous, tantalizing, perceptive ambiguity.

* * *

Now comes the time for reservations – the kind of reservations that one would expect to have to make about any play written so early in a dramatist's career and the first of its kind – *Love's Comedy* being Ibsen's first serious attempt at a modern drama.

My own sense of uneasiness about the weakness of the play is strongest when I consider one of the main antitheses on which it is founded: the antithesis between Love and Marriage. For if I subtract from Love, as the play insists that we should, all those qualities that it attaches exclusively to Marriage: affection, loyalty, devotion, self-sacrifice, durability – then I do not understand what Love can stand for. An overwhelming passion which can inspire poetry but cannot sustain a relationship with others, which cannot fight against material circumstances or contemplate its translation through the course of nature into something less intense but still valuable? Falk's love seems to me to be a merely theoretical emotion.

But, of course, Falk is moved not only by Love but also by poetry and a desire for the ideal, and the play makes better sense if we see him primarily as an idealist whose idealism happens to express itself partly through love;[10] the prime antithesis in the play then becomes that between the claim of the Ideal and the claims of Society. Put in these terms, we can see that this conflict, treated always with scrupulous sympathy towards both sides, offered as experience and not as judgement, explored with an open-mindedness that allows Ibsen to endorse both sets of values – this is the great formulation that served Ibsen throughout his maturity as a tragic poet of modern life. There is indeed a connexion between *Love's Comedy* and Ibsen's later plays; *Love's Comedy* contains the seed of the later plays more copiously than any other of the early plays. *Love's Comedy* throws light on the later plays, not they on it.

Another reservation that suggests itself concerns not a weakness in formulation so much as a lack of penetration. *Love's Comedy* contains a passage that has always fascinated me. Falk says to Strawman in Act III:

> FALK: (*humorously*) You mean you'll meet the justice you deserve.
> There is a Nemesis that walks through life;
> it may be slow, but it's enexorable,
> and no man can escape the fate it brings.
> If you have sinned against the high idea,
> (.../...) you must take the consequences.

This is impressive because it seems to show that even in this early work Ibsen has managed to formulate that concept of Nemesis in modern life that makes his plays tragedies rather than mere problem plays. In fact, when the lacuna is filled, the passage suggests a disturbing frivolity towards the concept:

> If you have sinned against the high idea,
> the press, its ever-watchful guardian, will
> speak out – and you must take the consequences.

The let-down – Nemesis equals the press – is breathtaking. It makes one realize that in this play at least Ibsen is not taking Nemesis seriously – perhaps cannot even see how there could seriously be a Nemesis at work in modern society. And indeed one of the marks of this play's immaturity is its lack of a sense of the way in which the past acts upon the present. The point deserves a little elaboration.

It is true that we are given tiny hints of the past when we hear that Falk has never known a home and that Svanhild has always felt a solitary in her parental home, but they are hints that are not developed and which do not enter into the dynamics of the play. One could put the matter simply by saying that Falk is potentially a Gregers Werle and Svanhild an Ellida, and leave the implied comparisons to make their point. The characters in this play remain virtually untouched by their pasts.

This is also true of Guldstad, though in a different way. Guldstad is a man of wealth, but he shows none of the signs of what the acquisition of wealth means to the character of a man. Again, a comparison or two is useful – in Bernick and in Borkman particularly Ibsen showed that he knew what concentration and sacrifice were required. In Guldstad there is no hint of these frustrations; he is so simply amiable that one cannot understand how he came to be rich. Guldstad has no past, and in consequence has no effective present. He is an embodiment rather than a person.

This lack of a sense of Nemesis concerns the future, too; Ibsen is able to turn this play into comedy because he does not seriously contemplate the effects that these various sacrifices and frustrations will have upon the future personalities of Falk and Svanhild. Falk is liberated into an uncomplicated future of idealistic and ecstatic freedom; we are not asked to consider whether he will, in the long run, turn out to be a second Rubek. Svanhild will be sad but content with her chosen life, no second Irene. Ibsen confines his vision in point of time.

To ignore the depth of time, the endlessness of the dialectic between past, present, and future, is to ignore, or to fail to see, the full size of the obstacle in the way of human happiness. And to do that is to diminish the size of the heroism needed to face that obstacle. Just as it lacks a sense of Nemesis, so the play fails to present a convincing portrait of modern heroism.

Svanhild, in Act I, asks the question to which I conceive Ibsen's later plays to be answers:

Who is prepared to fight for truth these days?
Who is content to stand or fall alone?
Where are the heroes?

A question which we could well put to this play. Where are its heroes?

Present in not much more than name alone, is the answer. 'Svanhild' is clearly used for its heroic connotations, and 'Falk', though lacking in such richness of reference, is heroic enough, but beyond that these characters are not faced, because of Ibsen's limitation of perspective, by any situation big enough, mysterious, compelling, eneluctable enough to make us feel their stature in withstanding it. Falk and Svanhild remain small in scale in spite of their pretensions otherwise.

When Ibsen had got his scale right, when he was able to perceive, as he watched modern life in action about him, both the operations of a Nemesis in modern society and, in consequence, the truly heroic stature of modern men and woman in conflict with it, he was able to write his great modern tragedies. *Love's Comedy* is clearly not one of them, but it was an essential step in their direction. We should look forward from *Love's Comedy*, not back on it; but above all I suggest, still tentatively, the need to look at it.

Notes

1. Jens Arup's admirable translation contains some dubious passages, the most serious of them occurring here. The lines bracketed above represent my own amateur attempt to translate what I think Mr Arup has misunderstood – though it is to be noticed that the editor endorses his reading on page 16 of the Oxford introduction. I give below, so that readers can decide for themselves, the Norwegian text beside the Oxford version:

    > Nej, midt i Lykkens vilde Jubeljagt
    > Hun maatte gaa til Evighedens Urland

    > no, here where everyone is wildly riding
    > the roundabout of pleasure, she and I
    > would tread the deserts of infinity.

2. 'For Hvor findes Helten?' 'Where are the heroes?' seems a little nearer to the text and avoids the impression of romantic whimsicality.

3. The *Oxford Ibsen* seems to lose its grip on the imagery here:

    > Tilhobe staar de, som de sorte Stammer,
    > En Skogbrand levned paa den øde Mo; –

4. Mr McFarlane seems to get the emphasis wrong in his analysis (p. 16) where he refers to Svanhild's indignantly rejecting the role of songbird.

5. For all indications to the contrary, the weather is as it was in Act I.

6. A point obscured by the Oxford translation's 'natural children' for "Elskovsbørn'.

7. The Oxford translation makes a minor difficulty here. Guldstad says: 'Last night I was planning a sort of poem'. This refers back to Act I: 'I also have a little theme in mind'. It is hard to see any justification for translating the Norwegian 'Digtning' as 'theme' if by so doing the reference is weakened; particularly since even in Act I Guldstad's line 'Jeg ogsaa gaar og grunder paa en Digtning' is clearly meant to echo an earlier line 'N aa, staar man her og grunder paa et Digt?' Which Mr Arup translates as: 'Well, are you meditating on a poem?'

8. It is here that the mistranslation mentioned earlier (p. 18) becomes most serious. The sense of the fulfilment of a prayer is lost by it.

9. The *Oxford Ibsen* introduces a slight nuance of gloomy compulsion by translating as 'must' the phrase 'jeg er færdig' – 'I am ready'!

10. As Brand's does through religion.

Originally published May 1964 (Vol. 3, No. 1).

Ideolectic Characterisation in
A Doll's House

Kristian Smidt

For the purpose of what we shall consider in the following pages we must posit an awareness of Ibsen's determined realism as evidenced in his plays from *The Pillars of Society* onwards. Useful pointers may be found in Daniel Haakonsen's *Henrik Ibsens realisme* (1957).[1]

Regarding 'certain of those dramas of contemporary life that fill the later years of [Ibsen's] authorship', Haakonsen points out the way in which we are entertained, even without listening to the dialogue, by the busy activities of the characters on stage relating to everyday occupations – private, domestic or social, but definitely ordinary. Then turning his attention to the dialogue of the plays, Haakonsen emphasises 'its *conversational* stamp'. He quotes a number of passages to exemplify this quality, among them the following exchange between Nora and Mrs Linde (in McFarlane's translation):

> NORA: ...Oh, Kristine, I'm so happy and relieved. I must say it's lovely to have plenty of money and not have to worry. Isn't it?
> MRS LINDE: Yes, it must be nice to have enough, at any rate.
> NORA: No, not just enough, but pots and pots of money!
> MRS LINDE: (*smiling*). Nora, Nora, haven't you learned any sense yet? At school you used to be an awful spendthrift.
> NORA: Yes, Torvald still says I am. (*Wags her finger.*) But little Nora isn't as stupid as everybody thinks...

Ibsen himself declared in a letter to the actress Lucie Wolf dated from Rome in May 1883, that he had given up writing in verse and for the past 7-8 years had exclusively practised 'the far more difficult art of writing in plain, truthful, realistic language' (at digte i jævnt sandfærdigt virkelighedssprog). It is important to realise, says Haakonsen, that:

> conversation is not, as one might be tempted to suppose, something commonplace in the theatre; on the contrary it is one of the characteristic features of Ibsen's drama. One could hardly say that Hamlet converses with his father's ghost, or that Racine's Phèdre converses with her stepson Hippolyte about the passion she feels for him and cannot subdue. But in Ibsen's plays there is, so to speak, no dialogue that is not adapted in some form or other to conversation.

Later playwrights have learnt from Ibsen. But in the twentieth century there was a veering away from the allegedly narrow realism which he represented and a lack of understanding of how he managed to convey a sense of important issues hidden by the trivialities of domestic life. Haakonsen shows how such higher issues may be powerfully at work under the deceptive surface of everyday objects and words and how they eventually break up the patterns of conformity and respectability on which the observable behaviour of the characters has been based. Ibsen's detailed realism, including his verbal realism, is not the be-all and end-all of his art, but the medium in which he works out the larger moral and psychological drama of his characters.

The typical setting of Ibsen's plays of modern life is the home of what in England might be called a middle-class couple. The husband is most often a professional man or academic. And the speech of the main characters is the standard educated Norwegian of the mid-nineteenth century, no doubt to some extent influenced in pronunciation by the orthography which Norway long shared with Denmark. Regional accents were obviously common then as they still are, but are hardly noticeable in printed words. This is what may be called the characters' sociolect, and it is basic to the dialogue of the plays in so far as it is spoken by persons who may be presumed to have had at least a modicum of education.

In using this sociolect Ibsen aims, then, at natural conversational speech, including such things as exclamations and repetitions. He even occasionally, in soliloquies, chooses to present something like a stream of consciousness rather than a formal monologue in the old dramatic tradition. Here, for example, is Nora anguishing over the threats from Krogstad:

A, hvis jeg turde gå ud. Hvis bare ingen kom. Hvis her bare ikke hendte noget herhjemme imens. Dum snak; der kommer ingen. Bare ikke tamke. Børste af muffen. Dejlige handsker, dejlige handsker. Slå det hen; slå det hen! En, to, tre, fire, fem, sex –

Some characters speak the bourgeois urban sociolect without any very noticeable deviations or idiosyncracies. They often play subsidiary roles as persons of common sense whom the author presents as reliable observers and critics. People like Lona Hessel in *The Pillars of Society*, Petra Stockmann in *An Enemy of the People* (admittedly a small part) and to some extent assessor Brack in *Hedda Gabler*. These people probably come as close to representing the author's voice as Ibsen's characters ever do. Lona, Petra and Brack have the last word in their respective plays. In *A Doll's House* Kristine Linde belongs to the same category. She is a practical woman with a cool head and a warm heart and a sense of responsibility tending to self-sacrifice. She has learnt to manage her life the hard way and speaks the plain, educated language of ordinary intercourse.

Others have their speeches interlarded with recurrent phrases or exclamations personal to these individuals, and Ibsen often contents himself with a few such idioms in otherwise quite ordinary speech in order to reveal a temperamental or mental peculiarity in a person and give him or her a kind of recognisable badge. Their iterations are often used for comic effect, as when Hilmar Tønnesen in *The Pillars of Society* constantly utters an 'Uff, uff!'. Poor Jørgen Tesman is ridiculed by his frequent 'Hvad' and 'Tænk det': 'Og jeg, som var så viss på, at du lå og sov endnu. Tænk det, Hedda!'. Jørgen's aunt, Miss Tesman, is in the habit of invoking God purely for emphasis. So, curiously enough, is Pastor Manders in *Ghosts*, though I am not convinced that Ibsen was completely familiar with clerical strictness in these matters when he makes a devout clergyman frequently utter such things as 'Nå du min Gud!', 'Men Gud bevare os vel!' and 'Nei, du gode Gud, det vilde jo være forfærdelig!'.

There is a certain attempt, not systematic, at imitating a distinct sociolect of the lower, or uneducated, order. It mostly consists in introducing here and there certain word forms and turns of speech which by educated standards would be regarded as incorrect. Regine in *Ghosts* has worked hard to acquire polite speech, but she betrays her background in her use of 'sanse' for 'erindre' or 'minnes' ('Å, jeg sanser nok hva ord du brugte') and in expressions like 'Vi hadde ikke ventet ham før som i dag' and 'kjære herr pastor, – tænk ialfald på mig dersom at – '. Engstrand, of course, is also given to swearing – his speech is peppered with 'Nei Gu'' and 'fan'', even 'Fan' ete mig – '. Servant girls have milder oaths. 'Ja kors, hun er ovenpå,' says Regine. 'Jøsses,' exclaims Berte in *Hedda Gabler*. The mildest expletive of all is probably 'Bevares', which is also in Ibsen's practice a lower-class indicator. It is used, for instance, by the Nurse in *A Doll's House*.

'Idiolect' seems to be a recently invented word (as, probably, is 'sociolect', and both probably of American provenance). It has not yet got into many dictionaries. It denotes the individual speech habits of particular persons, but I am not entirely confident as to how much it may include. I do not consider Tesman's 'Tænk det' as part of his idiolect, I see it rather as a mannerism tagged onto his generally unremarkable speech patterns. As for various characters' concern with 'mådehold' or 'skønhed' or 'home' this is a matter of topics, what they need to talk about, not of how they talk. And then there is affected speech, like the way in which Engstrand hypocritically assumes a pious air when it suits him – 'og fristelsene er mangfoldige i denne verden, ser du' – or Regine gives herself airs by putting in French words every now and then – her 'rendez-vouses' and 'pardons' and 'mercis', even 'pied de mouton'. These affectations I take to be extraneous to the natural speech of the two characters and essentially insignificant in relation to their sociolect. (In Regine's case I think the French is a little overdone, like Gina Ekdal's malapropisms – Ibsen had a tendency, perhaps, to overdo his comic touches.)

There are of course differences of style and different levels of formality and folksiness within a normal educated sociolect which perhaps might qualify as idiolectic features. Pastor Manders and Mrs Alving, for instance, do not talk in the same way. Manders tends to use old-fashioned words like 'såre' and 'blot' for 'meget' and 'kun': 'Det er et såre omtvisteligt spørsmål, fru Alving', 'Tænk blot på alle min embedsbroders tilhængere!' Manders talks stuffily, while Mrs Alving uses plain language. An interesting example of such qualitative speech differences is that of the two Stockmann brothers in *An Enemy of the People*, the doctor and the mayor ('byfogeden'). Here is the mayor:

> Men rimeligvis vil direksjonen i sin tid ikke være utilbøjelig til at ta under overvejelse hvorvidt det med overkommelige pekuniære offere skulde være muligt at få indført visse forbedringer.

And here the doctor:

> Min fremstilling er så slående sand og rigtig, det ved jeg! Og du skjenner det meget godt, Peter; men du vil bare ikke være ved det.

Idiolect is perhaps most simply and generally understood as a matter of peculiar or abnormal usage, like individual non-standard morphology, or of a predilection for rare words, nonce words, arbitrary word forms and syntax, and the like. Verbal idiosyncracies, more or less. But as I understand it, or at least choose to understand it for my present purpose, it is more important to see idiolect as a matter of statistics, the frequency with which certain words or word groups or sentence patterns occur in a person's speech in comparison with the speech of other persons in the same environment or comparable circumstances. The two Stockmann brothers use different vocabularies and different speech rhythms, which mark them out individually and so define their idiolects, though both are products of the same sociolect. It is also important to emphasise that the words which may serve to define an idiolect by their peculiar frequency need not be in themselves attention-attracting – rare or odd words or even polysyllabic monsters like 'vederstyggelighed' or 'gåseleverpostejer'. They may just as well be seemingly unassuming little creatures like 'and' and 'if' ('much virtue in an 'if',' as Shakespeare's Touchstone said, and perhaps we remember the importance of the little word 'nok' in *Peer Gynt*). As I also understand it, idiolect is a matter of liking for words conveying certain kinds of meaning or emotion and thence reflecting the intellectual and temperamental characteristics of the speaker. We may call this the generic dominance of certain word families.

We shall use these two criteria, relative frequency and generic dominance in considering the dialogue of *A Doll's House*. And it is natural to concentrate chiefly on Nora. She is not only unquestionably the main character but also the person with by far the largest speaking part. We find her talking to all the other characters in turn, while Torvald never talks to the children or their nurse or even to Mr Krogstad in our hearing. And the first phenomenon we shall consider is the occurrence in her speech of two of the smallest words in the language.

One is the interjection 'å', i.e. not the infinitive sign (as in 'å gjøre', 'to do') but the word corresponding to the English 'oh'.

It may seem surprising that this should be of any interest. You might think the 'å' so ubiquitous and unremarkable in anybody's conversation that you can hardly draw conclusions from a particular person's use of it. But this is not a matter of the singularity of the word per se but of its singular frequency in Nora's utterances. Nora uses this exclamatory 'å' far more frequently in proportion to her speaking part than some other characters in Ibsen with whom it may be relevant to compare her. Nora Helmer says 'å' by my count 82 times, Helene Alving, in the play which followed *A Doll's House*, only 18. Nora Helmer and Hedda Gabler have a great deal in common – foreign travel, unimaginative husbands, unfulfilled aspirations, both receive visits from old female friends and gentlemen admirers, and both have suicidal impulses when they are disappointed in their heroes. Hedda Gabler says 'å' only 30 times (plus twelve times 'ah') compared to Nora's 82. I know that statistics often lie, and I must confess that I have simply not had the time to consider all the relevant circumstances that would make a comparison of Nora's word counts with those of Mrs. Alving or Hedda Gabler strictly reliable. Mrs. Alving certainly has a smaller speaking part than Nora. But even so, 82-18, I submit, is suggestive. Nora is in a state of excitement, even euphoria, owing to the Helmers' sudden affluence, while Hedda is in a state of depression from general dissatisfaction aggravated by an unwanted pregnancy. So their present circumstances are different. But even so, 82-30 is indicative of something more fundamental. Nora's personality is different from both Helene Alving's and Hedda Gabler's. I would think Ibsen very intentionally gave Nora all these 'å's to speak. In Nora's penultimate speech, 'Å, Torvald, jeg tror ikke længer på noget vidunderligt', the 'Å' in the printed version replaced an 'ak' in the complete draft. It goes to show how conscious he was of the word.

Now 'å' is an emotional signifier. And consider its semantic potentials. You can fill it like a carrier bag with twenty different senses and a hundred different shades of meaning, all dependent on context, emphasis and tonal accent. It can express anything from indifference to comprehension, incomprehension, query, rebuttal, rebuke, indignation, impatience, disappointment, surprise, admiration, disgust and delight in any number of degrees. Different Norwegian dialects may also add a quota of various intonations. The little 'å' is actually an important pointer to emotions. Just think of the challenge to actors who just have Ibsen's 'å' to read with only very rare instructions as to how to interpret it vocally.

Unless it stands alone, as often happens, the 'å' is usually at the head of a semantic unit, an incomplete utterance, perhaps, or a full sentence. Here are some of Nora's uses of it.

Making light of something: 'Å pyt; til mig? Jeg bryr mig slet ikke om noget.'
Reprimand: 'Å ved De hvad, doktor Rank, – De vil såmæn også gerne leve.'
Appeal: 'Å, du må ikke være vred på mig!' 'Å, Torvald, kald det tilbage!'
Pity: 'Å, du stakker, hvor meget du visst har gået igennem.' Gratitude: 'Å hvor det er snilt af dig.'
Regret: 'Å det gør mig så ondt, Torvald; for du har altid været så snil imod mig.'
Realisation: 'Å, jeg forstår dig. Du mener, Torvald kunde kanske gøre noget for dig.'
Sudden recollection: 'Å, men jeg tankeløse menneske, som sidder her og snakker!'
Surprise: 'Å, der ringer det.'
Delight: 'Å, hvor det er vidunderlig dejligt at høre!' 'Å, du kan tro, vi glæder os!'
Sorrow: 'Å, det er det tungeste jeg har oplevet siden jeg blev gift.' Fear: 'Å, jeg er så ængstelig. Det store selskab – .' 'Å, det iskolde sorte vand. Å, det bundløse – ; dette – .'

Nora's use of 'å' is an admirably subtle way of revealing her emotion-al nature and nervous state of mind. In her conversations with Torvald in the first two acts she says 'å' three times as often as her husband. Most of Torvald's 'å's are in the third act when he is seriously upset and actually utters this sound twice as often as Nora, who eventually becomes resolute and strangely composed. Nora perhaps reveals more of herself in conversations with Mrs Linde, Krogstad and Rank than with Torvald – more 'å's here altogether than in her exchanges with her husband. One may wonder whether Hedda Gabler has less strong emotions than Nora? Hedda has a turbulent disposition, but she is less easily moved from moment to moment, less vivacious, or she represses her emotions under a surface of boredom. She may be compared in her own play to her old friend Thea, Løvborg's guardian angel, who exclaims 'å' about three times as often as Hedda.

'Å' is a typical conversational word, as is the corresponding 'oh' in English. There may be slight differences in the uses of 'å' and 'oh' in the two languages, but 'å' may in most cases be translated as 'oh' without affecting the sense. It is another matter with another small word which also frequently occurs in Norwegian conversation. It belongs to a group of words indicating modal qualifications which have no direct counterpart in English, words like 'jo', 'vel', 'nok'. Inga-Stina Ewbank has in several of her excellent essays drawn attention not only to the difficulty of translating these words, but also to the importance of not just ignoring them.

That little word is 'jo'. Not the answering 'jo' contradicting a negative statement or question, as in 'Han gjør det ikke' – 'Jo, han gjør det', but an adverbial modifier inserted into a statement like 'Han gjør det jo'.

Nora says 'jo' 71 times, most often in conversation with others than Torvald, Torvald only 20 times altogether and mostly, as in the case of 'å', in the third act. Helene Alving says 'jo' only 17 times and Hedda Gabler only 27 times, as against Nora's 71. But there is one character who practically equals Nora in the frequency of 'jo's – Hjalmar Ekdal – and probably for similar reasons.

This 'jo' basically and typically serves to verify, confirm or remind one of some undisputed factual circumstance, like 'Ibsen skrev jo *Catilina* i Grimstad'. But if the little 'å' may be said to be a maid of all work, so in its tricky way is 'jo'. It can mean things like 'as we all know', 'you must understand', 'remember', 'of course', 'isn't that right', 'this being so', 'oh dear, sorry', 'how odd', 'but listen' and even just 'oh'. The significance of the 'jo' in each case is so much a matter of context and situation that it is hard to pin it down to anyone exact message. But it does always communicate *something*, which may be lost if the 'jo' is omitted. 'Han gjør det jo' can express things as different as surprise – 'He's doing it after all' – and correction – 'He's doing it, so you're wrong', while 'Han gjør det' without the 'jo' is bare statement. 'Han er her' is mere information, while 'Han er jo her' may suggest 'I'm pleased to see' or 'as you ought to know' or 'so we may feel safe' or a great many other things depending on the context (and of course on the stress on different words – 'han', 'er', 'her').

'Jo' has been found such a difficult word to translate that in the great majority of cases where it occurs in *Et Dukkehjem* the translators, each and all, have simply ignored it. Out of Nora's 71 'jo's, only 12 are represented by some kind of explicit equivalent in Archer's translation, 15 in McFarlane's and 6 in Meyer's. The results of this – shall we call it timidity? – are such as these:

> NORA: 'Pyt, vi kan jo låne så lenge.' Sharp: 'Pooh! we can borrow till then.' A little 'please' is hidden somewhere in Nora's 'jo', and the little bit of appeal or persuasion is lost in the translation.
> NORA: 'Ja, nu har du jo dit gamle ansigt igjen', meaning 'I'm pleased to see'. Sharp's 'Now you look like your old self again' misses the element of pleasant recognition.
> NORA: 'Og han efterlod dig jo ikke noget at leve af?' McFarlane: 'And didn't he leave you anything?' The message that Nora has prior knowledge of her friend's circumstances is lost.
> NORA: 'Ja; da havde vi jo pengene.' Watts simply: 'We had the money then.' Something

like 'you must understand' is implied, but Nora's need to explain is ignored.

NORA: 'Af husholdningspengene kunde jeg jo ikke lægge noget videre tilside, for Torvald måtte jo leve godt.' 'Don't you see?' is implied. Meyer: 'I haven't been able to save much on the housekeeping money, because Torvald likes to live well.' Nora is trying to justify her behaviour, but her wish to make it seem obviously right is obscured in the translation.

NORA: 'Han underskrev jo.' Archer: 'He did sign it.' Similarly McFarlane and Meyer. This becomes a mere assertion and ignores Nora's urgent wish to make it a recognised fact.

NORA: 'Nej, men det er jo umuligt!' Archer: 'No, it's impossible!'.

NORA: 'Det k a n jo ikke ske noget sligt.' Meyer: 'It couldn't happen.' This in both cases is too unemotional – Nora's attempt to reassure herself is ignored.

NORA: 'Men du vilde jo ha'e det så.' McFarlane: 'But that's the way you wanted it.' Nora is trying to make Torvald see his fault. Her 'jo' implies something like 'you must admit'.

NORA: 'Jeg ved jo slet ikke, hvad der blir ud af mig.' Watts: 'I've no idea what will become of me,' which makes Nora sound indifferent rather than perplexed.

Both Nora and Hjalmar Ekdal are ridden by a sense of insecurity, Nora because of her money problems and her secret debt to Krogstad, later by threats of blackmail and her fear of exposure, Hjalmar because of the shame attaching to his father and his inability to get on with his great inventions. And the 'jo', which so often relates to facts and certainties, is a way of persuading themselves that things are all right. Both also feel a need to justify their actions (or inaction in Hjalmar's case) to themselves and others, though Nora in particular has to explain her behaviour and justify it without revealing too much. I take her frequent use of 'jo' to be in part an indication of this need.

As Inga-Stina Ewbank remarks: 'to the non-Scandinavian there is bound to be an element of surrealism in the behaviour of the Norwegian language itself: in its handling of pronouns, in those little modal adverbs – 'nok', 'vel', 'jo' – which so crucially affect tone and meaning.' 'The quintessence,' she says,

> (call it structure, action, theme or characterisation) of any Ibsen play is intimately connected with - indeed, is in - his language, in his handling of the vernacular. It follows, then, that any translation which does not at least attempt to render something of the verbal qualities of the original gives us that much less of Ibsen.[2]

Perhaps in the case of 'jo' that much less of Ibsen is sometimes inevitable. I wouldn't like to say that 'jo' always has to be represented by recognisable verbal equivalents. There is obviously a danger of making the implications over-explicit, and in any case the actors may supply what is mute in the text. But a little more effort on behalf of Norwegian surrealism might be desirable. Sometimes a simple 'of course' or a question-tab like 'isn't it?' or 'aren't they?' would do the job.

Another very noticeable feature of Nora's speech is the way she repeats or doubles, even triples, many of her words, especially the affirmative 'ja' and the negative 'nej', as well as adjectives and adverbs: 'Ja, ja, som du vil, Torvald', 'Nej, nej, det kan du have ret i', 'Nej, nej, nej; De får bare se fodbladet', 'du [...] kommer til at tjene mange, mange penge', 'Ak, jeg var mangengang så træt, sa træt'.

Exclamations, too, like 'Å Gud, å Gud, Kristine', 'Vås, vås, vås!', and more complete syntagmas like 'Lad mig om det! Lad mig om det!', 'Slå det hen, slå det hen!', 'De skal få se; De skal få se!'

Nora's idiolect obviously contains an unusual amount of repetitive utterances. They indicate again that she is temperamentally highly-strung. She speaks as if in a constant state of agitation. And this links up with another feature of her idiolect, the generic dominance of certain word groups. One may notice how often she uses words conveying a sense of the immeasurable, like 'umådelig(t)' (fourteen times), 'uhyre' (four times) and 'ubeskrivelig' (twice). 'Jeg har en sådan umådelig lyst til at sige: død og pine', 'Jeg glæder mig så umådeligt til kostumeballet', 'jeg synes altid her blir så uhyre fornøjeligt når De kommer', 'Torvald holder jo så ubeskrivelig meget af mig'.

Nora loves adjectives and adverbs suggesting extraordinary pleasure and expresses her fear or disgust in correspondingly strong terms. Her favourite word is probably 'dejlig (dejligt, dejlige)', which she uses seventeen times in the first two acts, most often about enjoying freedom from pecuniary worries ('det er dog dejligt at have dygtig mange penge'), repeatedly about her children ('Jeg har tre dejlige børn'), about clothes ('det er dog dejligt at gå fint klædt'), about the Helmers' home ('Ja, Torvald forstår rigtignok at gøre hjemmet fint og dejligt'), about the Christmas tree ('Juletræet skal blive dejligt'), about her gloves ('Dejlige handsker, dejlige handsker') and about her stockings ('Kødfarvede. Er ikke de dejlige!'). She even reinforces 'dejlig' with an adverbial 'vidunderlig' from time to time, as if she cannot express her pleasure strongly enough: 'Å, hvor det er vidunderlig dejligt at høre', 'Å, det var en vidunderlig dejlig rejse', 'det er dog vidunderlig dejlig at leve og være lykkelig!'

'Vidunderlig' is another favourite word. And in view of the importance which it assumes towards the end of the play it is essential to see how Nora uses it from the beginning. It does not take long to appear in the dialogue. Towards the end of the opening conversation between Torvald and Nora, Torvald remarks, 'Ak, det er dog herligt at tænke på at man har fåt en sikker, betrygget stilling.' And Nora answers, heightening his expression, 'Å, det er vidunderlig!' Then in quick succession in her next few speeches: 'Ja, det er rigtignok vidunderligt' and 'Å, hvor det er vidunderlig dejligt at høre!' Three times more she uses this word in Act I, talking to Mrs Linde, once about the journey to Italy and twice about her present happiness. It is an ordinary enough word, particularly perhaps as used by women to express delight in such things as material comfort, just as 'dejlig' in ordinary usage is – and was in the nineteenth century, as far as I can judge – a more feminine than masculine word and by its frequency helps to bring out Nora's femininity. And 'vidunderlig' has a contrasting, almost twin word in Nora's vocabulary, which helps to establish its emphatic and purely sublunary sense: 'forfærdelig(t)'. Nora uses this word four times in Act I about perfectly empiric conditions: 'Men i det første år overanstrængte han sig så aldeles forfærdeligt', 'og de [afdrag] er altid så forfærdelig vanskelige at skaffe tilveje'. There is actually a key passage in which the two words are juxtaposed: 'Ja, det vidunderlige. Men det er så forfærdeligt, Kristine.'

It is interesting to note that in revising the draft of *Et Dukkehjem* for his final version Ibsen several times omitted 'forfærdelig(t)' and passages containing that word and added a 'vidunderlig' three times. 'Vidunderlig' thus came into considerable prominence and now pointed forward clearly to its appearance as 'det vidunderlige' in Acts II and III.

In Act II both 'vidunderlig' and 'forfærdelig' appear in the absolute forms 'det vidunderlige' and 'det forfærdelige': 'Det forfærdelige sker' (Nora to herself as Krogstad is announced) and a little later 'Det er jo det vidunderlige, som nu vil ske' (to Mrs Linde after Krogstad's departure). These absolute forms are hard to match completely in English, and a majority of translators – Archer, Mencken, McFarlane, Watts, Meyer, Fjelde, Hampton and MacLeish – have rendered 'det vidunderlige' as 'the miracle' or 'a miracle'. (Sharp and Le Gallienne have chosen 'a (or the) wonderful thing' and Reinert simply 'the wonderful'.) But 'miracle' introduces a sense which is not in Nora's mind until possibly at the very end of the play. Nora may be naïve in some ways but she is definitely not superstitious and she says herself that she has no understanding of religion beyond what pastor Hansen once taught her in confirmation classes. What Nora has been waiting for for eight years is not a miraculous transformation of Torvald from lover to saint but the wonderful moment when not only will she be free of all money obligations but above all when Torvald will at last recognise that she is something more than a doll woman. Then when Krogstad reveals his knowledge of her forgery and threatens to expose her, her confidence in Torvald's nobility is such that she needs no miraculous transformation to see him as her saviour but merely a proof of his natural magnanimity, taking all guilt upon himself. A sacrifice which she will not let him perform, but his bid to do so is the wonderful event which she now expects. Only at the end, when she realises that a true marriage may be beyond realistic expectation and she speaks of 'det vidunderligste' does she hint at something miraculous. And even then the superlative 'det vidunderligste' recalls Torvald's 'Skulde det forfærdeligste – !' spoken only a little earlier when he thinks Krogstad may be implementing his threat. It undercuts the supernatural dimension.[3] It is interesting to see that in Ibsen's draft of the play Nora's penultimate speech is: 'ak, Thorvald, jeg tror ikke længere på mirakler'. Ibsen changed this in the final version to: 'Å, Torvald, jeg tror ikke længer på noget vidunderligt' (the change from 'ak' to 'å' is noted above). The play in fact has no metaphysical dimension. Its ethos is wholly secular. The ordinary 'vidunderlig' does assume extraordinary importance in being grammatically stepped up, but my point is that it is still part of Nora's idiolect and takes its colouring from that fact.

Nora's 'umådelig' and 'dejlig' and 'vidunderlig' are hyperbolic. It is not that she is so truly delighted with things as the words imply. She uses them to convince herself and to convince other people that she is happy. But deep down she is dissatisfied and unhappy. She is irked by Torvald's constant schooling and by the fact that she is not thought capable of anything serious. And she is unhappy in being treated as a plaything. The truth comes out in her final reckoning with Torvald. Nora is capable of acting decisively and independently when guided by her feelings, but has to do so in secret and is not allowed to be truly independent in her own house. There is a great deal in her personality which is unfulfilled. So she pretends a happiness which is at least in part factitious, and her exaggerated enthusiasm in wording her delights may possibly arouse our suspicion of something deeply amiss.

Torvald is a man of principle, a lawyer and a believer in rules. No sweetmeats, no borrowing. He likes the word 'Nå', introducing a concession or a doubt – 'Nå, man må tage dig som du er' – and his admonitions to Nora are often preceded by a 'Nå, nå' or 'Så, så!' or even 'Nå, nå, nå' and 'Så, så, så' – 'Nå, nå, hvad er det? Ræk mig hånden', 'Så, så, så; ikke disse forskræmte dueøjne.'

Torvald does not usually give way to verbal exuberance. Where Nora may say 'dejligt' or 'vidunderligt' he uses on a couple of occasions the more masculine word 'herligt': 'Ak, det er dog herligt at tænke på at man har fåt en sikker betrygget stilling!' 'Dejlig(t)' is exclusively Nora's word in the first two acts. In the third act it oddly enough becomes Torvald's word, but now with a special sense, a mouthwatering sexual sense, in which Nora does not use it. It is Nora who is 'dejlig' to the slightly tipsy and very much sexually aroused Torvald: 'Er hun ikke dejlig, fru Linde?', 'Er hun ikke mærkværdig dejlig?', 'Å du henrivende dejlige unge kvinde!'

Torvald needs to feel superior, not only to people like Krogstad, but perhaps above all to his wife. He uses the word 'lille' so frequently in addressing her (27 times in all) that it obviously serves as a way of asserting his inflated ego. And it is typically coupled with pet names such as 'lille sanglærken', 'min velsignede lille sangfugl', which are hardly objectionable, but occasionally, too, with less flattering names: 'du lille ødeland', 'du lille galning', 'den søde lille tingest', 'du lille hjælpeløse tingest', 'du lille rådvilde, hjælpeløse væsen'. He repeatedly calls her 'den lille egensindige' or 'du lille letsindige' and even 'min lille fru stivnakke'.

It is questionable, perhaps, whether Torvald's use of 'lille' should be regarded as idiolect since it applies only to his relations with Nora, but it certainly helps to characterise him. Apart from Torvald's patronising attitude to Nora as shown in his admonitory 'nå's, bird names and eternal 'lille', Ibsen has not gifted this man with noticeable peculiarities of speech, there is no professional jargon, for instance. But this in itself defines his portrait. Torvald is a conventional, unimaginative person, a conscientious, even over-conscientious, worker, kindly, polite, sensual, self-important but on the whole to be regarded as an average kind of bourgeois husband, the kind which was all too common. Ibsen did not want to make him comical like Jørgen Tesman or Hjalmar Ekdal.

There is nothing very remarkable in Krogstad's language, but he does tend to speak in the formal style of business letters and legal documents: 'Fru Helmer, vil De være af den godhed at anvende Deres indflydelse til fordel for mig', 'at det ikke kan være Deres veninde behageligt at udsætte sig for at støde sammen med mig', 'Det er ganske rigtigt; det har jeg erkyndiget mig om'.

Then there is doctor Rank. He has a great deal of pain to hide, physical and emotional, and he hides it under a flippant, ironical manner which becomes a quality of his idiolect. He suggests Mrs Linde may be 'en lide smule bedærvet indvendig' when she says she finds it difficult climbing stairs. And the word 'bedærvet' is applied again to Krogstad, who, he says, is 'bedærvet i karakter-rødderne'. Krogstad is a 'moralsk hospitalslem' in Rank's parlance. Rank speaks in medical terms of people suffering from 'moralsk råddenskab' being 'indlagt til observation i en eller anden fordelagtig stilling' and of society as a 'sygehus'. He does not mince his words. Of his own prospects he says morbidly: 'Inden en måned ligger jeg kanske og rådner oppe på kirkegården', which elicits Nora's rebuke, 'Å fy, hvor stygt De taler'. He will let her know, he says with gallows humour, quoting Jesus on the end of the world, when 'ødeleggelsens vederstyggelighed' has begun. In somewhat lighter mood he speaks of the time when he will have 'fået forfald'. He declares in mock-professional terms that he can have no 'begrundet formening' of the fit of Nora's stockings and asks archly what 'andre herligheder' he is to be allowed to see.

I have briefly included the secondary characters Krogstad and Rank (and Mrs Linde I touched on above) to show that Ibsen not only gave distinct touches to the portraits of his protagonists by means of their speech habits but was also careful to differentiate the characterisation of his personae by the same means, making them very distinct individuals. But I hope I have made it clear that he lavished his attention on Nora and was not deterred from using the most insignificant-seeming constituents of her talk to add shades and dimensions to his portrait of her.

Notes

1. An excerpt from Haakonsen's book, excellently translated by James W. McFarlane and entitled 'Ibsen the Realist', is included in McFarlane, ed., *Discussions of Henrik Ibsen*. (Boston: D. C. Heath and Company, 1962), pp. 70-82. This is the source of my English quotations from Haakonsen.
2. 'Henrik Ibsen: National Language and International Drama', in Bjørn Hemmer and Vigdis Ystad, eds., *Contemporary Approaches to Ibsen*, Vol. IV, (Oslo: Norwegian University Press, 1988), pp.57-67. Quotes pp. 65, 58.
3. My daughter Katinka pointed out to me that Camilla Collett uses the term 'det vidunderligste' in her foreword to the third edition of *Amtmandens Døtre*. She uses it in exactly the same sense as in Ibsen's play, about the kind of ideal union of man and woman which was virtually impossible given the social and moral attitudes of the age. The edition was published in 1879 a few months before Ibsen completed his draft of *Et Dukkehjem*, and it would not be surprising if Ibsen had read Camilla Collett's feminist apologia while he was working on his own.

Originally published November 2000 (Vol. 41, No. 2).

Forms of Address in Ibsen's *Ghosts*

Harold C. Knutson

Even the most casual reading of Ibsen's realistic plays will show how much the playwright depends upon forms of address to establish the scene and reveal character. This is all the more true since Ibsen depicts a relatively high level of society, one attuned to title and hierarchy. Every one has an acknowledged place in the various strata, and interaction – whether through professional, business or family contacts – is ruled by strict, largely unwritten laws of propriety which dictate, among other things, how people should talk to one another. Does decorum impose 'De' (the formal pronoun) over 'du' (the intimate one)? 'Fru Alving' over 'Helene'? 'Herr ('Mr') Pastor' over 'Manders'? For it is principally through pronouns, names and titles that people in Ibsen's plays signify their place in society.

Forms of address not only show how given personages fit in the various levels but to what degree characters may flout existing custom; to use the intimate form, for instance, where only the formal one is fitting conveys a striking dramatic effect that goes far beyond mere social portrayal. As Robert Amundsen points out in his essay on pronoun use in Ibsen,[1] a memorable example occurs in the third act of *The Lady from the Sea*. Here the heroine's former sailor lover, picking up the intimacy of the past, uses the 'du' form to entice her back into his sea world. Her husband, a witness to this scene, is outraged at such a breach of decorum from some one who is ostensibly a stranger, and low-born in the bargain. Ibsen uses forms of address, then, not only to depict a largely conformist society but to underscore powerful anarchical forces at odds with custom which rumble beneath a seemingly secure and enduring edifice.

While many realistic plays show this distinctive Ibsenian tension between the dictates of society and the affirmation of the individual, none surpasses *Ghosts* in its bleak, brooding meditation on the sterility of conventional morality and the betrayals it forces upon any aspiration to authentic selfhood. The following pages are intended to explore these murky realms as they are revealed by the seemingly simple ways in which characters address each other in direct speech.

Ghosts[2] takes place on an estate in Western Norway. It opens with an expository scene between Regine, the seventeen-year-old servant girl, and 'Snekker' ('Carpenter'[3]) Engstrand,[4] her putative father, who has slipped in through the kitchen door. He has been employed in the now finished orphanage which the lady of the house, fru Alving, has had built as a memorial to her late husband Kaptein Alving, a distinguished military officer who had acquired the honorary title 'kammerherre'

('Chamberlain').[5] Engstrand has his own project in mind, a seamen's home where Regine is to be the main attraction, a role that Regine vehemently refuses. Though the scene is between father and daughter, hostility and contempt dominate their exchange, as is conveyed eloquently by the way they address each other. They use 'du', for they are part, ostensibly, of a nuclear family. But Regine never uses 'far' ('father') in addressing Engstrand; he has told her often enough that she is another's daughter. The only word she does actually use in addressing him is an angry 'menneske!' thrown out twice (pp.93, 98), a dismissive neuter word – half expletive – signifying 'man'.

In the face of her stubbornness, Engstrand is alternately cajoling, whining and enraged. He gives in to spite when he addresses her as 'tøs' (p.95), a word meaning, literally, 'girl', but carrying as well the notion of 'wanton' and sometimes translated by 'wench'. Although he calls Regine by her first name once or twice, his most frequent form of address (eight times), usually in a sarcastic tone, is 'barnet mit' ('my child'). The phrase carries, of course, a heavy ironic weight, given Engstrand's doubtful paternity.

The scene is interrupted by the pastor's arrival, and Regine pushes Engstrand out the back way. However, Ibsen perpetuates the troubled mood, the subtle conflict between text and subtext, in the subsequent dialogue between Manders and Regine. Regine hurriedly primps before the mirror, then feigns surprise as Manders comes on scene. She greets him effusively with the respectful 'De' form and 'herr pastor', the way he will be addressed generally by every one during the entire play. (In fact, we never learn his Christian name.) Manders shows equal formality by speaking to her as 'jomfru Engstrand' (and with the 'De' pronoun, naturally).

'Jomfru' was used mainly to address and refer to women in domestic service.[6] Already by Ibsen's time it had a somewhat archaic ring, and it is not surprising that the term is part of Manders' vocabulary. But apart from confirming the pastor's old-fashioned and stuffy formality, the word has more general connotations which resonate darkly in *Ghosts*. Like its German cognate *Jungfrau*, it also conveyed a suggestion of virginity. Now Regine may still be a maiden, but she certainly is a precocious and manipulative young woman, only too aware of her earthy attractiveness and the impact it has on Manders and, as we learn later, on Osvald. Thus 'jomfru' carries a sardonic subliminal message typical of the author.

Regine has beautified herself in the mirror to good effect. The pastor 'looks her over' and remarks that she has grown since their previous meeting. It is she who speaks the subtext of Manders' observation, what he really has in mind: 'Madam says that I have filled out as well.' Characteristically, Manders backs away with 'Filled out? ... Yes, maybe a little' (p.99). His interest in her goes beyond pastoral solicitude, for an embarrassed silence follows the discussion of Regine's physical maturity.

The fact that Regine has turned rapidly into a woman has already been noted in the previous scene by her father, albeit in a more down-to-earth way: 'What a beautiful girl ['tøs'] you have become these past two years' (p.97). (Here 'tøs' probably has its neutral meaning.) As if to underscore the point, Pastor Manders himself will tell Mrs Alving in Act II, as he remembers teaching Regine the catechism in preparation for Confirmation, that she was 'considerably developed from a physical standpoint' (p.139). As it was customary to be confirmed at fifteen, his observation dates from only two years before the time of the play, the same reference point as for Engstrand's similar comment. We may assume that the fifteen-year-old Regine was more aware of Manders' special interest than he himself and has made it a point to play on this attraction during Manders' occasional visits to the Estate.

Manders has come to see fru Alving on business matters but takes advantage of her temporary absence to lecture Regine on filial piety. He urges the girl to return to her father and help with Engstrand's planned seamen's shelter. Artfully, Regine avoids dealing directly with this issue. She has her own opportunistic plans. It is clear from the beginning, for instance, that she has designs on Osvald, the young master of the house. Her coy conduct with Pastor Manders is part, perhaps, of a second-best scheme. Having built up a relationship of sorts with Manders she hopes to enter his service as a kind of foster daughter (p.100), Manders being unmarried and childless. She voices her aspiration, of course, with the greatest circumspection. During the ensuing rather comic dialogue of the deaf, in such contrast to the coarse exchange in the previous scene between Regine and her father, Regine holds to the deferential 'herr pastor' in addressing him. But curiously enough, he moves to a much more familiar range of address words (while avoiding 'du', however): 'Min gode Regine', 'min gode kære pige' ('my good dear girl') and, most significantly, 'mitt kære barn' (p.100), Ibsen's mocking echo of Engstrand's sardonic 'barnet mit'. As his nature is to fear physical intimacy and suppress any natural impulse, Manders frequently drops these endearing terms to return to the formal 'jomfru' appropriate for a young servant. However, he belatedly realizes that he is not only failing to help Engstrand but being wooed indirectly by a dangerously alluring young woman. He rises, coldly asserts his dignity and authority, and orders 'jomfru Engstrand' (p.101) to fetch her mistress. And once again, a heavy silence falls.

These hesitations and inconsistencies in address forms tell us much about Manders' character, and in later scenes we will see the same kind of uncertainties, especially with fru Alving. His forbidding clerical propriety, his homiletic strictures hide a repressed sexuality which Regine unerringly senses. His unconscious wishes have found partial expression with his fatherly terms of endearment, but he now thrusts his lurking carnal interest aside with a brusque dismissal.

By devices of this sort, Ibsen takes pains to make us aware as soon as dramatically possible of Manders' complex character at the centre of which lies his essential self-blindness. Only then can we proceed to the two unforgettable scenes which Manders shares in Acts I and II with fru Alving. There too, how they address each other will give us precious clues as to character and relationships.

In these two acts various facets of Manders' personality, several revelations of his hidden self, come to the fore as past events are relived, past feelings revived. At the very beginning, significantly, Manders addresses his interlocutor, not as 'fru Alving' but as 'frue', a slightly more distant, more courtly mode of address from a man to a woman. But Ibsen makes it clear that fear, rather than high respect, lies behind this formality. Manders, we learn, has taken the precaution of spending the night in town rather than on the Estate in dangerous proximity to fru Alving. Only when he is reassured by the latter's quiet aplomb will he adopt the more appropriate 'fru Alving'. As for the lady of the house, she maintains, for the time being, the respect of title: 'herr pastor.' It goes without saying that the pronoun used by both is 'De'.

The scene begins with a matter-of-fact discussion of rather tedious business questions. But Manders cannot subdue the voice of conventional morality. He breaks the train of thought suddenly by questioning the propriety of Mrs Alving's reading tastes, having already noted unspecified but presumably dangerous books displayed on a nearby table. As her soul-guide he solemnly admonishes her: 'Just be careful, dear Madam!' ['kære frue'] (p.104). Once again, 'frue' and its hint of courtly distance.

Osvald appears for the first time. Like the others, he adopts the deferential 'herr pastor'. However, Manders, obviously more at ease with men, allows himself some familiarity. He calls him 'my dear young friend' (p.129) and asks – with characteristic formality – if he may use his first name. There is of course no question of 'du' here. This fatherly affection is expressed repeatedly by 'min kære Osvald' but then gives way to cold formality when Osvald defends the Bohemian way of life of his Paris friends. The indignant Manders shifts reprovingly to 'herr Alving', and Osvald leaves in dismay.

The conversation between Manders and fru Alving becomes again a business *tête-à-tête*, but the pastor is still simmering over Osvald's iconoclasm. Using the coldly formal 'frue', the cleric finally dispenses with his other roles: it is no longer, he warns her, the business advisor or the childhood friend who is speaking, but ... 'the minister' ['presten'] (p.114) – the solemn guardian of divine law. His speech is now permeated with the grandiloquence of pulpit oratory as, 'with a raised index finger', to emphasize the stage direction, he condemns the lady for dereliction of duty to both husband and son. 'Fru Alving', he concludes with heavy opprobrium, 'you are a guilty mother' (p.117). To make his point more tellingly, Manders uses the archaic, Biblical term for mother ('moder'),[7] rather than the standard form 'mor'.

Stung by Manders' pitiless judgement, fru Alving takes the initiative and moves against her interlocutor. To signify this change of dynamics, she shifts her mode of address from 'herr pastor' to 'Manders'. This use of surname alone was often the way a wife spoke to her husband, and it obviously revives here what was probably an earlier familiarity that Manders wants to banish from memory. On the defensive, stripped of his professional armour, he will be an unwilling confidant, the family friend, the former object of affection; for the text strongly suggests that in her youth fru Alving was in love with Manders (a reciprocal love, we assume), but family interests compelled her to accept a marriage of convenience with the respected and wealthy Kaptein Alving.

Manders betrays his unease by a striking change in the way he himself addresses fru Alving. The latter reminds him that, after she had fled in desperation to him during her first disastrous year of marriage, he had never again set foot in the Alving house until the Kaptein's death. Stung by this memory, Manders lapses unconsciously into a long-forgotten way of addressing her: 'Helene – is that a reproach?' (p.117). As Amundsen points out (p.45), there is an incongruity here between the spontaneous 'Helene' and the pastor's habitual formality. As the most that would be appropriate is 'fru Helene', we have a good indicator of the emotions they shared in the past. Fru Alving bitterly parodies the moral lesson – 'go back to your wifely duty!' – with which her despair was met at that distant moment, and Manders nearly falls back into the past of their near-betrothal. 'Kære ... fru Alving' comes out (p.117), but 'kære Helene' is on the tip of his tongue.

Fru Alving then reveals to Manders the appalling truth about her husband, and Manders is shaken to the depths of his being: not only did Alving continue his dissolute life all through his marriage, but he fathered a child by the then servant Johanne, a child revealed at the end of Act I to be Regine herself.

Interrupted by the midday dinner, an ordeal during which Manders ponders the horrible revelations of Act I, the discussion continues in the second act. Twice more the ashes of Manders' former affection for fru Alving will glow briefly as the terrible *Urszene* comes back to their memories: fru Alving's hysterical 'take me!' to Manders, his stern and terrified order that she return to her lawful husband, whatever the cost. It was then, asserts fru Alving, that Manders' teaching turned out to be so ill-sewn that it came apart utterly, as she reveals in her powerful 'gengangeraktig' speech (p.127).

Shocked, bewildered, Manders, addressing his companion again as 'Helene' (p.128), insists that his action was the greatest victory of his life, 'victory over himself', a phrase we assume to mean a victory over his lingering love for fru Alving. 'It was a crime against both of us' (p.128), bitterly retorts fru Alving, knowing that there was still, at this moment in the past, a vestige of passion between them, a possibility of fulfilled love. Denying now the meaning of his 'victory', he protests that after her marriage he never considered her as any other but another man's wife. 'Really?' (p.128), comments the other with muted scepticism. As if to prove her right unwittingly, Manders uses her Christian name for the third time: 'Helene!' 'One forgets so easily', she observes. 'Not I', proclaims Manders with suspiciously categorical finality. 'Not I ... I am the same person I have always been' (p.128). This declaration encapsulates the utter self-blindness of the pastor as he thrusts an event so dangerously exposed to awareness back into the murky recesses of his unconscious. It is no accident that of all the characters in *Ghosts*, Manders uses the greatest range of forms of address. Unaware of who he truly is, he can only respond successively to the various roles that circumstances impose upon him within the limits of his conscious and hidden life. Of exceptional significance is his thrice-heard cry 'Helene', so at odds with his formal and cold mask.

As if to prove his point in a comic register, Ibsen assigns a bit of harmless mischief to fru Alving in Act II. Engstrand has just left after explaining to Manders with egregious hypocrisy his lofty self-sacrifice in marrying the fallen woman Johanne, Regine's mother. Fru Alving can only marvel at Manders' naiveté; using the familiar surname form of address she says: 'You are and remain a grown-up child, Manders'. And, putting both hands on his shoulders, she adds: 'And I say that I could feel like putting both arms around your neck'. With a bristling 'desslike lyster' ('such impulses'), he pulls away with ruffled dignity (p.135).

So far, our study of forms of address has highlighted psychological ambivalence, uncertainty in motivation. But modes of address may also hint at mysteries built into the dramatic action itself. We touch upon the most distinctive trait of Ibsen's realistic drama, obliquity: the haunting echoes of the unspoken. Though brief and subtle, such a hint occurs, as Amundsen notes (p.46), at the very end of the first act. As the midday dinner is about to be served in the off-stage dining room, Regine asks Osvald (who has regained his composure after his altercation with Manders) about beverages for the meal. Her question is phrased with utmost third-person propriety: 'Does Mr Alving desire white or red wine?' 'Both, jomfru Engstrand' (p.121), replies the young man with the proper formality and distance. 'Bien – meget vel, herr Alving', Regine responds deferentially ('very good'). Up to this point, in one of Ibsen's own bits of mischief, we have not been informed as to why Regine uses French so pretentiously. Only at the end of the second act will we find out.

Having settled the wine question, Osvald goes into the dining room, ostensibly to help Regine uncork the bottles. But then the lady of the house hears the terrible words: 'Osvald da! Er du gal! Slip mig' ('Osvald, are you mad? Let me go' [p.121]). 'Gengangere', murmurs Mrs Alving to the baffled pastor.

This is not the first ghost we have met in the play. For Pastor Manders the late Kammerherre Alving has already come back in the form of his son. When Osvald comes on stage for the first time, smoking his father's pipe, such is his resemblance to the late kaptein that Manders is stunned. It is as if, he exclaims, Kaptein Alving stood before his very eyes (p.108).

However, nothing can compare in dramatic force to Regine's 'slip mig' carrying as it does a massive weight of Ibsenian irony. Fru Alving has just told Manders about her husband's pursuit of Johanne, the maidservant whom he finally made pregnant. She has recalled to memory Johanne's indignant words as Alving made advances to her: 'Slip mig, herr kammerherre! Lad mig være!' ('Let me go, Mr Chamberlain, let me be') (p.119). That the same two words 'slip mig' could occur in the same situation at one generation's remove underlines forcefully the brooding theme of inescapable destiny.

Yet, even this phrase is a ghost, in that we have already heard it in the time of the play, and from an unlikely source. In the very first scene Engstrand attempted to explain his mistreatment of Regine's mother by complaining that she denied him his conjugal rights. Mimicking her protests he whines: 'Slip mig, Engstrand, lad mig være!' (p.95).

However, there are significant contextual differences between Johanne's protest as recalled by fru Alving and Regine's indignant outburst just heard. In fending off Alving Johanne kept her formality even under duress – 'Mr Chamberlain.' As concerns Regine, not only does she address Osvald by his Christian name, but she uses 'du' as well. There could be no greater clash with the deference shown by Regine to Osvald while fru Alving and Manders were within earshot and this indecorous familiarity of a servant toward a young master.

This is typical Ibsen, a rapier-like slash across our expectations. What does this surprising 'du' mean? Is there, as fru Alving fears, already a relationship? But Osvald has been home for less than forty-eight hours. Yet, the girl – this 'splendid, beautiful, fresh young girl' (p.143), as Osvald admiringly describes her – has completely overwhelmed him. Or can we assume the continuation of simple childhood habits? In the ten years since Alving's death, at which time Regine was seven, Osvald sixteen or so. Osvald has been back to see his mother several times; as Regine grew up on the Estate, it would be natural for the two young people to use 'du' and their first names.

Yet, even this is put in doubt later. Toward the end of Act II, Osvald confesses to his mother that two years before, during his last visit to his mother, he jokingly offered to take Regine back to Paris with him when he returned next to Norway (p.143). Now we learn why, having taken Osvald at his word, Regine is busy teaching herself French. It is possible, then, that in this bantering conversation about a possible trip together to Paris Regine and Osvald used the familiar form of address into which Regine inadvertently falls when Osvald approaches her at the end of Act I. Yet, as Osvald repeats his words from that previous visit, he uses 'De': 'Wouldn't you yourself ['De selv'] like to come down [to Paris]?' (p.143). He may then have indeed used the formal 'De' to the fifteen-year-old servant. Or is he editing his own recalled words, knowing that the use of 'du' might make his mother wary? We remember that Osvald plans to have Regine give him the 'helping hand' of administering the fatal dose of morphine when his collapse comes.

Indeed, doubt hangs over Regine's very outburst. We know from the very first scene of the play that she has designs on Osvald, as Engstrand himself has surmised: 'It is amazing how much you bother about the young Mr Alving. – Oho! Could it be that he – ?' (p.98). The vehemence of her reaction and the absence of denial leaves no doubt that her father is right on this count. Thus, when Osvald fondles her at the end of the first act, is she really so indignant that her beauty has drawn this spontaneous gesture of desire? Might not she simply be afraid that such lack of decorum within earshot of authority figures might prejudice her own chances?

In any event, Regine's shock phrase introduces a new set of tensions signalled by forms of address. When Regine returns with the champagne fru Alving has ordered, Osvald, now intent upon making Regine his wife, tells her to get a glass for herself – 'til dig', the accusative of the 'du' form. Fru Alving has used 'du' to Regine quite naturally, as a kind of mother figure. But for the master of the house to be so familiar with a servant, and to invite that servant to share the champagne bottle with himself and his mother, such conduct flies in the face of accepted social norms. With a typical calculation of effect, Ibsen brings Manders back on stage at that very moment. He is almost speechless as he sees Regine: 'What? Here and with a glass in your hand?' (p.145). And when Osvald announces that he plans to leave with Regine as his wife, the pastor, knowing of course that they have the same father, is thunderstruck. But Ibsen then pulls his *pièce bien faite* strings: the fire that has broken out in the orphanage draws all the characters off-stage, and the act ends.

After the interval, the same characters reconvene, and the same forms of address are picked up. Regine is still ill at ease with the informality Osvald seeks to impose on her, especially as she invariably addresses fru Alving by the deferential third-person 'fruen' ('the lady'). Hearing Regine once more refer to him as 'herr Alving', Osvald upbraids the girl: 'Why can't you say "du" to me? Why can't you call me

Osvald?' (p.152). As Amundsen observes (p.46), Osvald here demands two degrees of closeness at once: being addressed by his Christian name and the far greater intimacy betokened by the 'du' form. However, fru Alving's shattering revelations – that Osvald is a sick man and that he and Regine are half-siblings – bring out Regine's cynical, self-interested and opportunistic nature. She will not be a nursemaid to an invalid, and considers Osvald forbidden to her on any account. Her sarcastic parting shot as she leaves the house forever concerns, significantly, the whole question of address propriety (with a mocking French word tossed in for good measure): 'Merci, Mr Alving; oh, now I can say Osvald – but it certainly was not in *that* way that I would have meant it' (p.154). In other words the intimacy should have been between spouses, not between half-brother and half-sister.

The subtleties and ambiguities just analyzed underline the suggestive force carried by modes of address when they are set against the norms of propriety or hint at events over which hovers a cloud of uncertainty. However, one last relationship, while straightforward, remains to be studied in terms of how people talk to one another: mother and son.

In Osvald's case, of course, the range of choice is limited to 'mor' or variations thereof. Yet there can be valid indicators of character even within this limited range. Frequency of use and tone of voice can tell us much. Moreover, Osvald is not limited to the unadorned monosyllable 'mor'. There are a whole gamut of conventionalized adjectives by which characters fill out their address discourse: 'min gode', 'snille', and above all, 'kære'. What is more striking about Osvald is that only once does he couple 'mor' with one of these words: 'kære mor' (p.109), and that very soon after appearing in Act I. On the other hand, he uses 'mor' by itself very often, almost obsessively; it occurs virtually in each speech, however short, sometimes more than once.

Thus his very form of address confirms his painful ambivalence regarding his mother. Not knowing why she sent him away so early in his life, he has felt rejected and resentful for years. Yet, in his bitter distress he longs for a principle of security, a moral support and an understanding confidant. Such is his anguish that he imagines a person as shallow and self-serving as Regine able to fulfil those roles. His resentment toward his mother comes out in his refusal to use more extended terms of endearment like 'kære mor', but his insecurity is revealed in the recurrence of the single word for mother. The more he reveals his terror in the secrets he imparts to his mother, the more urgently he addresses her by the term of family relationship. Indeed, the word begins the phrase by which his mental collapse sets in: 'Mother, give me the sun' (p.160).

Osvald's way of talking to his mother cannot of course be dissociated from her way of addressing him. Ibsen has built into this relationship some powerful effects of contrast. In response to Osvald's reserve, fru Alving is effusive, even maudlin in her glowing treatment of her son. Conventionalized adjectives abound in combination with the word 'gut' ('boy'). We constantly hear endearing phrases like: 'min kære gut', 'min kære, velsignede ('blessed') gut,' 'min stakkars ('poor') gut' and the like.

Ibsen intends us of course to be reminded of Engstrand's 'barnet mit' from the first scene of the play. As if to make his point yet more obvious, he has the carpenter return in Act III, between the two mother-son conversations. Engstrand has attained his goal of obtaining Manders' moral and financial support for his shelter, now that the orphanage is but smoking embers. He triumphantly takes leave of the Alvings and 'barnet mit', as he again calls Regine. But *sotto voce* he tells her, echoing another address word from the first scene, 'come along with me, girl [tøs]' (p.151). With her hopes of marrying into the Alving family dashed, she will this time obey her father and become truly a 'tøs' in the most pejorative sense.

Fru Alving's endearing words to her son occur, then, in a powerfully ironic context. She has the choice, of course, of using his given name with whatever adjective she wishes. She does so frequently but generally in a specific context. Fru Alving tends to use 'Osvald' whenever there is a certain formality between them, as when she delicately warns him not to drink too much: 'Dear Osvald, you should watch out for the liquor. It is strong' (p.135). But more importantly, she exclaims 'Osvald' typically during the most shocking moments of his two scenes with her. And Ibsen almost always emphasizes the tone with an exclamation point. 'You aren't sick, Osvald!' (p.137). 'Osvald! Look at me. No, no, that isn't true' (p.137). And in the second, when Osvald, virtually mad with terror, locks the door on his mother: 'Osvald! Let me get out!' (p.160).

Here, obviously, Mrs Alving is imposing a distance that is really denial. 'Osvald' is the shadow emerging in monstrous stages from her familiar, beloved son. Even at the very end she blindly reassures him, as the sun rises on the prospect of a beautiful day, that he is subject to mere fantasy. 'This has been a dreadful nightmare for you, Osvald' (p.160).[8]

On the other hand, such phrases as 'min gut' occur as expressions of sympathy, solidarity, understanding. Thus when Osvald asks her if she would do anything in the world for him should he ask, she responds that he can count on her, 'my dear only boy' (p.157). But these expressions diminish Osvald at the same time, for they place this twenty-six-year-old man at a stage of early adolescence. Indeed, we may read here an unconscious desire in fru Alving to recapture the past as she would have longed to have lived it, in an affectionate, close tie with her young son whom she felt forced to send away to protect him from seeing Kammerherre Alving in his irreversible slide to imbecility. This denial of her son's manhood comes out powerfully in the wish that she formulates at the very end of the play. During the calm moment at sunrise she assures him: 'Now you will be able to rest. Home with your own mother, you my blessed boy. Anything you point at you will have, as when you were a little child' (p.160).

Taking her at her word, Osvald asks for the sun.

From the foregoing it will be apparent that forms of address contribute in no small measure to the dramatic power of *Ghosts*. To be sure, we behold a rather typical Ibsen world, narrow, hierarchical, formal, proper. At the top in the professional elite we find Manders and the late Kaptein Alving, as well as the Kaptein's widow and son. These are the 'konditionerte folk' (p.155) ('high-class people') to use Regine's contemptuous phase. The lower classes are represented by the lame schemer, Snekker Engstrand, his adopted daughter, and, in memory like the ghost of Alving, Johanne, the carpenter's late wife. In general and on the surface, these people interact as they should. All due respect is shown to 'herr pastor' and to the late 'kammerherre'. Manders addresses fru Alving and her son fittingly as they do him. In talking to Engstrand they use the last name to signal his social inferiority, while he says 'fruen' to fru Alving and 'herr pastor' to Manders. In terms of outward form, all know their place.

However, forces contrary to the social order are at work, signalled in part by the way characters address each other. For Manders and fru Alving, their past lurks behind their awareness as disturbing intrusions: their early affection for each other, and above all, the *Urszene* where Manders turned back the distraught newlywed after her first miserable year of marriage. For Osvald it is a passion for a low-born person on whom he insists on imposing an equal first-name and 'du' relationship. For Regine an instinct of crass self-interest is inhibited by social form itself; she has designs on Osvald but finds it difficult to forget she is a household servant. And she turns back, partly out of propriety, the chance to marry her half-brother.

Even within close and forthright relationships, as with fru Alving and Osvald, hidden desires and fears originating in the past influence how they address each other. Osvald reveals long-suppressed resentment and distrust in the formal, inhibited way he talks to his mother, in his habitual, cold 'mor'. Fru Alving's effusive references to her 'boy' betray a smothering side to her personality, a wish to hold a twenty-six-year-old man in dependency, to deny him autonomous adulthood.

In many respects, these tensions on the verbal level are emblematic of a greater social malaise. And as if to underline the hollowness and fragility of his world, Ibsen allows the law of the jungle to prevail in *Ghosts*. Because of Manders' childlike gullibility and Engstrand's guile and ruthlessness, a brothel will be built, with the Church's blessing, on the ashes of the orphanage. Engstrand proudly assures every one that his enterprise will be called 'Kammerherre Alvings Hjem' ('Chamberlain Alving's Home') and, in a final stiletto thrust from the playwright, the triumphant carpenter adds: 'I can assure you that it will be fully worthy of the late Chamberlain' (p.151).

Notes

1. Robert Olav le Maire Amundsen, 'Ibsen's Use of the Pronouns of Address in Some of his Prose Plays', *Scandinavica*, vol.20, no.1 (May 1981), pp.48-9 (reprinted as chapter 3 of the present volume).
2. All quotations are from Henrik Ibsen: *Samlede Værker*, Gyldendalske Boghandel: København, 1914, VI Band.
3. All translations from the Norwegian are mine. I have tried to make them as close to the text as possible.
4. It was common at the time to address a person by business or trade as well as profession. Thus 'herr grosserer' ('Mr Wholesale Merchant') by which old Werle is addressed in *The*

Wild Duck. Engstrand does not merit a 'herr', but he is often referred to by his trade.

5. Ibsen depicted a number of 'kammerherrer' in his plays. It is the title carried by the elder Bratsberg in *The League of Youth*, and many of the smug and self-satisfied guests we see in the first act of *The Wild Duck* are referred to as 'kammerherrer'. It was obviously a coveted title, although its holders, as Ibsen depicts them, tend to be less than exemplary.

6. Thus Gina in *The Wild Duck* is mentioned as having been a 'husjomfru' Hansen.

7. Curiously enough, while Ibsen has Manders speak as if he were standing in his pulpit, his words contain no direct reference to the Bible or to accepted Lutheran dogma (except the general notion of guilt). Ironically, it is the arrant hypocrite Engstrand who resorts to Biblical language in order better to dupe the pastor. Examples: 'Tvi ... mammon, det er syndens sold' ('No ... mammon, those are the wages of sin') (p.133). Or the more egregious: 'I know some one who took the guilt of others upon himself before, I do' (p.150). We recall as well the Paris doctor's words to Osvald, as reported by Osvald himself: he is sick because 'fædrenes synder hjemsøges på børnene' ('the sins of the fathers are visited upon the sons'), a partial paraphrase of *Exodus* 25:5.

8. Ibsen's words translated by 'dreadful nightmare' are 'en forfærdelig indbildning' – 'indbildning' carrying the idea of 'illusion'.

Originally published November 1994 (Vol. 33, No. 2).

The Poetry of
An Enemy of the People

Brian Johnston

> For I do nothing but go about persuading you all, old and young alike, not to take thought for your persons or your properties but first and chiefly to care about the greatest improvement of the soul.
>
> (Sokrates: *Apology*)

> ...received the decisive thought as to how a philosopher ought to behave towards men from the apology of Sokrates; as their physician, as a gadfly on the neck of man.
>
> (Friedrich Nietzsche: quoted by Walter Kaufmann)

Hegel's account of the disintegration of the spiritual life of the Greek *polis* describes the evolution of the ethical spirit from the communal to the individual, from the objective to the subjective and from the physical to the spiritual. In the *Phenomenology of Spirit* the philosopher somewhat fancifully draws upon the conflict of two brothers who contest each other for control of the community, the outcome of their struggle being that one brother is honoured while the other is treated as an enemy of the community. Hegel's model obviously is the conflict between Eteokles and Polyneikes, dramatized in Aeschylus's *Seven Against Thebes*, and actually belonging to a period of Greek history greatly antedating the spiritual phase under analysis. In the *Philosophy of History* and in the *Philosophy of Fine Art* (or *Aesthetics*)[1] Hegel more appropriately draws upon the figures of Sokrates and of Aristophanes, radical and conservative opponents, to illustrate the divisions within the Greek (predominantly Athenian) *polis* that led to the overthrow of this phase of spirit thus preparing the way for the Roman and Christian phases to follow.

The parallels between Hegel's account of the decline of the *polis* and Ibsen's *An Enemy of the People* are striking: equally striking is the presence of other Athenian details beneath the imagery of modern realism of Ibsen's play. In Hegel's account, it was the very repression of the ethical individuality represented by Sokrates that further created this individualism, which then proved to be inimical to the old spirit upon which the city-state was founded. In Sokrates-Plato (*The Republic*) the Greek spirit turned from the *polis*, as no longer an adequate abode, to construct an ideal alternative at the same time that Aristophanes, in his comedies, presented the fatally divisive factions within the city-state, before the Athenian public. Thomas Stockmann's little Norwegian community is no Athens and Peter, certainly, is no Perikles, but these Greek patterns do erupt, ironically reduced and hilariously distorted, in the modern drama. Ibsen's method is a form of *galskap* which is as playful as it is learned and it quite outrageously exploits the possibilities of such archetypal clusters as Eteokles/Polyneikes, Perikles/Sokrates, the disciples Peter and Thomas and the conflict of Christ and Luther with Satan.[2]

The main argument of the play, for which the richest metaphors are created, is that we as individuals must look for truth and freedom not as citizens within the structure of the sustaining community but through a hard-won individualism that entails a more lonely and more desolating spiritual commitment. The play does not *state* this idea but *enacts* it, as a human drama on many levels, and with a great deal of energetic, Aristophanic humour. This argument involves a decisive shift in metaphors from the physical to the spiritual, from the objective to the subjective, from the communal to the individual, and from conditions of comfortable material enclosure to conditions of more alarming but more invigorating desolation. The movement of *liberation*, more gravely effected in the three preceding plays, now takes on comedic rhythms.

The dialectical action of the play is less subterranean than that of *Ghosts*, but the order of artistry is no less accomplished: for the art of brilliant comedic surface detail and of eloquently overt expression requires as much skill and imagination as the art of subtle and ironic tragic implication – just as the art of Aristophanic political comedy is as poetically accomplished, in its very different way, as the art of Sophoclean tragedy.

The theme of the individual, passionately committed to the well-being of his community, which he loves, who is set upon and branded its enemy for speaking unwelcome truth, goes back at least to the classic instance of Sokrates, that first 'enemy of the people'. The intellectual explorer of new and unwelcome truths, Sokrates, in Hegel's account (as in Nietzsche's *Birth of Tragedy*) was to prove fatal to the spirit of the community that he sought to save. After being condemned by the community, Sokrates was offered the opportunity of exile, but stayed his ground just as Stockmann will consider, then reject the opportunity of exile.

The parallels between Stockmann and the historical Sokrates are those of situation and character. Sokrates, through his 'inner voice' continually generated more and more alarming ideas. Like Stockmann he could see what other men could not see. His abstraction of mind, his love of the company of young men, his delight in feasting and drinking, his *naïveté* and ebullience, are traits we find also in Thomas Stockmann. Mrs Stockmann's alarmed disapproval of her husband's actions in the first half of the play echoes the notorious attitude of poor Xantippe and Stockmann is given the same number of children as Sokrates: one adult and two young boys.[3]

In the nineteenth century the scientist was the closest equivalent to the philosopher of ancient Greece, similarly transforming the world we conceive we inhabit, similarly arousing controversy by overthrowing conventional ideas. Stockmann begins by detecting the microbes within physical reality that are undetectable by ordinary seeing, then discovers the spiritual forces of disease that are undetectable by ordinary thinking. The pollution that descends upon the town from the surrounding hills is seen as insignificant compared to the pollution entering the community from the spiritual past. As long as society gains obvious advantage from the thinker or from the doctor-scientist, so it sees him as its friend (*folkevenn*); as soon as this same intellectual heroism engages with unwelcome problems, such heroism is seen as dangerous and inimical and the same individual becomes the people's enemy (*folkefiende*).

Thomas Stockmann is an eternal doubter and questioner, while his brother Peter is the rock of orthodoxy upon which the spirit is petrified. Thomas, the scientist, is the investigator of reality while *Peter* is its established codification. The two brothers, therefore, represent the extremes of their community's intellectual life and fight for control of it: a contest comically enacted in the brief capture and repossession of the mayor's hat and stick. Between these two extremes Ibsen creates a brilliant portrait gallery of political types: Aslaksen, the printer and chairman of the small property owners, bold in his defiance of the distant national government but pusillanimous before local power; Hovstad, the 'radical' journalist who can be bought for the right price; Billing, who claims he is taking part in a revolution while at the same time applying for a public office; and, finally, the townspeople who are furious at being told they have the mentality of a mob just as they are perfectly exemplifying Plato's description of the mob.

Outside this political portraiture, which is more developed than that of *Pillars of Society*, is a separate group, Stockmann's family, which is a more meticulously rendered image of everyday familial life than in the earlier plays of this group. Aloof from both the political and the familial spheres is Captain Horster, the sea-voyager who, like a Joseph Conrad hero, remains detached from the squabbling political life of the communities he drops in upon on his voyages.

In the beginning of the play Thomas is the doctor of *physical* life. He loves his new material prosperity, his home comforts of feasting and drinking, the burgeoning new life that he imagines flourishing in his community, the presence of healthy young bodies, at his dinner table, devouring roast beef and drinking toddy. At the end of the play his home comforts are shattered, he is ostracized, his young friends are spiritual cowards incapable of new ideas, he sees his task not as a physical, but as a spiritual doctor and he envisages setting up a school to feed growing young *minds*. This major transition from physical to spiritual is amplified by many details in the play and if, as I believe, *An Enemy of the People* also is recollecting the development of the life of the *polis*, Stockmann's development from ministering to bodies to ministering to minds can be seen as a recollection of the evolution of Athens from the physical *gymnasia* and baths to the founding of Plato's Academy and Aristotle's Lyceum – a major 'moment' in the advance of the human spirit.

The central and appropriately Hellenic metaphor of the play is that of the baths, and it is to this metaphor that detractors of the play point to justify their low opinion of its poetry.[4] The metaphor, it is said, states its themes, makes its analogies and points its lesson so obviously that it is not able imaginatively to *expand*, to become a symbol instigating the deepest reflection on our part. This, I believe, is to do it considerably less than justice, to see only its obvious aspects. The metaphor is perfectly suited to the purposes of political comedy, instigating violent action and reaction. Ibsen's metaphors, in all his plays, have the excellent quality of being at the same time clusters of meanings, of *ideas*, and of being palpable, functioning *things* in the reality of the play. While, in the nature of poetic metaphor, the baths illuminate the larger spiritual reality of the play, they also define the motives and the characters of individuals in the story *and* instigate actions and speeches on their parts. The history of the origins and development of the baths is the history of the community itself so that, so to speak, the community has itself created the living metaphor by which it will be judged.

The baths originate as a spiritual or intellectual reality, as the 'idea' or intangible vision of Thomas Stockmann in his exile in the north. He impresses this vision upon his fellow-citizens who then appropriate it, make it a tangible reality set up for personal profit, at the same time bungling the work against the doctor's warnings.[5] The baths now become a centre of struggle for political power and when the doctor reveals their calamitous defects the radicals and liberals envision the institution becoming the means to a political revolution, by sweeping out the board of governors and installing a new one. But the baths also have become the source of the community's wealth so that whole streets of doll houses have been built round their existence. The owners of these doll houses have a representative, Aslaksen, who articulates the moral compromises they assent to when their interests are threatened by the publication of truth.

The sources of the baths, the springs, go back to nature, before the human community existed, but the pipelines do not go back far and high enough (a delicious little subsymbol) so that the waters become contaminated by intervening human action – the tanneries and the bungling work of the profit-motivated governors. As Rolf Fjelde observes, water, in the Bible, is associated with life and with the spirit. In the play the waters that were intended to bring physical health instead bring sickness – but as Thomas Stockmann ponders their significance so they become metaphors for spiritual illness and the poetic elements of his new vision of spiritual health. His microscope detects swarming bacteria invisible to the ordinary vision and, as his community becomes as agitated and active as the bacteria it refuses to acknowledge, so he observes this new spiritual agitation and once again makes of the baths what they were in the beginning: an idea not perceptible to the ordinary ethical vision. When he first thought up the idea of the baths Thomas was lonely and separated from his beloved community, longing to rejoin it and to share in its life. When the baths once again become an idea, a metaphor, he is once again lonely and seriously contemplates exiling himself permanently from his community.

The baths, usually named after Herakles, were a central institution in Hellenic life. In Aristophanes' *The Clouds*, the play in which that enemy of the people, Sokrates, is mocked and physically attacked, a debate on the baths, in which Philosophy attacks and Sophistry defends the institution, is a major part of the young man Pheidippides' initiation into the Sokratic mysteries. References to the public baths constantly appear in Hellenic literature: in Aristophanes, in Plato, in Plutarch. In Act II of *Emperor and Galilean* the new students arriving in Athens are immediately escorted to the baths with great ceremony by the venal philosophers, increasing Julian's disenchantment with Hellenic learning. Not only do the baths signify the idea of physical well-being, therefore: they also call to mind aspects of Hellenic culture.

The baths metaphor, therefore, is poetry: a very jaunty, humorous, energetic poetry not unlike what the Elizabethans called 'conceits' (from *concetti*, or concepts) and Ibsen's method here, as in his other plays, could be termed 'conceptual poetry' – a poetry that insists its metaphors be intellectually thought out and physically established. Early in the play Peter Stockmann declared, 'these baths will become the very life-principle of our town', and Ibsen develops the conceit of the baths until they are shown to be just that!

The play opens in Thomas Stockmann's living room and there is immediate emphasis upon *physical* well-being. Figures from the community come to the house to eat and drink heartily and the word 'smake' (taste) is used three times in the few opening lines of dialogue, while the conversation turns upon the subjects of food and digestion. Thomas's brother, Peter, has a poor digestion – for food and for ideas-and takes no pleasure in feasting nor in domestic well-being.[6] Thomas, on the contrary, rejoices in his new physical well-being as much as in the new intellectual order that he naïvely sees as transforming the world. He is delighted with his good salary, a comfortable home, an elegant lamp which 'concentrates the light' so well and with the spectacle of the bodies of the healthy young men eating at his table. The baths themselves will bring material benefits to the town: land values are increasing, property taxes are being lowered and the expense of public welfare has been diminished. It is a picture of the good life in purely physical/material terms: a town prospering, invalids being cured, young people gathering strength and the good doctor ministering to the physical and material well-being of his fellow-citizens.[7] After leaving the supper table the young 'radical', Billing, declares that the meal has made him feel like 'a new man' – a condition that will prove intellectually more difficult to achieve than he is aware.

Thomas senses that he is on the brink of a discovery that will make him even more of a hero to his beloved town, for his investigations into the conditions of the baths have alerted him to a danger imperilling the community. He conceived of his task as, like Herakles, overcoming the physical peril and being honoured by his community. But his early quarrel with his brother, Peter, alerts *us*, even before the discovery is known, to the possibility of a contest ensuing between the brothers for the intellectual and ethical control of this community. In Act I, Thomas happily assents to Billing's rhapsody on the democratic nature of society, but Captain Horster somewhat deflates this account by observing that democracy would not work on a ship – as Plato famously observes in Book VI of *The Republic*. The discovery of physical danger, and the resolve to rescue the community from this danger culminates in happy physical action, as Thomas whirls his wife around the living-room.

In Act II Thomas's idea of himself as the old-style, Heraklean hero of his community seems to be confirmed. Hovstad and Aslaksen see Thomas as their champion and the people's friend (*folkevenn*) who will help to shake up the political life of the community and they hint at organizing a public demonstration to express the community's gratitude to its saviour. The innocent euphoria of Thomas who is living in a dreamworld ironically at odds with his scientific vocation, is effectively deflated by his brother, Peter, who indicates that the world by which Thomas so happily defines himself and his vocation, is capable of striking back. This is still mainly a family action – the quarrel between the two brothers in which Peter is supported by Thomas's wife – so that the setting is still that of Thomas's home: but in this Act Thomas's eyes partially are opened and he realizes that he is engaged in a war in which he will need allies. His understanding of his community has advanced to the point at which he sees factions where first he saw only happy unity. He sides with what he conceives are the forces of truth and freedom, the liberals, which means that he no longer is the Heraklean saviour of the whole community but only one force in its total structure – the progressive force. Thus he already has moved to a relatively more isolated stance, that of progress against reaction, and this is only a stage on the journey towards a more complete isolation.

When the fraternal conflict moves beyond the bounds of the family to become divisive of the community, in Act III, the setting changes to the *public* location of the office of the *People's Courier* which conceives of itself as engaging in bold intellectual warfare within society. The very title of the paper, *Folkebudet*, warns us that its radicalism is less bold than it proclaims, for a 'courier' or messenger merely carries other people's ideas and messages and does not initiate its own: a forewarning thoroughly confirmed by subsequent events in which the paper reveals that, far from being a pathbreaker of ideas, it dare not go against its reader's prejudices and opinions. In the cluster, *folkevenn, folkebudet, folkefiende*, the messenger's is the least distinguished role.[8] The journalists excitedly proclaim they are engaged in a 'war' and a 'revolution' and the overthrow of the old oligarchy, but Ibsen supplies clues to indicate the self-serving and duplicitous nature of their commitment. Billing declares that when he read Thomas's manuscript 'it was exactly as if I could see the revolution breaking like the dawn' but his fellow radical turns and whispers, 'Shh! Don't say that so Aslaksen hears', and so Billing continues, *dropping his voice*, 'Aslaksen's a chicken-livered coward'.

These self-professed radicals cautiously whispering obviously are not the bold young minds that Stockmann believes he has enlisted to his cause, so that we are not surprised when, as they understand the forces they are up against, they betray him. They certainly are no match for the mayor, Peter who, however dense he may seem to his brother, at least understands the world of power better than Thomas and knows how to manipulate the pseudo-radicals of the liberal press.[9]

The climax of Act III is the beautifully symbolic action of Thomas's brief possession of the mayor's hat and stick, his humiliating defeat, and the repossession of the insignia of office by his furious brother, an action that comedically encapsules the Eteokles-Polyneikes conflict. Thomas paraded before his enraged brother imagining the forces of society marching behind him and endorsing this *coup d'état*: but the mayor's political mastery (Peter's main Periklean attribute) has effectively intimidated these forces, so that he can reclaim his hat and stick with the words, 'That was an abrupt end to your first term in office!' Deserted by the political leaders of society, Thomas still cherishes the rebel's last illusion: he can go directly to the people.

In this act there has taken place a significant shift from the physical (the condition of the polluted baths) to the spiritual (the nature of the community's political life), so that it is appropriate that the setting should be a newspaper office: a place of words, opinions, censorship and the interests of different political groups. When he confidently entered the office Thomas had declared that 'this isn't simply a matter of sewers and water mains anymore. No, it's the whole society that has to be purged and disinfected.' After his defeat and betrayal his mission will become more 'abstract' still – the cause of truth itself: and in this cause he will gain a significant disciple, his wife Katherine, a conversion that will make more plausible his final resolution to become the teacher of his community. This movement from material to spiritual affairs also is a move from happy involvement with his community to further and further alienation from it, from an emphatically *objective* idea of reality deriving from direct participation in the social structure, to a more *subjective* idea in which the social structure will increasingly be critically remoulded by Thomas's imagination, to illustrate new concepts of reality to which he is being led.

It is in Act IV that we see this unambiguously. The action is that of the most extreme dialectic confrontation: the community *v.* the individual, the seer and the blind, the unwelcome truth teller and the willingly deluded. One is reminded of Plato's parable of the prisoners in the cave who will turn in fury upon the man who returns to liberate them to light and truth. I think we also are meant to see the situation in which Thomas faces the swarming, violent crowd, seeing them now with the clarity of new spiritual perception, as analogous to the scientist first observing through his microscope the swarming and malignant bacteria in the spa's water: the bacteria, as it were, now have grown immensely and directly set upon the doctor. The scene is filled with animal imagery and references, reminiscent of such Aristophanic comedies as *The Wasps*, *The Birds*, *The Frogs*. One of the most outrageous animal references, one that infuriates the crowd, is Thomas's defence of eugenics by appeal to the example of the breeding of dogs and hens: precisely the same argument, with precisely the same illustrations (dogs and birds) used by Sokrates in *The Republic*.

The setting, an old-fashioned room in Captain Horster's house – the only space available for the meeting – points to the new spiritual isolation and individualism toward which Thomas is being impelled, for the young Captain is an aloof and detached character in the play, uninvolved in the community's political life. The movement from democratic involvement to greater intellectual individualism was, Hegel observed, a development within the ancient Greek *polis* that was to prove decisive for the spiritual life of the West: and one important stage of that development was the extreme anti-democratic argument of Plato's *The Republic*. Thomas's tactless denial of the 'belief 'that the common man, the ignorant, untrained, undeveloped member of society has the same right to judge and approve, 'to advise and to govern as the intellectually distinguished minority', is almost a transliteration of Plato's description of the common man and of his argument for an intellectual elite – the guardians – to govern the community. The crowd's reply, 'So only the accomplished should rule!' is the natural democratic response to Thomas's Platonic proposal.[10]

This extreme dialectic development, from altruistic doctor to dishonoured prophet, from the healer of physical ills to the fierce healer of spiritual ills, from the friend of the community to its designated enemy, and from the citizen to the individual, makes up too careful and controlled an aesthetic pattern and dramatic rhythm for us to agree to the consensus of opinion that the play is a somewhat hasty reaction on Ibsen's part to the public rejection of *Ghosts*.[11] Even Act IV is designed to do more than to read off to the audience a civics lesson. An image of extreme alienation between the increasingly individualist Thomas and the increasingly outraged community is needed for the argument of the play, and nothing could be comedically more appropriate than the spectacle of the rebel, before his infuriated audience, excitedly and naively proclaiming one outrageous 'discovery' after another, rising to an exaltation of naive sublimity and of total and hopeless estrangement from his hearers. The scene has much of the quality of the famous *parabases* in Aristophanic comedy, where the poet speaks out directly and provocatively to his audience-nowhere more so than in *The Clouds* where he directly reproaches the audience for preferring inferior poets. One is reminded, also, of Book V of *The Republic*, where Sokrates is aware that he is bringing forward a succession of proposals, each more outrageous than its predecessor, likening each proposal to a great wave striking against the side of a ship – the greatest wave being the concept of the philosopher-king, that summit of the intellectual *élite*. We are meant to look at Thomas more critically, more amusedly, than biographical interpretation suggests: the scene is very *funny*, with Katherine Stockmann desperately and continually coughing in a vain attempt to signal to her impetuous husband who infallibly sets about insulting the entire world before him.[12]

If Thomas and his community have taken up postures of extreme alienation from each other, then this suggests that *both* sides need to 'learn more' and are merely at one stage of a process of mutual spiritual evolution. Until this point, the archetypal identities of Stockmann had been Hellenic (notably Sokrates) but now he begins to shade off into the identity of another martyr, declaring as the meeting breaks up in chaos, 'I am not as meek as a certain person; I'm not saying, "I forgive them, for they know not what they do"'; and in Act V this combination of the Sokratic and the messianic is further developed, as the dialectic of the *polis* merges into a newer higher phase.

For Hegel, as, later, for Nietzsche, the collapse of the spiritual life of the *polis*, exemplified and in part caused by the critical individualism of Sokrates, and accompanied by the political divisions dramatized by Aristophanes, ended one phase of Hellenism. For Hegel it was the necessary tragic preparation, involving alienation from nature and society (the Fall) that would lead to spiritual subjectivity and the long, painful training of the spirit by Christianity. The playful conjunction of Hellenic and Christian archetypes in Act V is, therefore, appropriate to this last of the first four plays in the Cycle that have dealt with the *objective* world of political, social and ethical institutions (the community and the family). It prepares the way for the first play of the second group, *The Wild Duck*, with its more sombrely messianic patterns and its shift to the submerged, fallen and subjective condition of alienation.

In Act V we return to Stockmann's house and, in sharp contrast to the opening of the play with its scene of happy celebration of material and domestic comforts to which the citizens are welcomed, it is now a place under siege, its windows broken and stones and rocks strewing the floor. The image of the besieged house probably recollects the closing scene of *The Clouds*, in which Sokrates' house is attacked and burned and the philosopher is driven out. Thomas vows to collect the stones as 'holy relics' (*heligdom*) for his sons to contemplate every day, as if the veneration of martyrs was about to begin! The setting has shifted from the living room, with its emphasis upon material comfort and on feasting, to Stockmann's *study*, emphasizing the new programme of education (reminiscent of the founding of Plato's *Academy*) which Thomas will announce. From the *parabasis* method of direct confrontation of Act IV we return to the complex ethical comedy of the first three acts, beginning with Thomas's indignation as the pussillanimity of the citizens who dared throw only mediocre-sized rocks at the house. Sokratic themes of ostracism emerge. The family is to be evicted from its house, the daughter, Petra is dismissed from her teaching, and the sons, Egil and Morten, are dismissed from school. (The pedagogic details, here, in the setting of the study, build up the emphasis upon education). If this *total* hostility of the community, in which not one courageous soul, apart from Horster, emerges to support them, seems unrealistic – even at Sokrates' trial almost half the citizens voted against condemnation – we should remember that Ibsen is less concerned with creating slice-of-life naturalism than in fashioning a brilliant comedic argument whose situations, recollecting and re-enacting their archetypal models, are pushed to dialectic extremes.

The Sokratic themes continue when Thomas is offered the escape of exile by the mayor, and when Thomas vows to become a 'teacher' and gather round him 'at least a dozen' outcast ragamuffins – which also nicely announces his emerging messianism. The temptation of exile after which, if he is repentant, Thomas might be re-instated, now is followed by the satanic temptation, for old Morten Kiil, 'the badger' who once was hounded (*hundsvortete*) from the town council 'like a dog',[13] enters and offers Thomas wealth and power if he will retract his proclamation of the truth. Morton Kiil comments on the desolation of the room and, with the pile of rocks on the table between them, the temptation scene seems to parody that of Christ and Satan in the desert, where Christ is urged by Satan to convert the stones to bread. Kiil has brought up all available shares in the baths and offers these to Stockmann. This would place Thomas in complete control of the baths, thus able to dominate his community completely. To attain to this supreme power, Thomas must clear Kiil's name, for it is the latter's tanneries whose filth has most polluted the streams feeding into the community. Kiil sees himself, his father and grandfather as 'three murdering angels',[14] and he begs Thomas to make him 'clean' – that is, to clear his reputation, his merely external identity; but Thomas's new Brand-like mission, over which he momentarily wavers, involves a more intrinsic cleanliness, *within*. When Thomas overcomes Kiil's temptation he rejects worldly power for spiritual in the manner of Christ, and he tells his tempter, 'When I look at you it is as if I saw the devil'.

What succumbing to this satanic temptation would have entailed now is swiftly and comically illustrated as Hovstad and Aslaksen enter, demanding a part in Stockmann's collusion with Kiil and offering, in return, the support of public opinion. Stockmann's triumphant assumption of power, then, would be assured: he would become virtually the *tyrannos* of this society but would be the monarch of a kingdom of lies. Grabbing his umbrella, Stockmann drives out these traders of the spirit. His note to Kiil, in which he finally rejects the temptation, is the word 'No', repeated *three* times, recollecting Christ's threefold rejection of satanic temptation. As he resolves to stay his ground and fight within his community, Stockmann concludes:

> Well, if I haven't been visited today by all the devil's couriers, I don't know what! But now I shall sharpen my pen against them until it becomes an awl;[15] I will dip it in venom and gall; I shall hurl my inkstand at their skulls.

The references, here, to such rebels as Christ and Luther have the buoyant openness and directness suitable to the comedic rhythm of the play where the audience is meant to enjoy, immediately, the archetypal patterns it sees emerging through the realistic action. It is a method very different from that of the subtle and secretive archetypal patterns buried within the structure and texture of *Ghosts* and of *The Wild Duck*; plays in which the inwardness of the patterns calls for a more sombrely meditative response from us; but it is an equally difficult form of dramatic artistry. That it is not crassly obvious is evidenced by the fact that these patterns, as far as I know, mostly have gone unrecognized by interpreters of the drama. The present writer is conscious, too, that he has picked up only a fraction of the full range of cultural reference in this most cleverly poetic play.

Notes

1. The Hegelian titles vary with translations. *The Phenomenology of Mind* is, in its new translation, *The Phenomenology of Spirit*, The full titles of the other works are: *Lectures on the Philosophy of History* and *Lectures on the Philosophy of Fine Art*, the latter work now available in a fine new translation by T. M. Knox, Hegel's *Aesthetics: Lectures on Fine Art* (Oxford University Press, 1975). By happy coincidence an '*Oxford Hegel*' is now emerging to parallel the '*Oxford Ibsen*'.
2. Realism, of course, should not be committing such *galskap*: if Ibsen, nonetheless, is doing so we simply have to put aside, as inadequate, the conventional definitions of realism.
3. Sokrates' eldest child also is male. Ibsen puts Petra's femininity to useful dramatic effect *vis-à-vis* Hovstad and Horster.
4. 'Of all Ibsen's plays *An Enemy if the People* is the least poetical, the one that makes the least appeal to our sensibilities.' William Archer, *The Collected Works if Henrik Ibsen*, Vol. VIII (Charles Scribner's Sons, New York, 1922), p. xiii. Jennette Lee, whose *The Ibsen Secret* was astonishingly ahead of its time in its account of Ibsen's symbolism – her book was published in 1907 when nothing comparable was being done in literary criticism (Caroline Spurgeon's study of Shakespeare's imagery did not appear until many years later) – nevertheless slights the symbol of the baths, noting that 'it holds throughout, but it is not, artistically, as perfect as in *Ghosts*' (Putnam, New York, 1907), p. 63.
5. Thus the man of mere ideas also is more practical, ultimately, than the pragmatists.
6. As a Hellenophile I am dismayed to see these as, comically reductive, Periklean

attributes. The great Athenian statesman, according to Hegel, 'renounced private life, withdrew from all feasts and banquets and pursued without intermission his aim of being useful to the state' [*Philosophy if History* (Dover Publications, New York, 1956), p. 260].

7. The medical details also are appropriate to the Hellenic themes of the play for medicine was one of the supreme achievements of Hellenic culture.

8. The satiric depiction of the newspaper office brings to mind the chapter in James Joyce's *Ulysses* that is set in the offices of the Dublin newspaper and which draws upon the 'cave of winds' episode in *The Odyssey*. The office is a place of the noisy dissemination of conventional platitudes. Joyce's lifelong admiration for Ibsen might have derived from a recognition of shared methods between himself and 'the old masterbilker'.

9. We learn that Stensgaard, the comic villain of *The League if Youth*, used to sit in the office of *Folkebudet*: a clear hint, to attentive Ibsenites, of the ethical shortcomings of the place. As Mortensgaard, he will occupy another newspaper office in *Rosmersholm*.

10. Is it also Ibsen's proposal? He insisted his method, in *Ghosts*, precluded the obtrusion of his own opinions in his work and this, I believe, holds good for all his work. In *An Enemy of the People*, appropriately to the spiritual *gestalt* he is dramatizing, he presents us with the most audacious and unsettling dialectical conflict, but as an *aesthetic* idea or argument.

11. That *An Enemy if the People* was begun before *Ghosts* has not in the least disturbed this settled opinion which, like so many of the conventional notions of Ibsen's art, has contributed to the layers of critical dust under which these audacious works are smothered. Nothing is more dispiriting to those who are aware of the life of these plays than to encounter in the secondary critical literature (e.g. the theatre programme notes) the dismally familiar and pitifully inadequate, smug commentaries: *Ghosts* was written in answer to the reaction to *A Doll's House*; *An Enemy of the People* was written in answer to the reaction of *Ghosts*; in *The Wild Duck* Ibsen is having second thoughts about idealism – and so on, relentlessly trivializing the Cycle all the way to *When We Dead Awaken*.

12. Ibsen commented that, though he got on well with Stockmann, the doctor was 'more muddle-headed than I am' (letter to Friedrich Hegel, 9 September, 1882).

13. The dog-identity of the devil is a long tradition in European folklore and letters. Goethe's Mephistophelean poodle (*Faust*) actually reappears, with fatal effect, in Ibsen's account of his Skien childhood, killing a night watchman. This is a classic 'tall story' for, as the dead man was the only witness to the black poodle, its manifestation must have remained unknown!

14. It is difficult to see how the father and grandfather could be guilty of polluting the baths, which were built after their lifetimes. Obviously the image of the 'three murdering angels' (a reference to *Revelations*?) was important enough to Ibsen for him to overlook this incongruity.

15. I have kept 'awl' (*syl*) because, in this packed little speech, it seems to refer to a confrontation between a cobbler or carpenter and the devil which I have been unable to track down.

Originally published November 1979 (Vol. 18, No. 2).

Ghosts and White Horses: Ibsen's *Gengangere* and *Rosmersholm* Revisited

Marie Wells

Ibsen research has developed rapidly since 1966 when Raymond Williams wrote that by the time Ibsen reached maturity, 'the last source of liberal tragedy had appeared: the increasingly confident identification of a false society as man's real enemy'.[1] The hero in the battle against this false society was 'the individual liberator', who 'by an act of will [...] refused the role of victim and became a new kind of hero' (p.95). However, the protagonist is also a tragic hero not only because he 'is opposed and destroyed by a false society' (p.97), but because he finds 'that as a man he belongs to this world, and has its destructive inheritance in himself' (p.98).

Research published since Williams' book appeared has been less interested in the nexus of the individual locked in battle with a false society and more interested in the battle going on in the psyche of the liberating individual. This research has developed along several lines. One represented by Erik Østerud[2] concentrates on the psychological conflict between Christian and pagan/instinctual values often presented in folkloristic terms. Another for which Jørgen Haugan[3] could stand as representative argues that Ibsen's protagonists are driven by a dual motivation, which aims to *appear to be* in the service of liberation while concealing a less noble, more selfish, often sexual aim. Yet another line of criticism for which Errol Durbach and Bjørn Hemmer could be regarded as representatives concentrates on the moral quality and consequences of the liberation to which some of Ibsen's heroines (and they are mainly heroines) aspire.

In a paper delivered in 1983,[4] and based on the ideas of Erich Fromm and Guido de Ruggiero, Errol Durbach distinguished between a 'freedom from' and a 'freedom to'. He sees Nora and Mrs Alving as 'exemplars of the "free from" condition – naked, burdened and tormented in the very act of delivering themselves from the subjection of mind and spirit' (p.15) and Rebekka West, and Ellida Wangel as embodying the '"free to" state, with its central experience of joyful autonomy where the liberated heroine, reassumes her place in the world, with all its ties and burdens – but without eliminating her essential individuality' (p.98). More recently still, Bjørn Hemmer has explored 'the negative sides to Ibsen's depiction of man's struggle to take possession of and act on this individual freedom'.[5] The sexual passion which overwhelms Rebekka and drives her to sweep 'the unfortunate Beate into the mill-race' (p.180) Hemmer sees as an example of this negative aspect.

It is Durbach's and Hemmer's line of approach which I wish to follow and carry further in this article. What I hope to show is that while liberation from dead values in Ibsen's plays becomes ever more necessary, Ibsen makes the value of that liberation ever more ambiguous. The plays that will be considered are *Gengangere* (*Ghosts*) and *Rosmersholm*, with an occasional backward glance to *Et dukkehjem* (*A Doll's House*).

Mrs Alving is an obvious example of Williams's tragic, liberating hero, and in her speech about ghosts she reveals an acute awareness of how much her mental life has been infected by the 'destructive inheritance' of the world:

> jeg tror næsten, vi er gengangere allesammen, pastor Manders. Det er ikke bare det, vi har arvet fra far og mor, som går igen i os. Det er alleslags gamle afdøde meninger og alskens gammel afdød tro og sligt noget. Det er ikke levende i os; men det sidder i alligevel, og vi kan ikke bli' det kvit.[6]

> (I'm inclined to think that we are all ghosts, Pastor Manders, every one of us. It's not just what we inherit from our mothers and fathers that haunts us. It's all kinds of old defunct theories, all sorts of old defunct beliefs, and things like that. It's not that they actually *live* on in us; they are simply lodged there, and we cannot get rid of them.)[7]

She started her married life as someone who had been socialized through and through (by her mother and aunts), and who accepted the values of the society that formed her. However, she has developed a critical attitude to those values, and consequently has slowly been trying to free herself from them in order to achieve a more honest moral standpoint. The event that changed her life was not so much her marriage to Captain Alving, but the fact that when she fled from Alving to Pastor Manders he sent her back to her husband. As she says,

> ...da De tvang mig ind under det, som De kaldte pligt og skyldighed; da De lovpriste som ret og rigtigt hvad hele mit sind oprørte sig imod som imod noget vederstyggeligt. Da var det jeg begyndte at se Deres lærdomme efter i sømmene. Jeg vilde bare pille ved en eneste knude; men da jeg havde fåt den løst, så raknet det op altsammen (IX, p.92).

> (...when you forced me to submit to what you called my duty and my obligations. When you praised as right and proper what my whole mind revolted against, as against some loathsome thing. It was then I began to examine the fabric of your teachings. I began picking at one of the knots, but as soon as I'd got that undone, the whole thing came apart at the seams.) (V, p.385)

Mrs Alving's guide on her road to liberation since then and up to the opening of the play was the journals and magazines which Pastor Manders sees on her table and so disapproves of. Then in Act I she listens to Oswald telling Pastor Manders about his life in Paris and she believes that what he says expresses her ideal, and she decides that Oswald shall be her spokesman. When at the end of Act I Oswald reveals himself to be not only a spokesman for the future but a ghost of the past, this does not change anything for Fru Alving, for at the beginning of Act II, emboldened by her reading and Oswald's vision of the free life in Paris, she starts attacking all the conventions which have so far ruined her life. To take but one example: when Manders says that her marriage was arranged in strict accord with law and order, Mrs Alving, retorts, 'ja, dette med lov og orden! Jeg tror mangengang, det er det, som volder alle ulykkerne her i verden' / 'oh, all this law and order! I often think *that's* the cause of all the trouble in the world' (IX, p.89; V, p.381). A little later she says that if she thought Oswald were serious in his intentions towards Regine, she might even sanction a relationship between them even though he is her half brother. She believes it is her cowardice – the effect of her conditioning by society, in other words the ghosts that prevent her from saying this.

The final prompt in Mrs Alving's struggle for liberation comes at the end of Act II, when Oswald tells her how on a previous visit home he had half promised Regine a trip to Paris. She had taken him seriously and when he came home this time had reminded him of his promise. As he tells this to his mother, he says

> ...da jeg så den prægtige, smukke, kærnefriske pige stå der for mig – før havde jeg jo aldrig lagt videre mærke til hende – men nu, da hun stod her ligesom med åbne arme færdig til at ta' imod mig [...] da gik det op for mig, at i hende var der redning; for jeg så der var livsglæde i hende (IX, p.111).

> (...mother ... this girl looked so marvellous standing there, so good-looking and vital ... I'd never really noticed her very much before ... Then when she stood there, ready it seemed to take me in her arms [...] it was then I realized that she was my salvation. Because she was filled with the joy of life.) (V, p.401/2)

The word '*livsglæde*', 'joy of life', makes an instant impression on Mrs Alving and she immediately asks, 'Livsglæde – ? Kan der være redning i *den*?' (joy of life...? Can there be salvation in *that*?), and a few lines later she returns to the matter again and asks, 'Osvald, – hvad var det du sa' om livsglæden?' (Oswald ... what was that you were saying about the joy of life?) (IX, p.112; V, p.402). Oswald then goes on to contrast life in Norway where he believes no one knows anything about this concept with life elsewhere where he believes people do, in fact he argues that 'derude kan det kendes som noget så jublende lyksaligt, bare det at være til i verden' (in other countries they think it's tremendous fun just to be alive at all) (IX, p.112; V, p.403). This is the final clue for Mrs Alving, and it is the one she uses at the end of Act III to explain the misery of her marriage to Captain Alving. As she tells Oswald, she believes that Alving was full of '*livsglæde*', but that it got corrupted and perverted by life in small town Norway, and by the values she brought into the marriage.

In the course of the play Mrs Alving has gone from someone trying to liberate herself from a crippling sense of duty to someone who believes in the joy of life, but in doing so she has espoused an all-or-nothing concept of liberation. This may have been what Ibsen was referring to when in a letter written to Sophus Schandorph shortly after the publication of *Gengangere* he says,

> en pastor Manders vil altid ægge en eller anden fru Alving frem. Og just fordi hun er kvinde, vil hun, når hun engang er begyndt, gå til de yderste yderligheder (XVII, p.451).

> (A Pastor Manders will always provoke som Mrs Alving or other into being. And just because she is a woman, once she has begun she will go to the utmost extremes.) (V, p.476)

However, the consequences of this all-or-nothing approach become very clear at the end of the play when she is faced with the agonizing decision of whether or not to give Oswald the tablets that will end his life. She who has rejected all the values of society, everything that society has taught her, is suddenly faced with the most agonizing moral problem imaginable and has no source of moral authority to which she can turn for guidance, only her newly-acquired belief in '*livsglæde*'. It is at this point that one needs to take a second look at the role of Regine and how she functions as a foil in relation to Mrs Alving.

According to Oswald, Regine would have been willing to give him the tablets, and this is the reason why on this visit he wants a relationship with her. At the point in Act II when he first tells Mrs Alving about Regine and the joy of life he sees in her, Mrs Alving does not yet know what lies behind Oswald's statement, for he has not told her about the tablets he is carrying ready for the time when the final stage of his disease develops. When he does tell her in Act III, he again says 'Regine havde gjort det. Regine var så prægtig lethjertet. Og hun var snart bleven ked af at passe en slig syg, som jeg' (Regine would have done it. Regine was so marvellously light-hearted. And she'd soon have got bored with looking after an invalid like me) (IX, p. 129; V, p. 420). This seems highly likely for when she does leave in Act III after learning that she is Oswald's half sister she makes it quite clear that nursing the sick is certainly not something she wants to do:

> Havde jeg vidst, at Osvald var sygelig så – . Og så nu, da det ikke kan bli' til noget alvorligt mellem os – . Nej, jeg kan rigtig ikke gå her ude på landet og slide mig op for syge folk (IX, p.123).

> (If I'd known Oswald had something wrong with him ... And anyway, now that there can never by anything serious between us ... No, you don't catch me staying out here in the country, working myself to death looking after invalids.) (V, p.414)

Regine, it turns out, is associated with the introduction of two of the central issues in the play: '*livsglæde*' and the question of whether to give Oswald the tablets. The consequence of this is that when Mrs Alving espouses the concept of '*livsglæde*' and grapples with the problem of whether to give the tablets to Oswald she is relating to two issues that have in fact become tainted or at least questionable because of their association with Regine, (and Oswald's deceit in the way he introduces the matter). Regine is certainly not held up as a moral exemplar in the play. She is a darwinian survivor, who is all the time trying to find the most comfortable and advantageous position for herself, be it through Pastor Manders or through Oswald. If Mrs Alving were to give Oswald the tablets, she would not do it in the same spirit as Regine i.e. in order to relieve *herself* of a burden, but because Oswald's life had become a burden *to him*.[8] Nonetheless, the fact that two central issues are introduced in connection with Regine, must surely alert a reader or audience to the *dangers* inherent in a person who is not constrained by any social morality. Mrs Alving is not Regine, but the two women do have certain things in common. Neither accepts conventional morality. Both in different ways want something more out of life than they have had heretofore, both want to put the orphanage behind them, and for both personal happiness ('*livsglæde*') is a guideline in life. That they would interpret that happiness very differently only highlights the subjective nature of the feeling, and therefore its arbitrariness as a moral value.

Regine as an amoral person who would perhaps have no qualms about giving Oswald the tablets that would kill him is only a foil to Mrs Alving in *Gengangere*, but in *Rosmersholm* Ibsen returns to the issue and it becomes a major theme. In this play, Rebekka West, the representative of new, liberal ideas, is responsible for driving Beate to suicide. At the time she did this, she was not like Mrs Alving a woman struggling to free herself from a hypocritical morality. In fact if Mrs Alving is a woman who was socialized through and through, Rebekka is more like Nora, someone who has never been socialized (and in this sense one can ask how far she is liberated). Her mental baggage when she came to Rosmersholm consisted not of traditional ideas as did Mrs Alving's when she married, but of the radical ideas she inherited from Dr West. However, in the course of the play these ideas acquire an increasingly negative colour and for several reasons. Firstly, it becomes clear that Dr West, who was the mediator of these ideas to Rebekka, did not recognize the boundary line between radicalism and licence. It emerges that he had no qualms about having a sexual relationship with Rebekka whom he must have known was his biological daughter. Rebekka, on the other hand, does not realize this till Act III when Kroll tells her about the dates of Dr West's first visits to Nordland. The second point which casts a negative light on Rebekka's liberal ideas, is the fact that they provided no bulwark against the overwhelming sexual passion for Rosmer which arose in her shortly after she came to Rosmerholm and which drove her to lure Beate to suicide.

A further aspect of Rebekka's irresponsible radicalism and absolute sense of freedom, is the right she assumed to put her ideas into practice through Rosmer. In a letter to Theodor Caspari written in 1884 Ibsen wrote that:

> jeg har for længe siden ophørt at stille almengyldige fordringer, fordi jeg ikke længere tror på at sådanne med nogen indre ret kan opstilles. Jeg mener at vi har alle sammen ikke noget andet og bedre at gøre end i ånd og sandhed at realisere os selv. Dette er efter min mening det virkelige frisind, og derfor er de såkaldte liberale mig på mange punkter så hjertelig imod (XVIII, p.29).

> (I have long since given up making general demands, because I no longer believe that such things with any real justification can be imposed. I believe that none of us can do anything other or anything better than realize ourselves in truth and in spirit . This is in my opinion real free-thinking and this is the reason why I am so out of sympathy in many ways with so-called liberalism.) (VI, p.437)

At the time of writing to Caspari, Ibsen had just completed the rough draft of his play *Vildanden* (*The Wild Duck*), the first of several plays in which a character transgresses the principles expressed above with fatal consequences. Hedvig's death is a direct result of Gregers's meddling, just as Beate's death is a direct result of Rebekka's meddling and Løvborg's death a result of Hedda's. All three interferers precipitate a tragedy. Not only that, but as I hope to show below, Rebekka's interference also has fatal consequences for Rosmer.

In addition to the radical ideas with which she arrived at Rosmersholm and an unbridled sense of her right to put them into practice, Rebekka also arrived with a profound ignorance of her own nature, and was soon enslaved by the sexual passion for Rosmer which arose in her and swept her off her feet, som et vejr ved havet. Det var som et af de vejr, vi kan ha' ved vintertid der nordpå. Det tar en, – og bær' en med sig, du, – så langt det skal være. Ikke tanke om at stå imod (X, p. 426).

(like a storm at sea. Like one of those storms we sometimes get in the winter up North. It takes hold of you ... and carries you away with it ... for as long as it lasts. It never occurs to you to resist.) (VI, p.369)

The symbolic significance of Rebekka's background in all this has long been recognized. Not only does she come from northern Norway which in the 19th century was considered beyond the pale as far as civilized and polite society was concerned, and at the time represented everything wild and untamed, but her mother's name was Gamvik. This as Sandra Saari pointed out[9] suggests a lappish connection, as the word '*gamme*' is the word for a Lapp tent, and in the nineteenth century the Lapps were associated with shamanism and sorcery. This association is strengthened by casual references to her ability to bewitch – '*å forhekse*' – people. Kroll believes that years ago, she 'bewitched' him in order to gain admittance to Rosmerholm. Rebekka protests that it was Beata who begged her to come and stay, to which Kroll replies, 'ja, da De havde fåt forhekset hende også' (yes, after you had managed to bewitch her as well) (X, p.409; VI, p. 354). There are also references to her as '*tiltrekkende havfrue*' – 'an alluring mermaid'.

In his notes to *Et dukkehjem* Ibsen wrote of the conflict between the female protagonist's 'naturlige følelse på den ene side og autoritetstroen på den anden' (her natural instincts on the one side and her faith in authority on the other) (VIII, p. 368; V, p. 436). In this conflict between Nora's *instinctive, natural* sense of justice and the norms of society it is not difficult to see where Ibsen's sympathies lie. But in *Rosmersholm* we are no longer in the social world of *Et dukkehjem* or even *Gengangere* where Nora's and Mrs Alving's natural morality is set against the hypocritical values of bourgeois society. In *Rosmersholm* the *social* conflicts are represented in the clash between Rosmer's conservative brother-in-law, Rektor Kroll, and the liberal newspaper editor, Peder Mortensgaard, but this conflict plays no part after the end of Act II. In *Rosmersholm* 'the natural' is something far more primitive, powerful and overwhelming than it was in either *Et dukkehjem* or *Gengangere*. Nora's naturalness and uninhibitedness are benign – Rebekka's which allowed her to drive another person to her death is not, but it is also in touch with far deeper sources. Furthermore, because she had not been subject to the constraints of culture, when passion rose up in her she had no counterforces with which to resist.

However, Beate's suicide happened several years before the opening of the play, and since then Rebekka has been living quietly with Rosmer, who represents the very opposite of Rebekka. Rektor Kroll speaks of

Rosmerne til Rosmersholm, – prester og officerer. Højt betroede embedsmænd. Korrekte hædersmænd alle sammen, – en æt, som nu snart i et par hundrede år har siddet her som den første i distriktet (X, p.358).

(The Rosmers of Rosmersholm ... clergymen and soldiers ... high officials ... men of the highest principles, all of them ... the foremost family in the district with its seat here now for nearly two hundred years.) (VI, p.305)

It turns out that he is not quite as unimpeachable as Kroll's eulogy implies, at least in his relationship to his dead wife, but there is still much truth in what Kroll says. In fact one could say that Rosmer and the whole Rosmer tradition is suffering from excess of culture and repression, for as the maid Madam Helseth says, children at Rosmersholm never cry and when they grow up they never laugh. The Rosmer line is dying out because it has become over-civilized and devitalized.

This is the environment in which Rebekka has been living for the past few years, and from which she originally wanted to liberate Rosmer. She wanted to win him for the radical new ideas and either to marry him or to win him for a free-love relationship. As she says,

> det er ganske sandt at jeg engang la' mine garn ud for at vinde indpas her på Rosmersholm. For jeg mente som så, at jeg nok skulde komme til at gøre min lykke her. Enten på den ene måden eller på den anden, – skønner du (X, p. 425-6).

> (it's perfectly true I angled for admission here to Rosmersholm. Because I had the feeling I would succeed in doing rather well for myself here. In one way or another, if you see what I mean.) (VI, p. 368)

Passion , 'det vilde ubetvingelige begær', was *not* part of the original plan – in fact it was the eruption of passion that broke her will and frightened her, precisely because it was an irrational force she could not control, 'men så kom begyndelsen til det som har knækket viljen i mig – og skræmt mig så ynkelig for hele livet' (but then came the start of something that finally broke my will ... and turned me from then on into a poor frightened thing) (X, p.426; VI, p.369). Critics such as Jørgen Haugan see a correspondence between 'det ville livet i Finnmark, det ville, ubetvingelige begjær og en generell radikal livsholdning' (the wild life in the North, the wild, uncontrollable passion and a generally radical approach) (*op. cit.* p.135/ MW). However, they do not distinguish between free love which Rebekka knew about through her association with Dr West and passion as an irrational, chaoticising force, which disrupts her plans. Rosmer does not see a necessary link between political radicalism and free love, let alone passion, as becomes clear in Act II when Kroll imagines that because Rosmer has lost his faith he must be living in a sexual relationship with Rebekka. Rosmer's response to this is the rhetorical question, 'du tror altså ikke at der hos frafaldne og frigjorte mennesker kan findes renhedssind?' (so you don't think there is any sense of virtue to be found among free-thinkers?) (X, p.380; VI, p.327). Haugan cannot accept that Rosmer may have 'tilegnet seg nye, moderne meninger som radikalt bryter med kirkens tvang på det erotiske område, samtidig som han viderefører et kristelig-platonisk kyskhetskrav' (acquired new, modern views, which break radically with the teaching of the church on erotic matters, while at the same time he perpetuates a Christian-platonic demand for chastity) (p.129/MW), and he mocks this possibility when he says, 'det groteske ved Rosmers tornefulle vandring på jorden blir tydelig bare man forestiller seg hvordan det vil bli å banke på hos naboen og foreslå ham at han i stedet for å gå til sengs med sin kone bør sette seg i sofaen og drøfte muligheten for å bli et riktig adelsmenneske' (the grotesqueness of Rosmer's thorn-strewn path on earth becomes clear when one tries to imagine what it would be like to knock on one's neighbour's door and suggest to him that instead of going to bed with his wife he should sit in the sofa and discuss the possibility of becoming a real noble man (*ibid./* MW). This caricature seems to say more about Haugan writing in the climate of the late1970s than it does about Ibsen writing in the 1880s, when political radicalism and erotic liberation were making their presence felt in Christiania through the movement know as *Kristiania bohêmen.* This was a movement for which Ibsen had no sympathy, as is clear from a letter he wrote to Nils Lund in 1887. In this letter he asks for a copy of Arne Garborg's *Mannfolk,* which he says he feels he ought to read because he has heard that it has been 'rosende omtalt i flere henseender' (in many ways favourably discussed) (*ibid.* / MW), but he goes on to say that,

> det er nok ellers en tækkelig literatur, man er i færd med at grundlægge i Kristiania! Hans Jægers rå bog har man i sin tid sendt mig og jeg gennemlæste den så nogenlunde. 'Albertine' kender jeg ikke til og bryder mig heller ikke om at stifte bekendtskab med den. For resten er det umuligt andet end at alt dette literære pøbelvæsen kun er en forbigående forvildelse. Men det viser i hvert fald klarlig nok at vort folk endnu ikke på langt nær er modent for frihedens idéer (XVIII, p.129-30).

> (for the rest I must say that it is a fine literature that they are in the process of establishing in Kristiania! Some time ago someone sent me Hans Jæger's crude book, and I skimmed through it. *Albertine* I do not know and do not wish to become acquainted with. It is in any case inconceivable that this literary rabble phenomenon can be anything but a passing aberration. However, it shows clearly enough, that our nation is far from ready for the ideas of freedom.) (MW)

Given Rebekka's hidden passion for Rosmer, Rosmer's proposal of marriage in Act II should have been the fulfilment of Rebekka's dreams. However, as we know, she rejects him. While we can accept Freud's reason for this, namely the re-surfacing of an unconscious guilt at having replaced her mother in Dr West's affections, (a guilt that then becomes intensified in Act III when she learns that she has also had a sexual relationship with her father) this is an extratextual explanation as critics such as Hemmer (*op. cit.* p.178) and Willy Dahl[10] have pointed out. What we know from the text is that since Beate's death Rebekka has been living quietly with Rosmer and seems to have undergone a transformation which she does not describe fully till the final act when she confesses to the sexual passion which preceded it and which was the overwhelming force that caused her to drive Beate to suicide. As she says to Rosmer:

> men da jeg så fik leve sammen med dig her, – i stilhed, – i ensomhed – da du gav mig alle dine tanker så uforbeholdent, – hver en stemning, så blødt og så fint, som du følte den, – da gik det store omslag for sig. Lidt efter lidt, – skønner du. Næsten umærkelig, – men så overvældende til slut. Lige til bunden af mit sind. [...] Alt det andet, – dette stygge sansedrukne begær, det kom så langt, så langt bort fra mig. Alle disse opjagede magter slog sig stilfærdigt ned i taushed. Der faldt en sindshvile over mig, – en stilhed, som på et fugleberg under midnatsolen oppe hos os (X, p.428).

> (But when I began living here with you ... in peace ... in solitude ... when without any kind of reserve you shared all your thoughts with me ... all your feelings just as they came, so delicate and fine ... then I felt the great transformation taking place. Gradually, you understand. Almost imperceptibly ... but overwhelmingly in the end, and reaching right to the very depths of my soul. [...] All the rest ... that horrible, sensual passion ... faded far,

far away. My restless agitation subsided in peace and quiet. A feeling of tranquility came over me ... a stillness like that which comes over a colony of sea-birds on the Northern coast under the midnight sun.) (VI, p.370-1)

It seems that through living with Rosmer Rebekka has become subject to the ancient laws of culture and civilization, everything that is represented by Rosmer and Rosmersholm. In Hemmer's words Rosmer enables Rebekka 'to liberate herself and gain some kind of control of her own life', and he sees *this* as a 'process of emancipation' which 'has nothing to do with radicalism'(*op. cit.* p.180). This culture, however, is not an unmixed blessing for it is repressive, and part of Rosmer's project in the early part of the play was to undo some of its influence by bringing 'lidt lys og glæde her, hvor slægten Rosmer har skabt mørke og tyngsel gennem alle de lange, lange tider' (a little light and happiness into those places where the Rosmers have spread gloom and oppression all these long years) (X, p.382; VI, p.329).

A critic such as Jørgen Haugan would deny that the Rosmer tradition had any positive values whatsoever, and there are certainly elements of his argument that no subsequent interpretations of *Rosmersholm* can ignore. Firstly, he highlights the profoundly negative implications of Rosmer's description in Act II of his behaviour towards Beata after Rebekka had come to Rosmerholm and he had started to discuss his ideas with her. Rosmer begins to think that

> det har ikke undgåt hende, at vi læste de samme bøger. At vi søgte hinanden og talte sammen om alle de nye ting. Men jeg begriber det ikke. For jeg var da så omsorgsfuld for at skåne hende. Når jeg tænker tilbage, så synes jeg, jeg var som på mit liv for at holde hende udenfor alt vort (X, p. 393).

> (it didn't escape her notice that we read the same books. That we liked to get together and talk about all the recent developments. Yet I don't understand! Because I was so careful to spare her any unpleasantness. When I look back, I think I did my utmost to keep her away from anything we were interested in.) (VI, p.339)

Of this Haugan says

> Rosmers handlemåte er noe av det verste man kan tenke seg. Han har latt alt liv sirkulere utenom Beate og utsatt henne for seksuell askese, samtidig som han selv satt nede i stuen i halvmørket og hygget seg med Rebekka (*op. cit.* p.141).

> (Rosmer's conduct is some of the worst imagineable. He has let all activity circulate round Beate, and imposed sexual abstinence on her, while he himself has been sitting downstairs in the living-room in the twilight enjoying himself with Rebekka.) (MW)

In short he sees Rosmer as profoundly guilty in relation to Beata, something he must unconsciously be aware of since he cannot cross the bridge. This may be true, but it is also true that Rosmer's behaviour at this point was very much influenced by Rebekka, and when he becomes aware of the implications of his actions, this new insight or knowledge does not serve to liberate him but only to make him aware of his guilt. One should also say that were Rebekka to have succeeded in freeing any latent eroticism in Rosmer, the first thing he would have had to do would be revise his opinion of Beate. Instead of seeing her as sick, he would have had to recognize that it was his attitude that had made her sick. Again deeper knowledge or enlightenment would not bring liberation but guilt, much as Mrs Alving realizes her part in destroying Captain Alving because she did not bring '*søndagsvejr*' into their home.

Haugan's second and far more serious attack on Rosmer relates to Rosmer's behaviour in Act IV when he asks Rebekka if she could 'go the way that Beata went'. This Haugan sees as an expression of how repressed sexuality returns in a demonized form, 'den demoniserte eros vil sende en kvinne i døden for å få bekreftet en illusjon av idealitet' (the demonized eros wants to send a woman to her death in order that an illusion of idealism may be confirmed) (p.154/MW). Certainly this scene reveals a new and distinctly sinister side of Rosmer, which Ibsen himself indicated in his notes for the play:

> hun er intrigant og hun elsker ham. Hun vil bli' hans hustru og urokkelig forfølger hun dette mål. Da kommer han efter det og hun vedkender sig det åbent. Så er der ingen livslykke mere for ham. Det dæmoniske vækkes af smerten og bitterheden. Han vil dø, og hun skal dø med ham. Hun gør det. (X, p.485-6).

> (She is an intriguer and she loves him. She wants to become his wife and she pursues that aim unswervingly. Then he becomes aware of this, and she openly admits it. Now there is no more joy in life for him. The demonic in him is roused by pain and bitterness. He determines to die, and she is to die with him. This she does.) (VI, p.445)

About this several things need to be said. Firstly that any demonic element in Rosmer is aroused as a consequence of Rebekka's interference. Just as liberation unleashes both positive and negative forces in Rebekka, so it does when she tries to liberate Rosmer. Secondly it has to be said that Rebekka has been begging Rosmer to think of a way in which she can demonstrate that she has been changed. Furthermore, though Rosmer's question suggests some distinctly sinister unconscious motivation, Rebekka's response to it does not necessarily mean that she is under the immediate influence of it. In fact her action is ambiguous, for it would be the same action whether she goes as a result of being ennobled or as a result of Rosmer's sinister suggestion. The only thing that weights the balance and perhaps helps us decide which of the two motivations is most likely, is Rebekka's attitude and verbal response. For me, the deciding factor is Rebekka's statement that she regards her death as an act of atonement, 'hvad jeg har forbrudt, – det bør det sig at jeg soner' (where I have sinned . . . it is right that I should atone) (X, p.437; VI, p.379). This statement takes Rosmer aback and he asks rather incredulously 'er det der du står?' (Is *that* how you see it?). Rebekka's response here seems to me to be very much under the older Rosmer influence i.e. that which worked quietly and imperceptibly when Rosmer shared all his thoughts with her. What is more it is that scheme of values, for which Rebekka is at this moment the spokesperson, that rescues Rosmer from the despair and demonic possession into which he has fallen. Because Rebekka recognizes his values he is freed to go with Rebekka not as her judge and witness, but as her husband.

Rosmersholm is regarded by many as Ibsen's most searching exploration of the liberal dilemma and liberal tragedy. However, some such as Willy Dahl would argue that Rebekka herself embodies the whole dilemma:

hun rommer skuespillets egentlige tematikk. Hun er lyset, varmen, livet, det fruktbare, det spirende. Og hun er døden, skylden, tragedien. Hun er bæreren av de nye tanker og nye idéer – lysbringersken. Men for å kunne utbre disse tankene og idéene, for å finne et virkefelt for dem, har hun gjort seg til morderske. [...] Hun representerer en ennå uløst konflikt i europeisk radikalisme: kravet om sosial samhørighet og sosialt ansvar på den ene siden, og kravet om individuell frihet, om rett till fullstendig personlig utfoldelse, på den andre (*op. cit.* p.48).

(She embodies the play's central theme. She is the light, the warmth, the life, that which is fruitful, that which is growing. She is the bearer of the new thoughts and ideas – the lightbearer. But in order to spread these thoughts and ideas, in order to find a field in which she can work, she has become a murderer [...] She represents an as yet unresolved conflict in European radicalism; the demand for social solidarity and social responsibility on the one hand, and the demand for individual freedom and the right to complete personal development on the other.) (MW)

This seems to me to ignore not only the dangerous consequences of Rebekka's interfering on Rosmer, but also the part Rosmer plays in liberating Rebekka from a destructive passion. The natural person in Rosmersholm is no longer the innocent naïf that Nora in *Et dukkehjem* is. Ibsen himself was well aware that liberation on its own is a two-edged sword, for as he wrote in a letter to Bjørnson's nephew, Bjørn Kristensen, in 1887,

Men foruden dette handler stykket om den kamp, som ethvert alvorligt menneske har at bestå med sig selv for at bringe sin livsførelse i samklang med sin erkendelse.
De forskellige åndsfunktioner udvikler sig nemlig ikke jevnsides og ikke ligeligt i et og samme individ. Tilegnelsesdriften jager fremad fra vinding til vinding. Moralbevidstheden "samvittigheden", er derimod meget konservativ. Den har sine dybe rødder i traditionerne og i det fortidige overhovedet. Heraf kommer den individuelle konflikt (XVIII, p. 128).

(But apart from that, the play deals with the struggle that every serious-minded man must wage with himself to bring his way of life into harmony with his convictions.
The different functions of the spirit do not develop uniformly or comparably in any one individual. The acquisitive instinct rushes on from one conquest to the next. Moral consciousness, however, 'the conscience', is by comparison very conservative. It has its roots deep in tradition and in the past generally. From this comes the conflict within the individual.) (VI, p.447)

Vitality on its own can be ruthless and needs to be encultured. Culture on its own lacks vitality, and ends up devouring its own offspring. What is suggested in this play is that each needs the other. In *Gengangere* it would be hard to find anything good in the values Mrs Alving rejected, but this leaves her very exposed, and the value she espouses does not offer her a guideline on what to do about Oswald. If she were to give him the tablets out of compassion, that would have nothing to do with the joy of life which is the value she believes provides the key to her misery. In *Rosmersholm* the *social* values as represented by Kroll and Mortensgaard may not be much better than they were in *Gengangere*, but they cease to play any part after the end of Act II. Thereafter Ibsen only seems interested in the struggle between the dark, chaoticizing forces of the unconscious and the values that one can only define as as culture, tradition, civilization. These are separate from, and less tangible than, social values, but they are ones in which there may be an element of salvation.

Notes

1. Raymond Williams, *Modern Tragedy*, Chatto and Windus, 1966, p. 95
2. Erik Østerud, 'Syndefall og alveslag. Om samfunnskritikk og eksistensialisme i Henrik Ibsens Gengangere', *Norskrift*, No 28, 1980, 1-81 and 'Den rosmerske adelighet og dybdepsykologien. En studie in Henrik Ibsens *Rosmersholm*', *Norskrift*, No 34, 1982, 1-45.
3. Jørgen Haugan in *Henrik Ibsens metode. Den indre utvikling gjennom Ibsens dramatikk*, Gyldendal Norsk Forlag, 1977.
4. Errol Durbach, 'Ibsen's Liberated Heroines and the Fear of Freedom', in: *Contemporary Approaches to Ibsen*, Vol. 5, (Reports from the Fifth International Ibsen Seminar, Munich 1983), Oslo 1985, pp. 11-23.
5. Bjørn Hemmer, 'Ibsen and the Crisis of Individual Freedom: Nora Helmer versus Rebekka Gamvik', *Contemporary Approaches to Ibsen*, Vol. 7, pp. 171-183 (p.173).
6. Henrik Ibsen *Samlede verker* (Hundreårsutgave) ed. F. Bull, H. Koht and D.A. Seip, 1928-36, Vol IX, p.92. As all quotations are taken from this edition, all further references will be given in the text, simply quoting the volume and page number.
7. *The Oxford Ibsen*, translated and edited by J. W. McFarlane 1960-77, Vol. V, p.384. As all the English quotations are taken from this edition, all future references will be given in the text, simply quoting the volume and page number.
8. At this point Jørgen Haugan argues that Mrs Alving 'står delt mellom morskjærligheten som fikk henne til å love og hjelpe Osvald ut av angsten og et pinefullt sykeleie, og en mer besittelseslysten lidenskap som vil beholde Osvald i live for kunne pleie ham som en mor pleier sitt barn' (p.122). Østerud suggests something similar, arguing that Mrs Alving's action could either be motivated by maternal love or by fear and horror, 'fordi fru Alving slett ikke ser sønnen foran seg, men den betente erotikeren Alving i sønnens skikkelse' (p.77). An even more radical position is taken by Theoharis C. Theoharis in his recent study *Ibsen's Drama: Right Action and Tragic Joy*, Macmillan, 1996, in which he argues from a Nietzschean angle that all the intrigues of the play 'result in this last scene's demand that she kill her only son Oswald and that she transform that ultimate crime into exonerating, liberating service of what Oswald has called "joy of life"' (p.75), or as he puts it even more challengingly, 'to kill him would be to redefine duty, to become the avenger of joy against duty, to make the sun's appearance a provocation to the transvaluation of all values, that supreme willing of the past that Nietzsche argues supremely powerful spirits accomplish when they affirm the eternal return of the same' (p.90).
9. S. Saari, 'Rosenvold and Rosmersholm: Protagonist implies interpretation', *Contemporary Approaches to Ibsen*, Vol . 4. Reports from the Fourth International Ibsen Seminar, Skien, 1978, Oslo, 1979, p.108. I have used the word 'Lapp' here deliberately as the word 'Sami' has none of the connotations which 'Lapp' has in this context.
10. Willy Dahl, '*Rosmersholm* – i dag', in H. Noreng, (ed.), *Ibsen på festspillscenen*, Eide Forlag, Bergen, 1969, p.39.

Originally published November 1998 (Vol. 37, No. 2).

'Klistret fast med sort på hvitt': The Problems of Writing in Ibsen's *Rosmersholm* and *Hedda Gabler*

Sara Jan

Introduction

In Act 2 of *Enemy of the People*, in the course of an argument about Dr Thomas Stockmann's intention of publicising the polluted state of the town baths, the mayor Peter Stockmann reproaches his brother for his restless, rebellious nature, and furthermore, his inclination for 'rushing into print about everything under the sun'('at skrive offentligt om alle mulige og umulige sager'); 'No sooner do you get some idea or other into your head than you've got to write an article for the papers about it ... or even a whole pamphlet', he complains.[1] Thomas willingly concedes that he 'fought for the idea [of the baths] year after year, writing and writing' (VI, 57); and throughout the play, this man of action does demonstrate a remarkable obsession with writing. Rather than showing us Stockmann at his scientific work, the play is filled with Thomas's abundant writing and his threats to write. In Act 1 we quickly discover that Thomas is 'a prolific contributor to the *People's Herald*' (VI, 24); and before long he is recalling how 'I myself have written repeatedly, both in the *Herald* and in a number of pamphlets' (VI, 37) in support of the new baths. At the end of the act he announces he wishes to replace one of these articles which the newspaper editor Hovstad about to print, with a report detailing the baths' grave threat to public health; and his exuberant attachment to the written word is evident: '[*He goes into his room and comes back with a sheaf of papers.*] Look! Four closely written sheets!' (VI, 40). Act 3 sees him visiting and re-visiting the editorial office of the *Herald*, anxious and protective of his report: 'Take care of it as though it were gold. No misprints, every word is important. I'll look in again later on; perhaps I could check some of the proofs. –Yes, I can't tell you how I'm longing to get this thing in print ... slam it down' (VI, 66). At the point where the editor Hovstad refuses to publish the article after all, Thomas orders Aslaksen to print it anyway at the author's expense: 'I want four hundred copies – no, five ... six hundred' (VI, 84). Even at the end of the play, having been betrayed by the refusal of the 'progressive and independent press' to publish his discoveries, Stockmann quickly re-states his passion for writing in his threats to his enemies: 'now I'm going to sharpen up my pen; I'll impale them on it; I'll dip it in venom and gall; I'll chuck the inkpot right in their faces!' (VI, 122).

Stockmann's insistent and prolific writing, along with his attacks on the 'compact, liberal majority' and references to hidden social putrefaction, points, of course, to Dr Stockmann's status as Ibsen's parodic double. Responding to the fervid press denunciations of *Ghosts* in Scandinavia in 1881-2, *An Enemy of the People* resounds with a comic, euphoric conviction of the writer's power to disrupt the complacencies of his society, to become an enemy of the people by writing about 'all kinds of possible and impossible things'. At the same time, Ibsen's satire of the press in *An Enemy of the People* also acknowledges the real power of this institutional expression of public opinion to suppress and limit visionary writing. As in other of Ibsen's realist plays, the representation of the newspaper here engages with the historical phenomenon of the rise of mass journalism, its increasing significance in the developing democratic party politics of Norway, and more broadly in culture at large, in the later nineteenth century.[2]

Ghosts, *Rosmersholm* and *Hedda Gabler* also show a significant preoccupation with writing. *Ghosts*, whose opening stage directions mention the '*books, periodicals, and newspapers*' covering the table of Mrs Alving's living-room, initiates an interrogation of the emancipatory possibilities of radical writing; writing which, appositely for *Ghosts*, is described as articulating what 'most people think and believe already', but won't admit.[3] In *Rosmersholm*, which addresses the interdependence of problems of personal and political emancipation more fully, writing – again in the form of newspapers, books and letters – plays a more significant role in the characters' interaction and the unfolding of the narrative. In *Hedda Gabler*, of course, the writer Løvborg and his manuscript form a main focus of dramatic tension.

Ibsen's use of writings in these plays can be easily overlooked, or dismissed as the residue of stage traditions of using texts as props and mechanical components of plot machinery.[4] This tradition reaches its apogee in the nineteenth-century well-made play and melodrama, and Ibsen's mastery of the convention is evident in such plays as *Lady Inger of Østraat*, *The Pretenders* and *A Doll's House*, where a letter is pivotal to the plot. However, I believe that writing in itself, as process and product, is of especial thematic interest to Ibsen in the mature realist dramas, and demands exploration.

Paradoxically, Ibsen's concern with writing is most insistently expressed in plays which aim at naturalistic representation of speech. The realist playwright's desire to elude writing by means of writing is made more self-conscious in Ibsen's case by his early struggles to establish spoken Norwegian as a dramatic language, as opposed to stage Danish (a genre strongly associated with writing) and by the problem that 'in a framework of Danish spelling and grammar he had to give the effect of bourgeois Norwegian speech'.[5] Ibsen's aesthetic commitment to the 'difficult art of writing the straightforward, plain language spoken in real life' leads to intense exploration of the dramatic possibilities of colloquial utterance and of speech genres such as confession and narration.[6] However this technical and thematic focus on speech is counterpointed by the intervention of texts: letters, newspapers, books, articles, that disrupt and infiltrate the dialogues.

My aim here is to read *Rosmersholm* and *Hedda Gabler* in terms of their thematisation of writing. In doing so, I draw on Jacques Derrida's description and questioning of the dichotomies between speech and writing, particularly in his work *Of Grammatology*. Derrida argues here for a tendency in western intellectual tradition since Plato to privilege speech over writing, citing Aristotle's assertion that: "'spoken words [...] are the symbols of mental experience [...] and written words are the symbols of spoken words'" to illustrate this sense of writing's secondary, 'fallen' status; 'the voice, producer of *the first symbols*, has a relationship of essential and immediate proximity with the mind', whereas 'the written signifier is always technical and representative'.[7] While meaning in *all* language, spoken or written, is made possible by a restless play of difference and deferral (a movement termed *différance* by Derrida), it is in writing that the sign's problematic and indirect relationship with meaning is most obvious and threatening.[8] The spoken word seems to escape the play of différance, 'because the speaker and listener are both present to the utterance simultaneously. There is no spatial or temporal distance between speaker, speech and listener', thus apparently guaranteeing the speaker's intentions and the listener's understanding.[9] The identification of the voice with ideal presence, in particular the speaker's self-presence, is termed by Derrida phonocentrism, a notion assuming: 'absolute proximity of voice and being, of voice and the meaning of being, of voice and the ideality of being'.[10]

This phonocentric idealisation of the voice is expressed in Ibsen's 1871 *Rimbrev – Til Fru Heiberg*, which fancifully contrasts the immaterial, intuitive spirituality of the actress's art: 'Deres kunst er barn av duften,/av beånden,/av en stemning,/av person og fantasi, –' with the frustrating materiality of the writer's art, in which thought must be 'klistret fast med sort på hvitt'– stuck down fast in black on white.[11] The actress, working with voice and body, dramatically present to the meanings she produces, is able to communicate with organic immediacy. By contrast, the writer must commit meanings to the inert yet treacherous form of writing, which typically functions in his absence (the poem's *letter* form emphasises this). Ibsen's sense of tension between the play's textuality and the actor's voice is, later, key to his realist social dramas: for the actor's success in speaking Ibsen's text significantly depends on his or her ability to establish the very identity between voice and being which is assumed natural to 'real' speech, but which must be negotiated or struggled for in the theatre. This is all the more so given that, from *Ghosts*, dialogue ranges between naturalistic and poetic or symbolistic styles of utterance (albeit in a general context of realist discourse) and thereby threatens a return to literature, that is, to writing (examples are the white horse at Rosmersholm and Hedda's vine-leaves). This contest between speech and writing which must be played out in a performance, is also present within the imagined world of those plays concerned with the problem of writing; and it is the latter's ambiguous role in the worlds of *Rosmersholm* and *Hedda Gabler* which I concentrate on here.

Rosmersholm, writing and dialogue

There is broad critical agreement that *Rosmersholm*, written in the context of Ibsen's experience of the intense political rivalry between liberals and conservatives during his visit to Norway in 1885, is significantly concerned with the interaction between psychological and ideological forces in the struggle for emancipation of the self and society, for radical thinkers of the period. The dramatic and thematic role of forms of writing in this struggle, and the extent to which characters' relationships are determined by their interaction with various texts, have been largely overlooked in critical accounts of the play, however.

Writing is thematised in *Rosmersholm* in the course of the play's remarkable exploitation of the dramatic possibilities of speech genres. The characters themselves show a continuing reflexive sense of involvement in 'language games' such as inquest, persuasion, narration and confession. Kroll's attempt in Act 1 to recruit Rosmer to the conservative cause is punctuated by Rebecca's covert promptings of Rosmer to confess his political conversion, and in Act 2 Kroll formally questions his brother-in-law about the causes of his 'emancipation': 'Would you be willing to submit to a sort of interrogation?'('Vil du finde dig i at jeg holder et slags forhør – ?').[12] Kroll's similarly forensic questioning of Rebecca and her 'origins' in Act 3, instigates a series of confessions and narratives made to Rosmer and Kroll, framed formally as a story-telling session. 'Come, let's sit down [...] All three of us. Then I'll tell you everything'(VI, 359). The association between speech and action, thematically and technically crucial for the play, is forged in Rebecca's account of her removal of Beata in a series of cryptic conversations: 'So, I took action' (VI, 316) ('Og så handled jeg', X, 417) and in Rosmer's stunned reaction (the point is clearest in the original text): 'Dette er altså, hvad du har sagt og gjort [...] Det var det, som du kaldte at handle'(X, 418).[13] Act 4 is dominated by Rebecca's further confessions, until the dreadful potency of the speech act culminates in the couple's suicidal 'marriage', with Rosmer's: 'now I lay my hand on your head ... [*does so*] and take you to be my truly wedded wife'(VI, 380). As for Rebecca individually, speech is action for *Rosmersholm* as a whole. Indeed, the narrative excitement and psychic energy of characters' speeches will enable writing's apparent positioning, in accordance with Derrida's account of phonocentrism, as a 'dangerous supplement': alienated from truth and inner life, moribund; inert and threatening at once in its overt materiality and function of signifying in the absence of its author.

The most obvious and immediate negative figure of writing in *Rosmersholm* is the newspaper, a text typically associated with duplicity and divisiveness in Ibsen. In Kroll's opening duologue with Rebecca, where he deplores the political ascendancy of the Radicals, it is a newspaper – the left-wing *Beacon* (*Blinkfyret*) – on which his hostility is most intensely focused, and which he identifies absolutely with left-wing political ideology: 'There's not a scrap of difference between them [Radical opinions] and the precious words of wisdom the *Beacon* keeps putting out'(VI, 303). Kroll complains that though personally abusive of him, the *Beacon* is read secretly in his own school and family, introducing 'the spirit of defiance and revolt'(VI, 301) amongst his wife, children and students. His daughter has even embroidered a red cover to keep copies of the *Beacon* in, he explains angrily, raising a theme which will emerge more fully later: that of the great significance and appeal of radical writing to women in isolated or oppressed circumstances (a topic also addressed in *Ghosts*). In spite of this contempt for demagogic journalism, he reveals he now intends to fight the left 'with the written as well as the spoken word' (VI, 302) ('både i skrift og i tale',

X, 355). His conservative faction has purchased the local *County Times* (*Amtstidenden*) in which this battle will be fought. Kroll senses (as Rosmer will not) the critical role of mass journalism in shaping the new democracy, realising that the traditional hegemony of the clergyman, patriarch and schoolmaster can no longer be sustained purely through the exercise of personal influence in the pulpit, family or schoolroom. It is his demand that Rosmer edit the paper or at least allow it to be associated with his 'family name and all that that means'(VI, 305) that catalyses the split between Rosmer and Kroll by forcing Rosmer's revelation of his newly radical politics.[14] Rosmer, who Rebecca claims in any case 'dislikes that sort of thing'(VI, 302) rejects the editorship because of his political conversion; but equally the aggression and publicity of the writing Kroll proposes is antithetical to Rosmer's interpretation of ideological affiliation. Having revealed his conversion to a shocked Kroll, who reproaches his secrecy, Rosmer confesses that he has assumed his ideas concerned 'nobody but myself', and that he had intended to live out his emancipation through quiet private reading of 'all those works that had previously been closed books to me' (VI, 315).

Act 1 therefore articulates bourgeois conservative (Kroll) and liberal (Rosmer) anxieties about democracy in terms of anxieties about popular journalism, to the extent that political struggle in *Rosmersholm* is at first represented entirely as struggle over writing. As in *An Enemy of the People* and *Ghosts*, mass journalism's weaknesses – expediency, vindictiveness, duplicity – are made coincident with those of a democracy determined by public opinion. In *An Enemy of the People*, however, Stockmann figures as an exceptional newspaper writer, in that his copious texts are presented as extensions of his voluble speech. The parallel is humorously enforced in the scene where he instructs the printer Aslaksen to take good care of his report on the baths, and 'whatever you do, don't go leaving out any of my exclamation marks! If anything, put a few more in!' (VI, 68). When the paper refuses to publish the article, he threatens to hire a man with a drum and: 'proclaim it at every street corner' (VI, 85). The world of *Rosmersholm*, however, has no space for this comedic and optimistic vision of the unity of writing and the authentic voice. As much is clear in Act 2, where Mortensgaard approaches Rosmer offering to publicize the latter's sympathy with the left, on the condition that Rosmer's separation from the church remain a secret. Mortensgaard explains the urgent need for the radical cause to promote a respectable image: he will print not the truth, but only what 'the dear public needs to know'(VI, 337).

The role of the newspaper plot in shaping Kroll and Rosmer's relationship is clear at the start of Act 3, where Rebecca shows Rosmer the day's copy of the *County Times* in which Rosmer, though unnamed, is denounced as a 'Judas-like' traitor and apostate, while Rebecca herself is alluded to as a 'pernicious influence'(VI, 348-9). 'How can they write such things about me!' asks Rosmer naively, 'Things they don't even believe themselves. Things they know there isn't a single word of truth in – yet they write them all the same'(VI, 348). The answer is that they may do so precisely because they are able to write 'such things'; betrayal of truth is inherent in the genre of the newspaper as such, and its treacherous autonomy is cited by Kroll when he is subsequently confronted with the offensive article: 'I didn't write it' – to stop it 'would have been unjustifiable interference with the cause I serve. Nor was it in my power' (VI, 359). Rosmer and Kroll's reconciliation can only begin, in fact, from the point of Rebecca's symbolic destruction of the offending copy of the *County Times*, in a gesture which, we discover later, indicates also her own renunciation of Rosmer as a political instrument: '[*tears up the paper, crumples the pieces and throws them behind the stove*]. There. Now it's out of sight. And let it be out of mind as well. For there'll be no more of that kind of stuff, Johannes' (VI, 359).

Significantly, the tearing of the newspaper follows on the interview between Kroll and Rebecca where he questions her identity and political authenticity, a scene itself preceded by that in which Rebecca and Rosmer read the slanderous newspaper article. A key part of their confrontation centres on the radical literature in the library Rebecca inherited from Dr West. Previously in the play, Kroll had implied the pernicious influence of radical writing by asking Rosmer if Beata ever had access to any works 'dealing with the institution of marriage, giving the modern, advanced view'(VI, 324), a book which Rosmer admits, was lent to him by Rebecca. This suspiciousness echoes his previous dismay at the influence of the radical *Beacon* on the women and children he seeks to control, and he comes close to Pastor Manders in Ghosts, in expressing these traditional conservative anxieties about the moral and political subversiveness of women reading.[15] Kroll is more subtle than Manders, however, for he will challenge Rebecca not so much with writing's seductiveness, but with an (equally phonocentric) conviction of writing's limitation; its exteriority, as a supplement unable to touch the inner core of personality. Liberation achieved through reading and academic study is merely a form of theoretical knowledge (the point is clearest in the Norwegian text):

> De har læst Dem til en hel hob nye tanker og meninger. De har fåt vide et slags besked om forskninger på forskjellige områder, – forskninger, som synes at omstyrte adskilligt af det, der hidtil hos os har gjældt for uomstøteligt og uangribeligt. Men alt dette er bare ble't en viden hos Dem, frøken West. En kundskap. Det er ikke gåt Dem i blodet' (X, 413).[16]

She can only admit that perhaps he is right, fatally weakened as she is, by his previous suggestion that she is West's biological daughter.

Kroll recognises the fundamental importance of radical texts in Rebecca's ability to challenge the 'incontrovertible and inviolate' ('uomstøteligt og uangripeligt') truths of the dominant ideology, given her status as a dependent and isolated woman with little access to formal education or other discourses of power. It is crucial to his strategy of weakening Rebecca's hold over Rosmer to dismiss the intellectual inheritance of her father West, represented by the caseful of books he leaves Rebecca after his death, and replace it with an inexorable socio-biological inheritance: 'I consider your whole conduct derives from the circumstances of your birth' (VI, 356). Insofar as in the nineteenth century the private library continues to be seen as 'a masculine space, even a symbol of male power and rationality', Rebecca's possession of such a library is in itself transgressive, symbolically key to her status as an emancipated woman, and symptomatic of the social upheavals feared by Kroll.[17] By reducing Rebecca's politics to an effect of heredity, he invalidates her self-definition through radical ideology. Following this, it is possible to discern in her destruction of the newspaper immediately afterwards, a symbolic abandonment of writing as a political weapon.

Having established newspaper writing as a treacherous supplement to traditional vis-á-vis ideological discourse, the book is condemned, through Kroll's critique, as extrinsic to the human drives that reside in 'the blood' and delusory in its promises of emancipation. Insofar as *Rosmersholm*, like *Ghosts*, dramatises the resistance of the inherited and psychological past to emancipatory ideologies acquired by its heroine principally through texts, Kroll's scepticism converges with the story's ironization of the characters' struggle for freedom.

It is another figure of the text, however, which demonstrates most powerfully this obduracy of the past, and establishes the play's traumatic temporal depth. This text is the citation of Beata's words, both in Kroll's repetition of her utterances (which I will argue constitute a form of writing), and in her letter to the *Beacon*'s editor Mortensgaard, the contents of which he discloses to Rosmer in Act 2. Moreover, the interrelationship of public and private texts is suggested by Beata's anticipation and unconsciously willed activation of the power of the press over Rosmer's reputation, by writing to Mortensgaard begging him not to exploit his position as editor to spread scandalous rumours about her husband, and thus avenge Rosmer's former moral stigmatisation of Mortensgaard.

This letter dramatises what Derrida argues is the intrinsic relationship between writing and absence – this absence being most strikingly characterised as death: 'a letter which was not readable after my death would not be a letter'; 'it is necessary for you to be able to read me even if I am dead'; 'My mortality (my finitude) is thus inscribed in everything I inscribe'. Derrida continues, in terms fitting to Beata's situation, that this absence entails a problem as to 'whether what I write is really what I meant, fully *compos mentis*, at the moment of writing, etc. That there be this fundamental and irreducible uncertainty is part of the essential structure of writing'.[18] Ibsen is not, of course, using his plot to study the nature of writing, but rather exploiting writing's characteristics as traditionally understood, to dramatise conflicts within and between characters. This can be seen in the way Beata's letter establishes the traditional phonocentric theme of the connection between writing and death, based on assumption of writing as secondary to speech's vital, intimate proximity to the subject. It is a precursor to, and warning of Beata's suicide, and Mortensgaard's revelation of its contents and existence to Rosmer abruptly raises Beata's phantom. At the same time, it is the very uncertainty as to Beata's meaning and her mental state at the time of writing which will make its effect devastating.

Beata's words figure as a form of ghostly repetition (and hence as a form of text, repeatability being characteristic of writing and contrasting with speech's apparent evanescence) momentarily at the end of Act 1, where in response to Kroll's warning that he is 'not the man to hold out alone', Rosmer dissents: 'There are two of us to bear the loneliness' (VI, 316). Kroll exclaims 'Even that too! Beata's very words!', but quickly dismisses his suspicion. But the return of Beata's words proves inescapable in two parallel scenes in Act 2, where in the privacy of his study but overheard by Rebecca, Rosmer receives Kroll and then Mortensgaard.

In the first duologue, Kroll reveals how Beata visited him twice in the year leading up to her death. On the first occasion, pouring out her feelings of 'agony and despair' (VI, 325) she warns Kroll of Rosmer's impending 'apostasy' and he summarises this conversation briefly. Kroll recounts the second conversation in more detail. He directly quotes Beata's poetic prediction of death: 'They can expect to see the White Horses at Rosmersholm again soon' (VI, 326) and insists on the precise phraseology of Beata's utterances in order to force Rosmer's recognition of the implied meaning of her words:

> KROLL: [...] And now I ask you, Rosmer, what truth is there in that other accusation of hers? In the last one, I mean?
> ROSMER: Accusation? Was that an accusation?
> KROLL: Perhaps you didn't notice how it was phrased. She wanted to go, she said... Why? Well?
> ROSMER: So that I might marry Rebecca...
> KROLL: That wasn't quite the way it was put. Beata expressed herself rather differently. She said, I haven't much time left. Because now Johannes must marry Rebecca at once. (VI, 326-7)

In this passage, Beata's reported speech, at once opaque and subject to forensic repetition and exegesis, retains none of speech's supposedly 'natural' spontaneity and immediacy to meaning, instead taking on the ambiguity and permanence of a text. The dramatic function of Beata's reported speech in this scene is, indeed, identical to that of the letter discussed in Rosmer's subsequent interview with Mortensgaard. Here he gives Rosmer a detailed account of the 'strange' ('underlig'), but sane letter she sent to him before her death, delivered in secret and darkness. For the sake of dramatic subtlety Mortensgaard discusses the letter (which he says he has at home if Rosmer wishes to see it) from memory rather than brandishing it at Rosmer, yet Ibsen is careful nevertheless to stress its textuality. Mortensgaard speaks *as if* he has the letter in front of him (this is clearest in the Norwegian): 'Hun begynder' ... 'Og så kommer det underligste '... 'Det står i brevet' ... 'dernæst skriver hun, – og det er temmelig forvirret, – ' (X, 389). Mortensgaard explains he is telling Rosmer about the letter now to warn him that any personal scandal could jeopardise the liberal cause he has joined: but the impact of his disclosure extends far beyond Mortensgaard's immediate purposes.

The two scenes of repetition of Beata's words disrupt entirely Rosmer's ability to sustain his previous interpretation of the situation preceding her death, and his assertion to Mortensgaard, prior to the letter's revelation, that 'I feel secure against any attack on personal grounds [...] My conduct cannot be impugned' (VI, 333). Yet immediately after the interview he is in torment: 'How am I to explain Beata's terrible accusation?'. Rebecca, who has duplicated Rosmer's audience of Beata's duplicated words, now tries to silence Rosmer's own repetitions of the same: 'Oh, stop talking about Beata! Stop thinking about Beata any more! Just when you had begun to put her right out of your mind, now that she's dead'. But Rosmer: 'Since I heard about all this, she seems in some uncanny way to be back among the living again'(VI, 338) ('Siden jeg fik vide dette her, så er hun ble't ligesom så uhyggelig levende igen', X, 392). The uncertainties surrounding the real meaning of Beata's texts (Mortensgaard admits the most compromising passage of the letter is 'temmelig forvirret', 'rather confused') make these more terrible for Rosmer than any straightforward accusations of infidelity, while the ambiguity of Beata's phraseology tauntingly echoes the ambiguity of his relationship with Rebecca. 'There will always be some doubt remaining, some question'(VI, 340) ('Altid vil der bli' siddende igen en tvil. Et spørsmål', X, 394-5) to disturb the quiet, happy innocence that makes life worth living. This loss of certainty in interpretation will agonise the rest of the play, and secure the triumph of death: 'Oh, all these wild speculations. I'll never be rid of them. I'm sure of it. I know it. They'll always be there, ready to charge in and remind me of the dead' (VI, 340). In the form of texts read after her death, Beata's utterances retrieve the energy and power of signification denied them by her husband and brother while she lived, dismissed as voicings of 'hysterical' sexuality. Yet they answer to Derrida's description of writing as 'the dead letter, [...] the carrier of death [which] exhausts life'.[19]

So far then, it is possible to see to what extent writing, figured by the newspaper, book and letter, becomes an absorbing topic of speech, and furthermore, a catalyst and source for the intimate speech-act-based dialogue which constitutes the dramatic body of *Rosmersholm*. Whereas the Scribean drama confines writing to a prop or plot mechanism, in Ibsen's play, writing embeds itself in characters' speech, disrupting spoken discourse in the form of repetition, quotation, paraphrase, summary, readings aloud. However, there is also a metalanguage for speech in *Rosmersholm* which importantly develops the play's thematic engagement with the problem of writing. This metalanguage is used by Rosmer and Rebecca in their retrospective accounts of their early friendship, which is defined in terms of ideal, secluded conversation. These reminiscences form the basis of the couple's own narrative sense of their relationship, and shared ideological ambitions, and are cited at critical moments in the 'real time' of the play. In the discussion following Mortensgaard's visit, Rosmer guiltily recalls that Beata must have noticed that he and Rebecca 'read the same books' and 'liked to get together and talk about all the recent developments'(VI, 339). Rebecca then tries to distract Rosmer from his preoccupation with Beata, but her method is to continue the nostalgic narrative he has started: 'How lovely it was when we used to sit in the dusk downstairs in the living-room. Helping each other to plan our lives anew. You wanted to lay hold of life – the throbbing life of the day, you used to say'(VI, 340). Significantly, Rebecca imagines Rosmer's mission of ennobling the people as coming about in a domestic face-to-face context, through speech authenticated by Rosmer's personal presence and idealistic spirit, and a medium whose intimacy and integrity opposes it to the 'fallen' discourse of political writing: 'You wanted to go from house to house like a messenger of deliverance, winning the minds and the wills of men. Creating all about you a nobility ... in ever wider circles' (VI, 340).

In Act 4 Rebecca returns for the last time to their shared narrative, in order to explain the 'ennoblement' of her physical desire for Rosmer. In this crucial passage, she again develops the phenomenology of listening through which she has characteristically defined their relationship. She tells how Rosmer has weakened her sexuality and 'power to act' by means of the same intimate, platonic voice that was to spread ennoblement among the people: 'when I began living here with you ... in peace ... in solitude ... when without any kind of reserve you shared all your thoughts with me ... all your feelings just as they came, so delicate, so fine ... *then* I felt the great transformation taking place' (VI, 370).

It is thus Rebecca's sense of the 'absolute proximity of voice and being' in Rosmer's voice, an 'experience of the signifier producing itself spontaneously, from within the self' which seduces her and displaces the influence of the ideological texts which have formerly helped motivate her.[20] This coincidence between consciousness and utterance opposes Rosmer's voice to writing and to Beata's words; there is no interpretative struggle or temporal lapse between thought or mood, and expression. In their ideal exchanges, both characters have the illusory privilege of 'hearing (understanding) – oneself speak' [*s'entendre parler*]; it is as if Rebecca has heard her own voice speaking, and so she is 'broken' by Rosmersholm.[21]

In spite of Rebecca's sense of defeat at this point, the couple's fragmented allusions to their early discourse emit throughout the play a compelling romantic energy. Yet this phase of their relationship exists only as nostalgia in *Rosmersholm*, given the invasion of textuality, be it public (the newspaper, radical book) or private (the letter) into the pair's idyll, from the start of the play's action. Seen in this way, *Rosmersholm* seems to appeal to traditional phonocentric oppositions between speech and writing, stating what Derrida terms: 'a classical ideology according to which writing takes the status of a tragic fatality come to prey upon natural innocence, interrupting the golden age of the present and full speech'.[22] But if writing in *Rosmersholm* implies: 'repetition, absence, risk of loss, death'; it simultaneously suggests that, 'no speech would be possible without these values' as within Rosmer and Rebecca themselves is staged a progressive struggle to keep faith in the affective and spiritual authenticity of the voice in intimate dialogue.[23]

The ironic note is sounded as early as Act 1 in the figure of Brendel, 'a caricatured *alter ego* of Rosmer', going out in his cast-off clothes on an ineffectual mission to preach redemption to the people.[24] When Brendel explains why his 'really important works are known to nobody [...] unwritten' (VI, 309), he articulates a bombastic version of the phonocentric suspicion of writing and the materiality of writing. The audacious new ideas, the 'poems and visions and images', are formed only 'in rough outline, as it were, you understand'; 'But you never wrote it down?' Rosmer asks. 'Not a word!' he replies, 'I have always felt quite nauseated at the thought of solemnly writing it all out'(VI, 309-10); ('Dette platte skriverhåndværk har altid vakt en kvalmende ulyst i mig', X, 363). Moreover, committing himself to writing would compromise his auto-erotic enjoyment of solitary intellectual ecstasies. This argument parodies Rosmer's naive distaste for writing, and equally the couple's idealisation of their 'golden age' of speech. The disastrous consequence of Brendel's rejection of writing is shown during his second brief visit to Rosmersholm in Act 4, where in answer to Rebecca's question about 'all those still unwritten works of yours' he explains that when he tried to recover this hoarded treasure, he found that 'The mills of time had ground it all to dust. Not a blessed thing left, *nichts*.'(VI, 374-5). It is the editor Mortensgaard, the proliferator of writing who can live without ideals, whom he names 'lord and master of the future'(VI, 375). Thus Brendel departs for the 'great void', after suggesting that Rebecca, who has been significantly identified as a listener throughout the play, 'cuts off her incomparably formed left ear'(VI, 376).

The retrospective discoveries progressively unfolded in *Rosmersholm* gradually undermine Rebecca and Rosmer's ability to sustain the 'illusion of full and present speech' in particular, the 'illusion of presence within a speech believed to be transparent and innocent'.[25] This disillusionment is suggested in Rosmer's eventual guilty acknowledgement of the eroticism of his early discourses with Rebecca. But the transparency and presence to meaning of speech is most strikingly challenged in Rebecca's series of confessions. As Freud pointed out in his discussion of *Rosmersholm*, each disclosure by Rebecca is partial, enigmatic, or effects a further concealment. In her intimate duologue with Kroll in Act 1, she claims she has nothing to live for apart from sacrificing herself 'for the sake of others'; that she was 'genuinely fond of Beata' (in a sense possible) and that while Beata lived she was 'only acting on her behalf, in the wife's name, as it were' (VI, 298). At the end of Act 2 she refuses to reveal why she can never marry Rosmer, and she is similarly incomprehensible to Kroll when she reacts with violent distress to the possibility of West being her biological father, in Act 3. Her subsequent initial confession to Rosmer and Kroll of her manipulations of Beata – how she convinced her 'that a childless wife had no right to stay on [...] it was her duty to [Rosmer] to make way for another' (VI, 362), are incomplete, and it is only under pressure from Kroll, mindful of Beata's words to him, that she admits the extent of her actions, still insisting, however, that her aims were political.

This trial of speech is brought to a head in Act 4 with Rebecca's final confession: that concerning the growth and death of her 'horrible, sensual passion'(VI, 370) for Rosmer, and his response to her revelations. Here we find at once the climax in the play of Ibsen's exploration of the dramatic and emotional potency of intimate speech naturalistically represented, and the impasse of this discourse. In her struggle to voice the unspeakably private, Rebecca's speech absorbs literary language, the language of Beata's symbolism to which the white horse belongs, that is, the language of death, to narrate the phases of her relationship with Rosmer, in three images powerfully suggestive of liminality and the uncanny: the northern winter 'storm at sea'; the stillness of a 'colony of seabirds under the midnight sun', and later the 'sea-troll slumped over the ship that is to carry you [Rosmer] forward' (VI, 369-70; 379). In their poetic opacity, elaborate extension, and allusion to supernatural folklore narratives resonant of oral tradition, Rebecca's similes expose the indeterminacy of the opposition between speech and writing. Her words claim poetry's archaic alliance with the voice, yet breach the bounds of 'natural' dialogue narrowly defined as 'the straightforward, plain language spoken in real life'.[26] Aware of a further unresolved enigma concerning Rebecca's past, which he declines to discuss, Rosmer for his part cannot believe the assertions expressed in these metaphors, namely that her love and 'transformation' are genuine. How can her last confession really be the last, or provide a closing interpretation of their history and stop the agonising proliferation of meanings: 'Oh Rebecca, how can I believe you ... after the furtive way you have gone on here! And now you come along with this new idea. If there's anything behind it, please tell me straight out'; 'I shall never be able to free myself from this doubt'. Her appeal to his intuitive sense of truth, based on their former communion of speech 'Doesn't something deep within you tell you of the change that has taken place in me!' – is fruitless: 'I have no faith in myself any more. No faith either in myself or you' (VI, 373). Even Rebecca finally concedes the defeat of the authenticity of speech. 'I'll take you at your word ... once more', Rosmer offers, vacillating, once she has agreed to his suggestion of suicide; she replies: 'How can you ever take my word for things after today?' (VI, 379).

The fatality of Rosmer's own speech (earlier suggested by Mrs Helseth's claim that he is incapable of laughter or weeping) is demonstrated in his final temptations of Rebecca to emulate Beata. The alliance between death and Rosmer's voice is rehearsed shortly before her agreement to his plan, in her account of Rosmer's moral influence, effected 'Gradually [...] Almost imperceptibly ... but overwhelmingly in the end, and reaching right to the very depths of my soul' (VI, 370). This description shows striking parallels with her earlier account of her murder of Beata, accomplished by pushing always 'Just one little bit further. And then a bit more. And then it happened' (VI, 363). Both seductions occur in intimate conversation, secretive, charged with suppressed eroticism: both lead to death at the mill-race.

By the end of Act 4, it has become clear to Rosmer and Rebecca that the only evidence for the authenticity of one confession, declaration or promise, can be a further, equally questionable utterance, and so on. This circularity is suggested in the verbal structure of the final riddle of the suicide pact: 'is it you who goes with me, or I with you'; 'That is something we shall never fathom' (VI, 380). The restless movement of meanings in the dialogues in which they struggle to authenticate their politics and love, is the movement of meaning as constituted by *différance*; that is, they speak what is, after all, a form of writing. But far from making his characters the victims of language's inherent treacheries, in accordance with a pessimistic scepticism as to the possibility of effective meaning, Ibsen continues to assert the social and political forces which have driven the couple into a labyrinth of signifiers. *Rosmersholm* has been characterised throughout as a site of paralysis in which political action and physical sexuality are disabled. Rebecca and Rosmer can only 'take action' sexually and politically, in terms of, confined to, their own discourse. Yet the only 'proof' ('vidnesbyrd') of this speech's truth outside of itself, will be in suicide.

Writing inspiration: forms of texuality in *Hedda Gabler*

In spite of *Rosmersholm*'s pessimistic account of writing, Ibsen returns to the theme more fully and explicitly than ever before in *Hedda Gabler*, a work significantly preoccupied with the possibility of cultural progress and emancipation through writing. At the same time, *Hedda Gabler* is notable for the technical and aesthetic mastery with which it represents spoken discourse. Edmund Gosse expressed this in his review of the Norwegian text in 1891, speaking of 'an unceasing display of hissing conversational fireworks' and praising Ibsen's 'feat of combining a story with a play, and combining both in meteoric bursts of extremely colloquial chat [...] on the stage, no doubt, this rapid broken utterance will give an extraordinary sense of reality'.[27] The ellipsis and fragmentation of *Hedda Gabler*'s dialogue, its intense orientation to the theatrical present, even in the brief passages of retrospective narrative and poetic symbolism, distinguishes it from the speech in *Ghosts* and *Rosmersholm* which is challenged from within by writing, or else heavily shaped by genres orienting speech to the past.

Hedda Gabler can therefore be seen as polarising speech and writing more definitely than any previous Ibsen play: for alongside the (artfully and constructedly) naturalistic treatment of colloquial exchange is a deliberate thematic demarcation of writing. The radical writer Eilert Løvborg's manuscript is key to the plot and the theatrical impact of the play, and constitutes another example of Ibsen's placing his characters around a text through which their relationships will be negotiated. At the same time however, the play's orientation towards phonocentric oppositions between speech and writing is markedly new. One of Ibsen's preparatory notes to the play: 'The fear of hearing one's own voice. Something foreign, outside oneself', aptly expresses how the dialogue never even promises transparency to meaning and proximity to inner being, given the irony, innuendo and self-conscious role-playing of the more sophisticated speakers and the satirical deflation of the would-be sincere speakers.[*] Furthermore, writing itself is now represented doubly: as moribund and exterior (as before), and newly, as transcendent and ideal. Rather than exploiting the contest between speech and writing then, *Hedda Gabler* can be seen as engaging with a related phonocentric opposition identified by Derrida as that between 'bad writing', and writing as metaphor, 'the Platonic writing of the truth in the soul [...] a *natural*, eternal, and universal writing' understood as pure inscription of divine or natural truth.[29] Though Eilert Løvborg's manuscript has no pretentions to absolute truth, being by nature speculative and discursive, it answers to this account of 'writing as metaphor' in several powerful ways, as Ibsen explores the promises and limitations of the radical text by appealing to the myth of the Platonic book. The ideal of Platonic writing 'systematically contrasts divine or natural writing and the human and laborious, finite and artificial inscription'.[30] The motif of writing as these last, opposed to organic vitality is figured chiefly through Tesman, historian of the medieval domestic industries of Brabant whose very name means 'thesis-man'.[31] In the conversation with Aunt Julle early in the play, Tesman's commitment to moribund writing is made in his insistence on the volume of text accumulated on his honeymoon trip: 'for me it was a sort of academic trip too, you know. I had to look through all those old records. And the books I had to plough through!'; 'the whole of that case was crammed full of nothing but notes' (VII, 176). The same motif is apparent in the series of comic substitutions of textual for sexual generation made in reply to his aunt's hints: Tesman's 'news' from the trip is the achievement of his doctorate rather than paternity; his 'expectations' are of professorship; the future use for his empty rooms will be to house his growing collection of books (VII, 177). Hedda's claustrophobic response to this mass of text is suggested in Act 2 where Tesman returns home with 'quite a number of unbound books under his arm and in his pockets'. In answer to Hedda's 'Do you need still more academic publications?' he replies: 'Oh yes my dear Hedda ... can't get too many of those. One must keep up with everything that's written' (VII, 208-9). Shortly before, Hedda has complained to Brack that Tesman is 'absolutely in his element if he's given leave to grub around in libraries. And sit copying out ancient parchments ... or whatever they are'(VII, 205). Tesman's writing is a process of sorting out, collecting and copying, obdurately material (he sweats under his huge pile of books in Act 2). For Hedda, his accumulation of written texts at the start of the play, is continuous with the September leaves visible outside the windows 'so yellow. And so withered' (VII, 183) and the 'odour of death. Like a bouquet the day after a ball' which she imagines permeates the house (VII, 212). In Hedda's imagination, Tesman's scholarship is tainted with obsolescence, death and obscurity from the start of their marriage.

Tesman therefore provides an obvious foil to the brilliant radical thinker Eilert Løvborg. Though we are forced to take Eilert's genius on trust, I believe it is a condition of our being able to take *Hedda Gabler* seriously 'to believe (and it makes the play more interesting to believe) that Lovberg's [sic] manuscript was truly "one of the most remarkable things ever written," as Tesman explains'.[32] As mentioned above, Ibsen's representation of Eilert's text accords strikingly with Derrida's description of western culture's imagination, within phonocentric paradigms, of a Platonic 'writing in the metaphoric sense, natural, divine, and living writing'. This ideal writing is conceived of as expressing a totality 'enveloped in a volume or a book'; this book being 'profoundly alien to the sense of writing' as understood in the 'common sense'.[33]

Løvborg's manuscript book initially appears to constitute a totality of this kind. Shortly after his first stage entrance in Act 2, Løvborg cuts short Tesman's enthusiasm for his previous acclaimed book, deliberately written, he says, to court approval and restore his reputation. Pulling a packet wrapped in paper from his pocket, he reveals a manuscript, telling Tesman that this is the work he must read: 'For det er først det rigtige. Det, som jeg selv er i'.[34] Leafing through the pages, he shows Tesman the sections dealing with future cultural forces: 'fremtidens kulturmagter' and the future course of civilisation 'fremtidens kulturgang'(408). Though Løvborg refers to the new book as the continuation ('fortsættelsen') of his previous study which extended to the present day, his dismissal of the earlier work makes the later one discontinuous with it and complete in itself. Furthermore, in writing of the future and therefore independently of a referent, Løvborg's book seems at this point to escape the mimetic restrictions, materiality and associated senescence thematically associated with Tesman's historical writing.[35] Unlike Tesman's suitcases of notes and bulky library, Løvborg's slight manuscript, all too easily carried in the pocket, figures on stage as a unique treasure.

In the same scene, Løvborg's writing is characterised through a related, also very significant theme: its closeness to the voice (Derrida argues that: 'Natural writing is immediately united to the voice and to breath').[36] On being shown the manuscript, Tesman observes immediately that it isn't in Løvborg's handwriting. Løvborg explains: 'I dictated it', and then, 'I brought it along so that I could read you a bit this evening'(VII, 216). Indeed, Tesman's excited response to the work is on hearing his friend read aloud. Later, after Brack's party and Eilert's loss of the papers, he will exclaim: 'Ejlert read to me [...] Oh Hedda, you've no idea, it's going to be ever so good! One of the most remarkable books ever written, I'd almost say. Think of that!' (VII, 236).

Løvborg's text is characterised as an extension of his voice from Mrs Elvsted's first interview with Hedda in which she describes how Løvborg 'made me into a sort of real person. Taught me to think' not through formal lessons but intimate speech: 'he talked to me. Talked of so fantastically many things'. It is this practice which leads directly to the composition of Løvborg's books: 'And then came that beautiful, happy time, when I shared his work! Was allowed to help him! [...] When he wrote anything, we always had to do it together'(VII, 194). This method of writing which unifies voice and text is the source of its much discussed 'inspiration' – 'he says I've inspired him'(VII, 225), Thea will later declare – which in turn, distances his text from writing in its debased, everyday sense. Where Tesman's writings are not only repeatable but, very often in themselves repetitions of archival texts, the uniqueness of Løvborg's manuscript derives from its status as a transcription of the inspired voice. In Act 3, finding out that Eilert's copy is the only one he has got, Hedda finds herself fascinated by the book's unrepeatability: 'But can't a thing like that be rewritten? Over again, I mean?'. Tesman replies that it couldn't, 'Because the inspiration... you see...' (VII, 238).

It is this belief in the manuscript as the uniquely precious and natural issue of genius that enables Thea to imagine Løvborg's supposed destruction of the text in terms of child murder; but it is in this image too, that the classical phonocentric characterisation of Løvborg's 'natural writing' takes an unpredictable turn. Thea has taken on the familiar female function of moral nurturer and amanuensis; but unlike the conventional muse who tactfully withdraws when the spark of male creativity has been lit, she demands recognition as co-creator. What is more surprising however, is that Løvborg passionately accepts the imagery and elaborates on it to Hedda after Mrs Elvsted has left: 'To kill his child ... that's not the worst thing a father can do' and he admits 'Thea's soul was in that book (VII, 249) ('Theas rene sjæl var i den bog', 374). He also uses the image, we hear, when he returns to Madame Diana's to look for the book yet again: Brack recounts, 'He was talking wildly about a child that had been lost' (VII, 263). Løvborg's recognition of the extent of Thea's claims not only opposes traditional romantic ideologies of male creativity which in other respects, closely define Løvborg's identity as writer, but also resists the distinctively fin-de-siècle (and anti-feminist) narratives of male literary autogenesis, in which the man fathers his own text in isolation, or else is inspired homoerotically by another male.[37]

While the begetting of this 'child' ironically parallels Tesman's own obtuse substitution of writing for paternity, and the displacement of sexuality achieved in Hedda and Eilert's own past tête-à-têtes, it is the image of Thea's intervention in Løvborg's writing that supremely inspires Hedda's jealousy. Charles Lyons points to Hedda's overt lack of intellectual aspirations and indifference to the content of Løvborg's manuscript as evidence of her motivation by class snobbery and sexual jealousy rather than frustrated vocation.[38] But Hedda's desire for power in the play, however vaguely conceptualised, is persistent; and though for social reasons she cannot even imagine herself culturally productive, she intuits the extent to which Løvborg's ('living') text is a discourse of power. It is the couple's mutual development of the child/writing trope, rather than the sexuality of Thea's relationship with Løvborg as such, that spurs Hedda to burn the manuscript. In the exchange where Løvborg tells Thea 'You're right. It was like killing a child' and Thea: 'But how could you then...! The child was mine, it was also mine', Hedda echoes '[*almost inaudibly*]. The child...' (VII, 248). She herself will ensure its actual destruction immediately after this confrontation between Thea and Løvborg, feeding the sheets into the fire of the stove: 'Now I'm burning your child, Thea! [...] Your child and Eijlert Lövborg's...' (VII, 250). Janet Garton has pointed out that in Hedda's final words of the scene she is burning 'the child': that is, her own as well as Eilert and Thea's.[39] The identity of authorship and childbearing established in the couple's rhetoric evokes their escape from mortality through the 'child' of their Platonic book, but can only sharpen Hedda's sense of futility.

Løvborg's fantasy of the book's destruction, ostensibly woven to conceal its sordid loss from Thea, announces once more the status of his book as 'natural writing', by asserting the text's identity with nature on the one hand, and his own personality on the other. He says he has torn it 'Into a thousand pieces. And scattered them out in the fjord. A long way out. At least the water's clean and salt out there. They'll drift with the current and the wind. And after a while they'll sink. Deeper and deeper. Like I will, Thea' (VII, 247). The immediate contrast is between the cleanliness of the elements and the impurity of Løvborg's haunts the previous night. This rhetoric of purity, along with the elaborate extravagance of Løvborg's excuse, suggests that the actual loss of the book has been unconsciously willed. Løvborg's narrative fantasises the text's immunity from the despised popular audience which has fêted his previous book, at the same time as effecting his release from Thea's embarrassing emotional demands. In any case, the book's transcendental status is preserved momentarily in this outburst of Løvborg's imagination.

The closing scene of *Hedda Gabler* shows the absurd transformation of Løvborg's total book, 'natural, eternal and universal' into the fallen writing against which it has been systematically contrasted. As Tesman laments that Eilert has ended his life without leaving behind 'the work that would have made his name immortal', Mrs Elvsted suddenly, incredibly, produces from her pockets the drafts: 'Look here. I kept the notes, all the notes he used when he dictated' (VII, 260). The inspired voice has had recourse to writing after all, then; and it is to the form of this '*handful of small papers*', not unlike one of Tesman's own 'collections', that Løvborg's work now reverts. If writing, understood as a supplement and as a treacherous mechanical copy of speech in phonocentric ideologies, is identified by its status as a repetition and by its overt repeatability, it is as writing in this sense that Løvborg's text now exists. The textuality of the work, that is, its necessary separation from a present 'father' who guarantees and protects its meaning, is realised only through the death of the author, and its burning and reconstruction. It is evident to Hedda that Tesman, the arch copier and editor, will be expert in this labour and that Thea will repeat her 'inspiration' of Løvborg with Tesman; given the devotion of the pair there is no reason to suppose that they are beginning work on a travesty of Løvborg's book, however limited their version. But Hedda now finds herself oppressed by Løvborg's writing rather than Tesman's, as her husband's obsession with repeating Løvborg abandons Hedda entirely to Brack's coercion; while the abrupt resuscitation of the text Hedda has ritually destroyed must be as much a disillusionment as Løvborg's failure to 'die beautifully'.

Løvborg is the last great writer in Ibsen's plays. Allmers' work in *Little Eyolf* is exposed as a self-regarding evasion; Foldal's aspirations to poetry in *John Gabriel Borkman* are a self-deluding fantasy. Ibsen's future heroes will aspire and achieve in fields outside of writing. The loss of Løvborg's manuscript therefore, can be seen as marking the close of Ibsen's problematisation of writing begun in *An Enemy of the People*, and worked through in *Rosmersholm* and *Hedda Gabler*. As I have tried to show in this essay, these plays explore at once the potent lure and the impossibility of the ideals of 'pure' speech and Platonic writing.

But however sharp the irony of Løvborg's end, Hedda will choose death over the dishonouring of his memory; and it is not least through Hedda's loyalty that Ibsen, himself the radical writer *par excellence*, has Løvborg's image retain some of the charisma of the radical intellectual who, in spite of his weakness, is sufficiently courageous to risk writing. In this way, Ibsen states again the seriousness of radical writing and its problems. After all, Løvborg's aspiration to inspired writing, unified with the voice and breath, ideally imagined floating in torn fragments on the sea, echoes the earlier dream expressed in the opening of Ibsen's '*Rimbrev – Til Fru Heiberg*', which fantasises a pure form of communication, free of the ludicrous and constricting mechanisms of writing: 'Kunne jeg på engang sendt,/uten bur av skrift og prent,/alle tankens løse fugle,/...'.[40]

Notes

1. *The Oxford Ibsen*, trans. and ed. by James McFarlane, 8 vols (Oxford: Oxford University Press, 1960-77), VI (1960), p.57; *En Folkefiende, Henrik Ibsen, Samlede Verker, Hundreårsutgave*, ed. by Francis Bull, Halvdan Koht and Didrik Arup Seip, 21 vols (Oslo: Gyldendal Norsk Forlag, 1928-57), IX (1932), p.237. All references to the English and Norwegian texts of Ibsen's plays are to these editions respectively.

2. In *Powers of the Press: Newspapers, Power and Public in Nineteenth-Century England* (London: Scolar Press, 1996) Aled Jones argues that 'Not only had the newspaper been transformed into the most dynamic and profitable of all products of the printing press by the end of the century, but it had also been securely implanted into the cultural landscape as an essential reference point in the daily lives of millions of people' (p.2); the description also applies to contemporary Norway. Ronald Popperwell has commented that during the 1850s, 'with the increasing polarization of the political parties [...] the dramatic improvement in communications, and a general upswing in the economic, social and cultural condition of the country, the Norwegian press and periodical literature entered a period of continuing expansion and increasing sophistication', *Norway* (London: Ernest Benn, 1972), p.40.

3. *Oxford Ibsen*, V (1961), pp. 349; 359.

4. See for example Theoharis Constantine Theoharis: 'the machinations of the struggle between Kroll and Mortensgaard for Rosmer's editorial service at one or the other newspaper never heat up. The obligatory incriminating letter figures in the play, but is only mentioned and plays a diminished role in the political and sexual story, corroborating rather than revealing crucial information', *Ibsen's Drama: Right Action and Tragic Joy* (London: Macmillan, 1996), p.95.

5. Einar Haugen, *Ibsen's Drama: Author to Audience* (Minneapolis: University of Minnesota

Press, 1979), p.100; see also Trygve Knudsen, 'Phases of Language and Style in the Plays of Henrik Ibsen', *Scandinavica* (May 1963), 1-20 (p.9) (reprinted as chapter 2 of the present volume) and Michael Meyer, *Henrik Ibsen: the Making of a Dramatist 1828-1864* (London: Rupert Hart-Davis, 1967) pp.164-5.

6. Letter from Ibsen to Lucie Wolf, 25 May, 1883, *Ibsen, Speeches and Letters*, ed. by Evert Sprinchorn (MA: MacGibbon and Kee, 1965) p.218. I am using the term 'speech genre' in M. M. Bakhtin's sense of 'relatively stable types' of utterance associated with particular activities and 'spheres of communication'. Such genres are characterised by distinctive 'thematic content, style and compositional structure', Bakhtin, 'Speech Genres and Other Late Essays', in *The Bakhtin Reader*, ed. by Pam Morris (London: Edward Arnold, 1994), pp.81-87 (p.81).

7. Jacques Derrida, *Of Grammatology*, trans. by Gayatri Chakravorty Spivak (Baltimore and London: Johns Hopkins University Press, 1976), p.11.

8. 'The signified concept is never present in and of itself, in a sufficient presence that would refer only to itself. Essentially and lawfully, every concept is inscribed in a chain or system within which it refers to the other, to other concepts, by means of the systematic play of differences. Such a play, *différance*, is [...] the possibility of conceptuality', Jacques Derrida, 'Différance', trans. by Alan Bass, in *A Derrida Reader: Between the Blinds*, ed. by Peggy Kamuf (Hemel Hempstead: Harvester Wheatsheaf, 1991), pp.59-79 (p.63).

9. Barbara Johnson, 'Translator's Introduction', in Jacques Derrida, *Dissemination*, trans. with an Introduction and Additional Notes, by Barbara Johnson (London: Athlone Press, 1981), p.viii.

10. Jacques Derrida, *Of Grammatology*, p.12.

11. Ibsen, *Samlede Verker*, ed. by Didrik Arup Seip, 6 vols (Oslo: Gyldendal Norsk Forlag, 1952), VI, p.420: 'Your art is the child of fragrance,/of inspiration,/of feeling,/of character and imagination'; (my translation).

12. *Oxford Ibsen*, VI, p.323; *Samlede Verker*, X (1932), p.377.

13. In McFarlane's *Oxford Ibsen* version: 'You actually said that? You did that? [...] So that's what you meant when you said you "took action."' (VI, 362).

14. Kroll's attempt to turn the clergyman into an editor aptly symbolises the anxiously perceived shift of influence from oral to print communication in the later nineteenth century, described by Aled Jones in *Powers of the Press*: 'while printed texts might be seen to lack the "social feeling" and the "accompaniment of look, gesture and intonation" that were associated with speech, the expansion of the popular press [...] had left the pulpit "helplessly, hopelessly, ignominiously in the shade". In the scale of persuasive effectiveness, newspapers were increasingly seen as the most immediate and influential of media.' Jones quotes here from James Leatham, 'The Press and the Pulpit', *Westminster Review* (June 1892), 602-07.

15. See Jacqueline Pearson, *Women's Reading in Britain 1750-1835: A Dangerous Recreation* (Cambridge: Cambridge University Press, 1999). Though Pearson is writing about British culture in a period prior to Ibsen's, I believe that many of her arguments about conservative attempts to police women's reading hold good for the society portrayed in Ibsen's realist prose dramas. Similar anxieties are expressed in Pastor Manders' attitude to the 'disgusting, free-thinking pamphlets!' (V, 384) which he believes have undermined Mrs Alving's morals in *Ghosts*.

16. 'You have read up a lot of new ideas and opinions. You have acquired a smattering of various ideas and theories – that somehow seem to upset a good many things that up to now we took for incontrovertible and inviolate. But in your case, Miss West, it never got beyond being anything but an abstraction. Book knowledge. It never got into your blood'(VI, 357).

17. *Women's Reading in Britain*, p.152.
18. Derrida in *Jacques Derrida*, by Geoffrey Bennington and Jacques Derrida, trans. by G. Bennington (Chicago: University of Chicago Press, 1993), p.51.
19. *Of Grammatology*, p. 17.
20. *Of Grammatology*, pp.12, 20.
21. *Of Grammatology*, p.12.
22. *Of Grammatology*, p.168.
23. Derrida, *Jacques Derrida*, p.49.
24. Janet Garton, 'The Middle Plays', in *The Cambridge Companion to Ibsen*, ed. by James McFarlane (Cambridge: Cambridge University Press, 1994), pp.106-125 (p.113).
25. *Of Grammatology*, p.140.
26. Inga-Stina Ewbank discusses in detail the interplay of metaphorical and colloquial language in female characters' dialogue in 'Ibsen and the Language of Women', in *Women Writing and Writing About Women*, ed. by Mary Jacobus (London: Croom Helm, 1979) pp.114-132.
27. *Hedda Gabler*, trans. by Jens Arup, *Oxford Ibsen*, VII (1966), p.510.
28. *Oxford Ibsen* VII, p.483. For discussion of the reflexive ironies of *Hedda Gabler* see Frode Helland, 'Irony and Experience in *Hedda Gabler*', *Contemporary Approaches to Ibsen*, 8, ed. by Bjørn Hemmer and Vigdis Ystad (Oslo: Scandinavian University Press, 1994).
29. *Of Grammatology*, p.15.
30. *Of Grammatology*, p.15.
31. Evert Sprinchorn, 'The Unspoken Text in *Hedda Gabler*', *Modern Drama*, 36 (1993), 353-67 (p.356).
32. Elinor Fuchs, *The Death of Character: Perspectives on Theater After Modernism* (Bloomington and Indianapolis: University of Indiana Press, 1996), p.65. c.f. Frode Helland (one of the few critics to discuss the manuscript in detail) who argues that Løvborg and his manuscript are over-rated and ironically negated in the play, 'Irony and Experience in *Hedda Gabler*', pp.111-112.
33. *Of Grammatology*, pp.17, 18.
34. *Samlede Verker*, XI, p.341. In the *Oxford Ibsen* translation Løvborg's line reads more casually: 'Because this is the real thing. I put some of myself into this one' (VII, 216).
35. Here it is interesting to consider also Charles R. Lyons' discussion of the two scholars' rivalry in terms of social class, in *Hedda Gabler: Gender, Role and World* (Boston: Twayne Publishers, 1991). Løvborg's 'disinterest in the kind of empirical research that marks Tesman's work – reflects the greater freedom of his class from material circumstances of production and the opportunity for reflection' (p.68).
36. *Of Grammatology*, p.17.
37. Elaine Showalter, *Sexual Anarchy: Gender and Culture at the "fin de siècle"* (London: Virago, 1992), p.78. In *Gender and Genius: Towards a Feminist Aesthetic* (London: Women's Press, 1989), Christine Battersby points out that by the mid-1880s Schopenhauer and Nietzsche had established influential formulations of the notion of artistic creativity as exclusively male and yet conceived of in terms of 'spiritual pregnancy', birth and maternity (pp.107-9; 121-2).
38. *Hedda Gabler: Gender, Role and World*, p.88.
39. 'The Middle Plays', p.123.
40. Ibsen, *Samlede Verker* (1952) VI, p.420: 'If only I could for once have sent/ without the cage of writing and print/ all the free birds of thought'; (my translation).

Originally published November 2000 (Vol. 39, No. 2).

A Woman's Place/Female Space in Ibsen's *Fruen fra Havet*

Anne-Marie V. Stanton-Ife

The triangular character constellations evident in the majority of Ibsen's dramas have been a dominant concern of critics. Ibsen positions his heroes between two women who represent radically different values and perspectives, for example, Furia and Aurelia in *Catilina*, Anitra and Solveig in *Peer Gynt* and Maja and Irene in *Når vi Døde Vågner*. These women function not so much as characters in their own right, but as symbolic articulations of internally conflicting and competing values, the tension between which, in his metaphysical struggle, the hero has somehow to resolve.[1] However, the application of this 'hero caught between two women' formula to the dramas in which women are caught in an apparently parallel conflict between two men (for example, *Fruen fra Havet* (1888) and *Hedda Gabler* (1890)) is problematic, for it tends to produce metaphysical readings in which the heroine's final resolution of her conflict is similarly reduced to the articulation of a choice between two competing values – a choice which finds its expression in such terms as 'the individual versus society'.[2] What this apparently innocuous terminology conceals is how notions of femininity and the social reality of women are conveniently collapsed into it, thus erasing questions of sexual difference and establishing a false parity between the men and women of the dramas.

The consequence of such an approach is two-fold. Firstly, as Luce Irigaray[3] and others have pointed out, the edifice of western metaphysics is one in which women are neither seen nor heard: the apparently ungendered labels, 'individual', 'agent' and 'subject' are always already gendered – in the masculine. Therefore, to impose a metaphysical reading on plays which explore the social reality of women is to perform the same operations of silencing on the plays as the patriarchal structures perform on the women in them. Secondly, it undermines the central tension on which these plays are predicated: that women's relationship to absolute values such as 'freedom' is necessarily even more relative and tenuous than men's, for the simple reason that women are denied any accession to selfhood or any status as responsible ethical agents: 'A woman cannot be herself in contemporary society', wrote Ibsen:

> ...it is an exclusively male society with laws drafted by men, and with counsels and judges who judge feminine conduct from the male point of view. (Preface to *A Doll's House*. Vol V:436)[4]

It can therefore be argued that the way into these plays and the way towards understanding the predicament of characters like Ellida and Hedda is not via the

Socratic question of *how* we should live, but, rather, via the more pressing Irigarayan question of *where* women should live within the patriarchal structures that constitute society – a society in which women are 'homeless'.

To argue that the women in Ibsen's plays are homeless, might well seem to be a perverse gesture, for women are strongly identified with their homes, particularly with their bourgeois drawing rooms. However, in *Fruen fra Havet*, Ibsen opens up the drawing room and releases Ellida from its confines, thus implicitly questioning her very being there. In fact, as this article aims to demonstrate, the play can be seen as a play about places and spaces, more precisely, female places and spaces. It will access the question of spatiality on two different yet interdependent levels: first of all it will offer a thematic analysis, using the work of Luce Irigaray (particularly *An Ethics of Sexual Difference*[5] and *Speculum of the Other Woman*) to provide a sharper focus for the discussion; it will then go on to show how Ibsen realizes this question of female space not only thematically, but also technically through his manipulation of dramatic space – the theatrical medium *par excellence*.

√ intro (rephrase for diss)

1

According to Irigaray, to 'inhabit is the fundamental trait of man's being... man is forever searching for, building, creating homes for himself everywhere: caves, huts, women, cities, language, concepts, theory, and so on' (E:141). As women are used as material for the structuring of the male symbolic,[6] clearly they cannot simultaneously inhabit it as men do (E:107), that is as subject, whether as the subject of discourse or as an ethical or legal agent: 'Tradition places [them] within the home... But that home, which is usually paid for by man's labour encloses [them], places them in *internal exile*' (E:65). The only place available to women in this 'internal exile' is that of the 'maternal-feminine'. The maternal-feminine is not a biological category in Irigaray's thought, but a social construct evolved by patriarchy in order to stave off male dereliction. Dereliction is the term applied to the state of being totally abandoned outside the symbolic, that is being denied representation. The structuring of the male symbolic depends on the dereliction of the female for its survival. For Irigaray, 'woman is place' (E:38), the place man uses as his point of *retour* (a point which itself will be returned to later in this article), a place which is a 'container', 'envelope' or 'vessel' (E:43).

In the socio-sexual economy, these containers function as objects of exchange between men and therefore as objects properly belonging to men. In order to establish sovereignty over the container, men have idealized it. 'If woman could be inside herself, she would have at least two things in her: herself and that for which she is a container: man and child' (E:41), but in the moment of appropriation/idealization, the place occupied by the child is privileged as the primary, proper place, in the passage to which the woman acts as container for the man, and in this passage to place, her 'self' as thing is forbidden. Thus women inhabit/become a place *for*-the-other and never for themselves. In her inscription into the maternal-feminine, the woman as *amante*, as lover is banished – and it is precisely this exile that is explored in *Fruen fra Havet*.

2

The identification of woman-as-place-for-men is made early on in the play by Ellida's doctor-husband, Wangel. Catching up on the past with Arnholm, an old family friend and tutor, he recounts how:

> We were so happy here, she and I... And now I live on here very happily with the woman who filled her place.

> Her har jeg levet så inderlig lykkelig med henne som gikk bort fra oss så tidlig... Og nu lever jeg her så lykkelig med henne som jeg fikk i stedet. (VII:38/335)

Wangel uses the (im)personal pronoun *henne* to refer to both wives, the living and the dead, even though he knows that both women were personally known to Arnholm. This has the effect of privileging place over person, and, moreover, suggests that one woman can easily re*place* another, thus guaranteeing man's survival. As Ellida later explains (and Wangel concurs in this), after the death of his first wife he could not bear the emptiness of his house and looked for a new wife and mother for his two daughters. He chose Ellida: 'Though you had absolutely no idea if I could fill that position or not' / 'Skjønt du visste jo slett ikke om jeg dudde til den stilling' (VII:98/368). It was simply taken for granted. However, as is evident from the first act, the place of the maternal-feminine is one that Ellida neither could nor would occupy, but being the only one available to her in the symbolic, she is left to construct an uncertain identity in its margins.

The play opens with Wangel's daughters, Bolette and Hilde, decorating the verandah with flowers and hoisting the flag in celebration of their dead mother's birthday, while Bolette tries to pretend that it is all in honour of Arnholm's visit. Implicit in this is a rejection of Ellida as mother and of the type of easy substitution described by Wangel. This rejection is later made explicit in this exchange between Lyngstrand, the aspiring sculptor, and Hilde:

> LYNGSTRAND: I saw your mother down there. She was going into her bathing hut.
> HILDE: Who did you say?
> LYNGSTRAND: Your mother.
> HILDE: Ah, I see what you mean.

> LYNGSTRAND: Jeg så Deres mor der nede. Hun gikk inn sitt badehus.
> HILDE: Hvem gjorde det?
> LYNGSTRAND: Deres mor.
> HILDE: Nå, så, nå. (VII:333/33)

When compared with the first, the second Mrs. Wangel has clearly failed as maternal-feminine. Bolette explains to Arnholm that she has to put domestic duties above her reading, as Ellida:

> isn't very good at all the things that Mother used to do so well... There are so many things that <u>this one</u> doesn't even *see*... or doesn't *care*...

> er slett ikke skikket til alt det som mor hadde så godt et grep på. Der er så mangt og meget

som <u>denne her</u> ikke ser. Eller som hun kanskje ikke vil se, – eller ikke bryr seg om. (VII:73/354, my underlining)

Not only has Ellida failed to assume her domestic duties, but she has also refused to live with Wangel 'as his wife' for many years. Having rejected the only role available to her, Ellida's exile is a double one: an exile from the always already exile of the maternal-feminine. A clear problem of representation arises from this fact. That those around her have great difficulty in referring to her because she has no apparent place in the scheme of things is evidenced in the following, which is an example of a finely tuned code of avoidance of direct reference:

WANGEL: Is anybody else at home?
HILDE: No, *she's* gone.

WANGEL: – Er – er vi *alene* i huset nu?
HILDE: Ja, *hun* er gått i – (VII:35/333, my italics)

Feeling her homelessness very acutely, Ellida has retreated into a private world represented by her relationship and identification with the sea and her excursions into memories of her Stranger whom she had met ten years before at her father's lighthouse and with whom she was symbolically wed to the sea. As Wangel says, the sea is 'all she seems to live for' / 'liksom hennes liv og lyst' (VII:38/336). The sea, with its associations of unboundedness, changeability and fluidity, (characteristics which, in Irigaray's thought, are closely linked to the female imaginary[7]) can be seen to represent the space in which Ellida can 'be inside herself', a container for-herself; a space in which her own pleasure and meanings can unfold.

However, Ellida's daily swim (whatever the weather) and her '*home*sickness for the sea' (or, rather, her homesickness for her*self*) (VII:59) is considered obsessive by Wangel and the community: 'The people round here don't really understand it at all. They call her "The Lady from the Sea"' / 'Folk her i byen kan slett ikke forstå det. De kaller henne "Fruen fra Havet"'(VII:39/336), thus marking off her difference in a semi-folkloric representation without attempting to interpret it.[8] Hilde and Wangel also have recourse to this description. Hilde uses it ironically, as one of many strategies of rejection and effacement; rejection of Ellida as mother and effacement of Ellida as a woman, for unlike Bolette, Hilde never refers to Ellida by name. Wangel uses the description in an attempt to romanticize his wife's difference, thus also failing to interpret it on its own terms.[9]

Ellida is only too aware of the vulnerability of her subject position when trying to communicate her desire of a self for-herself. This vulnerability is attributable to the fact of the impossibility of any representation in the symbolic of a female self that is not coterminous with the maternal-feminine. She also senses the 'unspeakability' of her experience and pre-empts her husband's subsequent construction of it around medical theory, explaining to Arnholm that:

...The whole thing's quite incomprehensible. I don't know how I could begin to describe it. You would only think I was ill. Or else completely mad...

...Det er noe så rent ubegripelig. Jeg vet ikke hvorledes jeg skulle kunne fortelle det. De ville bare tro at jeg var syk. Eller at jeg var rent gal. (VII:44/339)

182

A female self that cannot speak about itself is inevitably appropriated and 'spoken' by other discourses. In this case, the problem that a female self in touch with her own sexuality presents to the patriarchal order is 'resolved' through the 'diagnosis' of female sexuality as 'the manifestation of something wrong, an illness'.[10] That Ellida has, herself, to an extent, absorbed this patriarchal construction is evident from the fact that when discussing her relationship with the Stranger she regularly interjects pronouncements on it as being 'utterly mad and meaningless' / 'rent galt og meningsløst' and repeatedly begs Wangel to 'help me..save me!' / 'hjelp meg! Frels meg!' (VII:81/358).

Wangel is wholly unable to understand Ellida's homesickness in all its apparent illogicality. He is, however, determined to respond to her plea, but his mode of operation serves more to heal the physician than it does the patient. By seeking sanctuary in medical theory he un-houses her in yet another language – the discourse of mental illness, which constructs her difference as a 'condition'. Wangel clearly feels the threat of the chaos and darkness traditionally read in female desire. He warns Ellida that this 'craving for the unattainable, for the limitless, the infinite.. will ultimately put your very mind in darkness' / '[k]ravet på det grenseløse og endeløse – og på det uoppnåelige, – det vil drive ditt sinn helt inn i nattemørket til slutt' (VII:120/380).

For him, her failure as *self*-sacrificing maternal-feminine signifies what he diagnoses as an illness – the nosology of which he cannot fully understand:

> This is no ordinary illness, either. No ordinary doctor is much help here. And no ordinary medicines either.
>
> ...dette her er jo ikke noen alminnelig sykdom. Her hjelper ingen alminnelig læge, – og ingen alminnelige lægemidler. (VII:92/364)

His medicalization of Ellida's 'condition' and his constant searching for 'cures' (medicines, which as Bolette points out, will do her very little good in the long run) and taking her back to live next to the sea are all an attempt to immobilize her difference in (albeit shaky) medical theory, and to naturalize her by restoring her to 'normality' and 'health'.

These gestures of immobilization are essential for Wangel's continuing survival. For, if, as Irigaray points out, woman is used as the material, the base of man's dwelling, then the illusion that she is immobile is essential. Ellida's identification with the sea, 'the bottomless', 'the unlimited', that which 'ebbs and flows', clearly refuses stasis. In this way she denies the possibility of his *retour*, the search for his 'original dwelling place', his 'unconditional first home' in the mother, which he returns to and through the maternal-feminine:

> He exists in his nostalgia for a return to the ONE WHOLE; his desire to go back toward and into the originary womb ... it is impossible unless he is sure of a foundation in which there is place. (E:100)

Ellida, in her fluidity, stands in direct contrast to Solveig, who accommodates Peer's *retour* to 'my mother, my wife, innocent woman' / 'min moder, min hustru, uskyldig kvinde'. She is not available to Wangel as a 'foundation in which there is place' as she represents *another* desire, which, clearly, is different from 'that o*f being as much as possible like the man's eternal object of desire* [the mother] and she does not correlate her desire with her success in this operation.' By refusing 'to join in this *first* male desire' she constitutes a threat, the threat of castration and dereliction, which is overcome by her inscription as 'crazy, disoriented, lost' (SP:32-3).

Although, as we have seen, Ellida has, to a degree, assimilated prevalent notions of difference as a form of dislocation, there are several moments in the play in which she mounts an instinctive resistance to immobilization in concept, theory and explanation. In Act II, Wangel tells her that he thinks he understands her, to which she counters '[*vehemently*] You don't! How can you say you understand...!' / '[*heftig*] Det gjør du ikke! Si ikke at du forstår – !' With his confidence rising in his theory, he claims to have seen 'through to the very depths' / 'helt til bunns', and reads Ellida's unrest as resulting from her inability to replace his former wife: ELLIDA: 'The depths you say. Not altogether, believe me' / 'Helt til bunns, sier du. Å tro bare ikke det' (VII:58/346).

Later, when Ellida recounts that although at one stage she had forgotten the Stranger, she explains how he seemed to 'come back' while she was expecting the child. Having internalized notions of guilt which are imputed onto the failed maternal-feminine (the quotation from *Peer Gynt* expressly locates 'innocence' in the *ewig-weibliche*) she in her delusion declares that the child had the Stranger's eyes, and she is therefore fearful of sleeping with Wangel. Wangel immediately seizes on this intelligence and constructs her 'illness' as a symptom of pregnancy – a time when women are supposed to be particularly vulnerable to inexplicable cravings. On this view, Ellida's present 'disorder' could be explained by the child's untimely death at about five months old, an explanation which conveniently erases the significance of the Stranger and his power over Ellida.

> WANGEL: Ah! It was then was it? Ellida, I am beginning to understand a lot of things.
> ELLIDA: No, you're wrong my dear! What it was that happened to me I don't think one can ever understand.
>
> WANGEL: På den tid altså? Ja, Ellida, – da begynner jeg jo å få rede på så mangt og meget.
> ELLIDA: Du tar feil kjære! Det som er kommet over meg – . Å, jeg tror det er aldri i verden til å få rede på. (VII:65/350)

Ellida is, of course, quite right. It cannot be understood because it cannot be represented. In spite of what she tells him, Wangel clings to his biological reading, (which reduces Ellida to a container for the child, as it implies that nothing else could be a source for her disquiet) even though he has to concede to Arnholm that:

> ...quite by chance ... she had a rather severe attack in that March of three years ago [but] that can be explained by the circumstances – the condition she was in at that time.
>
> ...[r]igtignok kom det – tilfeldigvis – nettopp i mars måned for tre år siden et temmelig voldsomt utbrudd hos henne ... det lar seg ganske simpelt hen forklare av den tilstand – de omstendigheter, – som hun nettopp på den tiden befant seg i. (VII:94/336)

Arnholm pronounces the conflicting evidence he hears to be 'sign against sign' / 'tegn imot tegn',[11] an opposition in which the female 'signs' will inevitably lose ground to the masculine ones erected over them. As Irigaray writes in *This Sex which is not One*:

> She is indefinitely other in herself. This is undoubtedly the reason she is called temperamental, incomprehensible, perturbed, capricious – not to mention her language in which 'she' goes off in all directions and in which 'he' is unable to discern the coherence of any meaning. Contradictory words seem a little crazy to the logic of reason, and inaudible to him who listens with ready-made grids, a code prepared in advance.[12]

At several points, Wangel tries to mould Ellida's discourse into coherent meanings, and is utterly bewildered by its resistance to them. In this scene from Act IV, following her first re-encounter with the Stranger, Ellida is typically elusive. Wangel is trying to ascertain why, if the Stranger had appeared to Ellida over the years looking exactly as he had the night before last, she had failed to recognize him:

> WANGEL: ...You said that he always appeared to you looking the same as he was when you parted. Ten years ago out there.
> ELLIDA: Did I say that? ... In that case he must have looked more or less as he looks now.
> WANGEL: No. The night before last as we were coming home, you gave a very different description of him. Ten years ago he had no beard, you said. And dressed quite differently. And what about the breast pin with the pearl? The man yesterday was wearing nothing of the sort.
> ELLIDA: No, he wasn't.

> WANGEL: ...oppe på Utsikten sa du at han alltid viste seg for deg slik som han var da I skiltes. Der ute for ti år siden ...
> ELLIDA: Sa jeg det? Så har han vel den gang sett ut omtrent som nu.
> WANGEL: Nei. Du ga en ganske annen skildring av ham i forgårs på hjemveien. For ti år siden var han uten skjegg, sa du. Ganske annerledes kledd var han også.. Og så brystnålen med perlen i – ? Den hadde jo slett ikke mannen i går.
> ELLIDA: Nei, den hadde han ikke. (VII:97/367)

Ellida thinks hard at Wangel's behest, trying to produce a clear image of the Stranger as he was ten years before, and declares 'No, today I can't. Isn't that strange?' / 'Nei, – i dag kan jeg det slett ikke. Er det ikke besynderlig?'. He does not think it at all 'strange': 'A new image hs presented itself ... Reality ... and it overshadows your morbid fancies' / 'Der er nu trådt et nytt virkelighetsbilde frem for deg. Og det skygger for det gamle, – så du ikke kan lenger se det' (VII:97/367). Wangel sees in the Stranger's arrival a possible 'recovery' for Ellida, in the form of 'reality'. But this is clearly a masculine version of reality, and, as such, 'overshadows' nothing for her.[13]

It is this version of reality and the structures that underpin it that the Stranger's arrival and his insistence that she come with him 'of her own free will' prompts Ellida to expose. In Act IV she begins the arduous process of *aletheia*.[14] She tells Wangel that they 'lie to each other ... or at least conceal the truth' / 'går her og lyver for hinannen ... – vi fordølger sannheten i alle fall' (VII:98/368). What follows is an indictment of their marriage as a 'transaction' in which she sold herself to Wangel and thereby renounced her a utonomy:

> Never ... Not at any price! I shouldn't have sold myself! Far better to have had the most menial of jobs, the most beggarly existence ... of my own free will ... and of my own choice!

> Aldri for noen pris skulle jeg ha ... solgt meg selv! Heller det usleste arbeide, – heller de fattigste vilkår i – frivillighet – og efter eget valg. (VII:99/369)

What she wants is not a legal divorce which would enable her to transfer from one man to another, but that they should agree, of their own free will, to release each other. She implores Wangel: 'Give me my full freedom again! I must have my freedom today' / 'Gi meg bare fri! Jeg må jo ha min frihet igjen i denne dag'.

Ellida is trying to negotiate a space in which she can confront the Stranger as a free agent, for in order for her decision to be a genuine one, she cannot 'dodge the issue by claiming to be another man's wife. Nor by claiming that I have no choice' / 'skyte meg inn under at jeg er en annen manns hustru. Ikke skyte meg inn under at jeg intet valg har'. This desperate plea for subjectivity appals Wangel, who remarks 'You speak of choice! Choice, Ellida! Choice in a matter like this!' / 'Du taler om valg! Valg, Ellida! Valg i denne sak!' (VII:101/369). The full ironic sweep of this statement is characteristic of Ibsen: clearly, in deciding 'denne sak' – the course of her life, a woman cannot be expected to have any choice. In Act V, during the final half hour of torture before the Stranger returns for the last time to hear Ellida's answer, Wangel reinvokes the standard of ownership and protection over Ellida by insisting that she has no choice. Until almost the last minute, Wangel continues to exercise his proprietorial rights over Ellida despite her clear articulation of her homelessness: 'I am completely without roots in your house ...there is nothing to hold me here...nothing to support me'/ '... så har jeg jo slett ingen ting å stå imot med! Her hjemme er der jo ingen verdens ting som drager og binder meg. Jeg er jo rent rotløs i ditt hus, Wangel' (VII:108/373). When his attempt to confront the Stranger alone and to speak for Ellida fails, he is forced to listen to her as she speaks with increasing vehemency and presents *her* version of reality, which includes an unequivocal statement of her *self*, that which, though exiled by Wangel, is nevertheless beyond the reaches of his ownership and control:

> Of course you can keep me here! ... But my mind ... my thoughts ... my desires and longings ... these you cannot bind! They will go on ranging..out into the unknown ... which I was made for ... and which you have shut me away from!

> Vel kan du holder meg tilbake her! Det har du jo makt og midler til! ... Men mitt sinn, – alle mine tanker, – alle mine dragende lengsler og begjær, – *dem* kan du ikke binde! De vil hige og jage – ut i det ukjente, – som jeg var skapt for – og som du har lukket for meg! (VII:120/380)

At this point, forced to listen and to accept that to keep her would be to lose her, and that none of his 'ready-made grids' can contain her, he cancels the transaction, freeing her:

> from me and all things mine. You can make of life what it properly ought to be. Now you can choose freely. And on your own responsibility, Ellida.

fra meg og mitt. Og fra mine. Nu kan ditt eget riktige liv – komme inn på sitt rette spor igjen. For nu kan du velge i frihet. Og under eget ansvar, Ellida. (VII:121/381)

This unprecedented representation of her as subject and agent changes everything for Ellida. It is the first time that any self to which she is responsible has been granted her. She chooses to remain in her marriage, 'for now I can. For now I come freely ..of my own free will and choice'/ '[n]u kan jeg det. For nu kommer jeg til deg i frihet, – frivillig – og under ansvar' (VII:122/381). In order to save Ellida, Wangel has had to abandon his project of saving himself, and only by completely cutting himself off, by performing true symbolic castration, from the maternal-feminine could this be achieved. Wangel thus proves he has the courage to apply the only and right remedy.

That Ellida chooses Wangel has often been seen by critics as a capitulation to bourgeois values,[15] or an affirmation of Kantian ethics.[16] However, what these interpretations neglect is the fact that Wangel offers her a genuine choice, at a point when he could not have foreseen a favourable outcome for himself. His decision to release Ellida into freedom and responsibility and thus elevate her from the pre-ethical status of a child to an ethical agent is motivated by his love for her, which now embraces her difference:

> ELLIDA: [*Stares at him for a moment as though speechless*] Is this true ... what you say!
> Do you mean it ... with all your heart?
> WANGEL: Yes I mean it ... with all my sad heart.
> ELLIDA: But can you? Can you bear this to happen?
> WANGEL: Yes I can. I can ... because I love you so much.

> ELLIDA: [*Stirrer en stund som målløs på ham*] Er det sant, sant hva du sier! Mener du det
> – av ditt innerste hjerte!
> WANGEL: Ja, – av hele mitt innerste, våndefulle hjerte mener jeg det...
> ELLIDA: Og kan du det også! Kan du la det skje!
> WANGEL: Ja, det kan jeg. Jeg kan det – fordi jeg elsker deg så høyt. (VII:121/380)

3

Fruen fra Havet is indeed an anomaly amongst the realist plays in that it explores the possibility of romantic/erotic love within marriage. Critics have perhaps for this reason tended to underestimate the importance of this love, or else cynically dismiss it. It is certainly an embarrassment to commentators who see it in terms of a Kantian ethics, for, as Martha Nussbaum points out, discourses on love have been largely banished from post-Kantian moral philosophy, as Kant had seen romantic (or 'pathological') love as something outside the domain of the will and therefore not the proper territory of ethical inquiry.[17] Luce Irigaray has done much to restore love to the realm of the ethical, and seen in the light of her work, the crucial role of love in this play can be accorded due importance.

Both Ellida and Wangel make unequivocal statements of love to each other. But by initially loving Ellida as the place of the maternal-feminine, or by fetishizing her difference, Wangel has immobilized both of them. He can no more move towards her than she can towards him. It is only by submitting his love to as radical a questioning as Ellida does that any movement is possible. The above quotation from Act V signals an extreme reformulation of the love he describes earlier in Act IV: 'I was so much in love with her. That's why I thought of myself first' / 'Jeg holdt jo så meget av henne ... Derfor tenkte jeg først og fremst på meg selv' (VII:92/365), the kind of love that needs to possess. His love has now been tested through its confrontation with Ellida as woman, as *other*. It proves equal to it, thus opening up a space Irigaray terms the 'interval', where two lovers can meet in mutual *wonder*, both as subjects, and in which their *telos* is *becoming* and not possessing (E:33).

Love thus acts as an intermediary, as a bridge across the boundaries of two people, rather than as a disguised gesture of appropriation. In this alternative exchange, the woman is a female subject and no more the immobilized point of *retour*. Neither is she reducible to the maternal function, for, as Irigaray insists, 'maternity is an extra' (E:43). This interval is the necessary condition for creative coupling (spiritual and possibly genetic too). The previous version of love opened up no such space for Ellida and Wangel, and therefore, no creative coupling was possible. Their child, who died not half a year old was the painful manifestation of this sterility.[18]

This play can be seen as Ibsen's second *Kjærlighedens Komedie*. But with a difference. In this play, order is not reestablished, but redefined. Jack certainly does get his Jill, but not without reconstituting the symbolic in order to properly accommodate her in it. Moreover, the final alliance between Hilde and Ellida suggests a new order in which Ellida, having acceded to subjectivity, is no longer implicitly competing for the dead mother's position, which had previously constituted *the* available position.

4

To conclude, this discussion will turn to a consideration of how Ellida's double exile and eventual attainment of subjectivity are underwritten on a technical level by Ibsen's manipulation of the scenic space. In his book, *Dramatic Space in Ibsen, Strindberg and Chekhov: Public Forms of Privacy*,[19] Freddie Rokem identifies a clear inside/outside dichotomy in the spatial organisation of Ibsen's social plays. He sees the domestic interiors shown on stage as representative of the private sphere inhabited by the characters, and as standing in contrast to the outside, that is to the public, social and moral world offstage. Rokem explains that although these two spheres, the inside/private and the outside/public are separate, they are by no means wholly distinct, for although not directly represented, the presence of the outside is indicated both structurally 'through the windows and doors that occasionally open on to it' and thematically 'in the form of a confrontation between the drive for individual satisfaction and the demands of morality and public, social good' (Rokem 1986:13). His analysis continues with an interesting demonstration of how Ibsen manipulates the scenic space to represent the dialectic between the inside/private and the outside/public spaces and the tensions that it produces in the characters.

Valid though this private/public distinction may be, in the context of the plays that examine a female social reality it needs further refinement as it overlooks the fact that the public sphere is constituted very differently for the Noras, Rebekkas, Ellidas and Heddas of Ibsen's stage world and for the Helmers, Rosmers, Wangels and Tesmans respectively, and is therefore productive of very different sets of tensions in them too. It is therefore useful to see these private and public spaces as gendered spaces: the public sphere as the 'outside' world of masculine projects and norms, a world which is both largely inaccessible to the female characters, and one which at the same time confines their activities to the 'inside' world of the bourgeois drawing room.

It is this restricted female space, (or, rather, 'woman's place') of domestic interiors that is directly represented on stage, that is *mimeticized* or shown, while the wider masculine space which circumscribes it is not usually shown on stage but is represented verbally through dialogue, that is *diegetically*.[20]

Characters who have an uneasy relationship with their mimetic existence overcome its restrictions in one of two ways: through departure (Nora) or through suicide (Hedda). These choices signal a rejection of the mimetic in favour of the diegetic, in that the characters either deliberately enter the unseen space or offer themselves up to inscription into narrative, as they can no longer talk but only be talked about. This shift from the mimetic to the diegetic is the movement that tends to obtain in tragedy.

But in order for *Fruen fra Havet* to work as comedy, Ellida cannot lose her mimetic status by entering the unseen space or dissolving into narrative, for in comedy, the mimetic to diegetic is necessarily reversed in this play, and as we shall see, the main way in which Ibsen achieves this is by abandoning the clearly asserted inside/outside dichotomy evident in most of the social plays.

5

What is immediately striking about this play is that only one-fifth of the action takes place inside the house, which usually constitutes the mimetic space of the social plays. The rest of the playing time unfolds outside (usually represented diegetically) and therefore spatial organization is inverted in that the normally diegetic constitutes the mimetic.

One consequence of this is that the motions of freedom and possibility generally connoted by the outside are automatically relativized. If Ibsen had wanted to dramatize the direct tensions between the inside and the outside, he could easily have incarcerated Ellida, along with Hedda and Nora, in the drawing room. But as Bolette's situation highlights, the 'der ute' with its possibilities and opportunities is not something that a woman can directly experience, and it will ultimately make little difference to her whether she stays by the carp pond or goes out into the world with Arnholm, who then, as before, will be her tutor.[21]

A further consequence of this is that the audience cannot make an identification between Ellida and the house, which in itself suggests her marginal position in it. This is highlighted by the fact that in the only act (IV) in which she appears inside the house she does two significant things: she locks herself in her room (which articulates her need for her own space and her desire for non-involvement in family life) and she gives an averredly Marxist reading of her marriage as a 'transaction' which she is determined to cancel.

Her marginality and exile are, however, spatially realized long before Act IV. In Act I, her position is communicated by the metatheatrical valorization[22] of the scenic division of Wangel's garden. She explains to Arnholm that the summer house is where she normally sits during the day, whereas 'the girls ... generally keep to the verandah ... my husband comes and goes between the two' / 'småpikene – de holder til på verandaen ...Wangel går så fra og til'. She considers that this 'arrangement suits all parties best. We can talk across to each other *if we fancy we have anything to say*' / 'alle parter finner seg best ved det på den måte. Vi kan jo tale over til hverandre – *når vi engang i mellem synes at vi har noe å si*' (VII:40/337, my italics).

However, even though it is known as '*my* summer house. I had it made' / 'mitt lysthus ... det er meg som har latt det innrette', she realizes that this space is not in fact an index of her autonomy, and she modifies her statement: 'Or rather my husband had it made ... for me' / 'Eller rettere Wangel – for min skyld'. Both her distance from the girls and her resistance to fixity are further emphasized in Act III when Bolette makes this friendly overture to her:

> BOLETTE: Won't you sit down?
> ELLIDA: No, thank you. I won't sit.
> BOLETTE: [*moving along the bench*] There's plenty of room here.
> ELLIDA: [*walking about*] No, no, no. I won't sit. Won't sit.
>
> BOLETTE: Vil du ikke sette deg?
> ELLIDA: Nej tak. Ikke sitte.
> BOLETTE: [*flytter seg på benken*] For her er god plass.
> ELLIDA: [*går omkring*] Nei, nei, nei. Ikke sitte. Ikke sitte. (VII:74/365)

As previously outlined, Ellida's subject position is compromised by the competing discourses of the play, which all contrive to appropriate her experience by fixing her in representation, be it on canvas (Ballested), in stone (Lyngstrand), in legend (the local community), or in medical theory (Wangel and Hilde). Ellida is more spoken about than speaking which has the effect of destabilizing her mimetic status, as her representation is not alignable with the here and now of the action. Because every attempt to speak herself is either appropriated or erased, Ellida's identity and desire remain in the realm of narrative, a narrative structured around the sea and the Stranger.

Narrative, or diegetic space and time offer Ellida infinitely more freedom than mimetic space and time, whose spatiality is static and its temporality linear: it can only move forward. Diegetic space on the other hand, because it is constituted verbally, is unlimited, unfixed and multiple, and can unfold on all three time levels: past recollection, present elsewhere and future projection. It is thus only natural that Ellida should cling to her sea-narrative as it is the only one that does not bind her in any way, and, furthermore, the sea as space is the only space which she can truly inhabit, which can truly contain herself. However, the danger of clinging to this narrative and unequivocally locating herself in the diegetic is that her desire will remain forever unsymbolized, that is unrepresented in the mimetic. (Diegetic space, it must be remembered, is one-dimensional – it can only be represented verbally.) Ellida is therefore caught in an impossible double bind; she cannot live without her narrative – in both the adverbial and prepositional senses of the word.

On the level of representation, the diegetic can be seen to correspond to the female imaginary, and the mimetic to the male symbolic or social order. The female imaginary and the diegetic have in common the characteristics of fluidity, multiplicity and unlimitedness. These are qualities that threaten, and therefore remain unrepresented in the symbolic and the mimetic: orders that depend on fixity and limit for their survival.

Seen in this light, the uni-dimensional choice that the Stranger offers Ellida (that is, to leave and utterly reject the mimetic/symbolic), would ultimately leave her in a state of dereliction, and it is for this reason that she feels so threatened by the sea and the Stranger. In order for any possible growth to occur, Ellida's choice cannot simply be that of an either-or, imaginary or symbolic, for in both cases she remains unrepresented. Therefore the only condition for growth has to involve the mimeticization of the diegetic and the intervention of the female imaginary in the symbolic order.

Ibsen's manipulation of what Rokem terms the 'focal point' is an enabling factor in this process. Rokem describes how Ibsen makes use of three stage areas: the front stage (usually the drawing room), where most of the action takes place; the middle-to-backstage area, which usually represents a variety of backrooms and verandahs, and the third area, the focal point 'where the perspective, as it were, ends':

> This point always relates to some *great emotional struggle* in the past, through which the characters have to pass again in the present tense of the play to achieve their freedom. At the focal point we in the audience and/or the characters see something that relates to or is a result of this struggle. While on the interpretive level the object situated at the focal point can be understood as a *symbol or metaphor for the hero's struggle*, on the plot level it is a *concrete physical object that has to be overcome.* (Rokem, 1986:17, my italics)

Examples of such focal points are the orphanage in *Gengangere*, General Gabler's pistols and the steeple in *Bygmester Solness*.

In *Fruen fra Havet*, the focal point is the sea, but it is never directly represented scenically; in fact Ibsen expressly states in the didascalia that the 'open sea cannot be seen'/'det åpne hav ses ikke'(Act II). It is always the 'point beyond' and constitutes the main diegetic space of the play. By excluding the sea from the mimetic, Ibsen destabilizes it as a 'concrete, physical object' because, unlike General Gabler's pistols and the Captain's orphanage, it does not have any existence independent of the protagonist's narrative.

This necessarily raises the question of why, or to what effect Ibsen chooses to reduce the physical dimensions of the focal point in this play. Clearly, by so doing, he gives greater weight to the metaphorical dimensions of the sea, which as we have seen, in all its multiplicity and fluidity is suggestive of the female imaginary: the sea, therefore, like the imaginary is denied mimetic/symbolic representation. The fact that the focal point is located in the diegetic is central to the definition of the 'great struggle' that Rokem refers to – Ellida's struggle is a struggle for representation; for adequate representation in the symbolic/mimetic, and a struggle against being abandoned outside it in the imaginary/diegetic.

As a necessary stage in this struggle, Ellida has gradually to abandon the narrative of displacement in which the sea functions as an external concrete reality and as her panacea, and instead project its possibilities. Wangel, too, reads the sea on the level of the literal:

> WANGEL: [*places his hand on her head*] And that is why my poor sick child shall go home again ... Somewhere by the open sea – a place where you can find a true home...
> ELLIDA: But what do you think we could gain by that?
> WANGEL: Your health and your peace of mind.
> ELLIDA: I doubt it.

> WANGEL: [*legger hånden på hennes hode*] Og derfor så skal det stakkars syke barn få komme hjem til sitt eget igjen ... Ut et steds ved åpne havet, – et steds hvor du kan finne et riktig hjem efter ditt sinn...
> ELLIDA: Men hva tror du da vel vi ville vinne ved det?
> WANGEL: Du ville vinne sunnhet og fred i sinnet igjen.
> ELLIDA: Knapt nok det. (VII:59/346-7)

By Act IV, this process of self-representation is well underway when Ellida states that there 'is no external power or force threatening me. The thing is much more deeply seated, Wangel! The pull is within my own mind' / 'er jo slett ikke noe vold og makt utenfra som truer meg. Det grufulle ligger dypere, Wangel! Det grufulle er dragningen i mitt eget sinn'(VII:102/349).

In Act V, the tension between the mimetic and the diegetic mounts in a tempo of intense urgency. Ellida is made painfully aware of the passage of time as represented by the changing seasons. Ballested quotes the tragic line '[s]oon the seaways will be locked and barred' / 'snart er alle sunde lukket', which reinforces the need for a quick decision whether or not to exit from the mimetic before it closes in on itself. With the arrival of the English boat, the diegetic is mimeticized acoustically by the ship's warning bells, which demand an instant answer from Ellida. Having established a place in which she and Wangel can *become* through the mediation of love, she is able to align herself once and for all in the mimetic and reject the diegetic, fully aware that the English ship will not return and that the seaways will soon lock. The Stranger takes his leave of the sea creature that has now become an unambiguously social animal – 'Farvel, Frue'. Ellida, whose desire has now been adequately symbolized, has avoided both death and dereliction. Moreover, her newly-acquired mimetic/symbolic status makes her resistant to one-dimensional narrative:

> ELLIDA: Once a creature has settled on dry land, there's no going back to the sea.
> BALLESTED: Why, that's just like the case of my mermaid! ... Except for one difference. The mermaid dies.

> ELLIDA: Når en nu engang er blitt fastlands-skapning, – så finner en ikke veien tilbake igjen – ut til havet ... Og ikke ut til havlivet heller.
> BALLESTED: Men det er akkurat som med min havfrue ... Bare med den forskjell at havfruen – hun dør av det. (VII:123/381)

The dialectic interplay between the mimetic and the diegetic and the symbolic and the imaginary is thus played out. But the symbolic/mimetic would never have triumphed had it not been for the considerable intervention of the imaginary/diegetic in it. On its very local level, this play suggests an answer to the Irigarayan question mentioned at the beginning of this article, of where women should live: – in the symbolic, but in the form of intervention, not unquestioned inscription.[23]

Notes

1. For example, Egil Törnqvist, 'Individualism in *The Master Builder*', *Contemporary Approaches to Ibsen*, vol. III (Oslo, 1975).
2. For the limits of this approach to the early plays, see Åse Hiorth Lervik, 'Mellom Furia og Solveig', in *Contemporary Approaches, op. cit.*
3. See the section 'Any Theory of the Subject Has Always Been Appropriated by the Masculine' in *Speculum of the Other Woman*, transl. C. G. Gill (Cornell University Press, 1985). All future references to this work will be indicated by the letters SP, followed by page number, in parentheses, and are to this edition.
4. All references are to *The Oxford Ibsen*, ed. James McFarlane, and will be indicated by volume number and page number. Where the references are followed by the original Norwegian text, the references are to the Fakkel edition, *Nutidsdramaer 1877-99* (Oslo: Gyldendal, 1962), and are indicated by page number in parentheses after /.
5. Transl. C. Burke and G .C. Gill (London: The Athlone Press, 1993). All references are to this edition and will be indicated by an E, followed by page number, in parentheses.
6. In Irigaray's thought, the symbolic and the social orders are definitionally very close. See Margaret Whitford, *Luce Irigaray Philososphy in the Feminine* (London: Routledge, 1991), ch.8.
7. In Irigaray's thought, the female imaginary is not equatable with the classical pre-Œdipal space, nor with unconscious phantasies, but has a projective dimension and should thus be seen more as a *process*, or an attempt at creating 'a space in which women, in all their multiplicity can *become*, i.e. accede to subjectivity'. However, until subjectivity has been achieved (which of course can only occur inside the symbolic) there is a sense in which the imaginary does not exist. See Whitford, *ibid.* pp. 90-91.
8. The English rendering, 'The Lady from the Sea' does not adequately communicate the word-play of the Norwegian 'Fruen fra Havet' which is immediately evocative of *havfruen*, the mermaid. *Havfruen* was in fact the title Ibsen originally gave to the play. Much painstaking research has been carried out to establish possible ballad sources. (See Per Schelde Jacobsen and Barbara Fass Levy, *Ibsen's Forsaken Merman: Folklore in the Late Plays*, (New York University Press, 1988).) However, I think one should be wary of overemphasizing Ellida's mermaid qualities for two reasons. Firstly, such emphasis diminishes the importance of the play's very social dimensions, and misses the clearly social identity of the title *frue* – Mrs. Secondly, it merely serves to reduplicate one of the many alien narratives that Ellida has forced upon her.
9. It might be argued that Wangel's use of this label and his characterization of Ellida as 'one of the sea people' does amount to a recognition of her difference, but only on a very superficial level, for it reduces it to a romantic formulation. Her sea qualities are indeed the source of his attraction to her, but only in his fetishized appropriation of them.
10. See A. Velissariou, 'Mental Illness and the problem of Female Identity in Ibsen', in

Themes in Drama, XV (Cambridge University Press, 1993), quoting Stephen Heath, *The Sexual Fix.*

11. James McFarlane has traced the broader significance of *tegn imot tegn* in Ibsen's dramas. See 'Meaning and Evidence in Ibsen's Drama', in *Ibsenårbok* VIII (Oslo, 1965).

12. Translated and reprinted in *Feminisms: an anthology of literary theory and criticism*, eds. R. R. Warhol and D. Price Herndl (Rutgers University Press, 1991), p.353.

13. Perhaps the beginnings of a female phenomenology?

14. *aletheia* – Greek – 'truth'; here used in the privative sense stressed by Heidegger, of 'unconcealment'.

15. See Sandra Saari, '"Hun som ikke selv har noe riktig livskall..." Women and the role of the Ideal Woman in Ibsen's Munich Trilogy' in *Contemporary Approaches*, V (Oslo, 1985).

16. See Brian Johnston, 'The Turning Point in *The Lady from the Sea*' in his book *Text and Supertext in Ibsen's Drama* (Penn State, 1989)

17. Martha C. Nussbaum, *Love's Knowledge: Essays on Philosophy and Literature* (OUP: New York, 1990), pp. 336-338

18. Irigaray develops the notion of spiritual coupling as a future vision of the spirit and the bride in *An Ethics*, section IV.

19. Freddie Rokem, *Dramatic Space in Ibsen, Strindberg and Chekhov: Public Forms of Privacy* (UMI Research Press, Michigan, 1986)

20. See Michael Issacharoff, *Discourse as Performance* (Stanford University Press, 1989), in which the quasi-Aristotelian terms 'mimetic' and 'diegetic' are used to denote 'space shown' and 'space narrated' respectively.

21. This article pays but scant attention to Hilde and Bolette, who offer alternative responses to the 'where to live' question: Bolette, whose story has distinct parallels with Ellida's, represents, in her decision to marry Arnholm, the lack of choices available to women, and shows how difficult it is not to perpetuate the prevailing system. Hilde, in her wedding-day-widow fantasy suggests another answer. In her fantasy it is the male, not the female who dies. However 'exciting' this prospect may be, it merely perpetuates, albeit in reverse, the phallocratic order.

22. 'Metatheatrical valorization' occurs when one theatrical mode comments on another. In this case, the verbal channel (dialogue) is used to comment on the visual channel (scenery). See Issacharoff, *op. cit.*, ch. 5.

23. 'In order for woman to reach the place where she can take her pleasure as a woman, a long detour by way of the analysis of the various systems of oppression brought to bear upon her is assuredly necessary. And claiming to fall back on the single solution of pleasure risks making her miss the process of going back through a social practice that *her* enjoyment requires'. *This Sex which is not One, ibid.*, p.335.

Originally published May 1996 (Vol. 35, No. 1).

The Illness Pattern in
The Master Builder

Egil Törnqvist

Illness figures as a motif in several Ibsen plays; we need only think of Rank in *A Doll's House* and Osvald in *Ghosts* with their (probably) *inherited syphilis, the blindness that threatens Old Werle and Hedvig in The Wild Duck*, and the dying Aunt Rina in *Hedda Gabler*. Some decades ago it was still a widespread idea that Ibsen introduced this motif primarily to heighten the realism of his plays; the arguments concerning whether the playwright's description of Osvald's illness is medically accurate or not reflects this attitude. Today we consider such an approach mistaken in its implied assumption that a major dramatist is ever concerned with scientific truths. Like so many other play elements once appreciated, or criticized, for their daring realism, Osvald's illness, we now realize, is dramatically arresting primarily because of its metaphoric connotations. On the realistic level, it concerns Osvald and his father, hardly more; as an image of how 'the sins of the fathers are visited upon the children' it illustrates not only the relationship of these two but various other relationships as well, in widening contexts; so that ultimately we end up with a metaphysical perspective: that mankind at large has gone astray, that there is something wrong with the world.

Compared to its central place in *Ghosts*, the illness motif in *The Master Builder* may seem peripheral. It is certainly not a motif which immediately strikes a reader of the play as of major importance. Yet a closer inspection reveals that it is one of the most pervading motives in the drama, branching out in various directions. Moreover, it is a motif which can tell us something about Ibsen's dramatic technique. By comparing a translation of the play with the Norwegian original we can see how many connotations suggested by the original are lost when the text is rendered in another language.[1]

The play opens sombrely in master builder Solness' '*plainly furnished*', dimly lit office. There we find, bent over their work, Knut Brovik, '*a thin old man, with white hair and beard*'; his son Ragnar, in his thirties, '*with a slight stoop*'; and Ragnar's fiancée Kaja Fosli, '*a slightly-built girl in her early twenties*', '*delicate looking*' (357). The first speech strikes the note of illness:

> KNUT BROVIK: (*suddenly gets up from the drawing table as though in distress and comes forward into the doorway, breathing heavily and with difficulty*)
> Oh, I can't stand this much longer! (357)

The three figures, all of the same family, clearly share a state of physical delicateness, least pronounced in the youngest one and most in the oldest one. What old Brovik suffers from, or how serious his illness is, we are not yet told; but we note that he finds it difficult to breathe. His moving away from the drawing office suggests perhaps, as Northam points out,[2] that he feels confined in there; there is indeed something suffocating in the dimly lit, windowless office. The feeling of suffocation is soon made explicit:

> RAGNAR: (*has risen and comes over*) You'd better go home, Father. Try and get some sleep...
> BROVIK: (*impatiently*) Go to bed, you mean? Do you want me to suffocate?

Soon 'the boss' enters from the outdoors:

> HALVARD SOLNESS [–] *is a man of mature years, strong and vigorous, with close-cut curly hair, dark moustache, and dark bushy eyebrows.* (358)

Here, obviously, is the master of the three 'slaves' we have just become familiar with.[3] Their physical weakness contrasting with his strength begins to take on a symbolic significance; but we do not yet know whether the contrast is primarily social or spiritual.

During the conversation between Solness and old Brovik the serious nature of the latter's illness is fully brought out:

> BROVIK: I won't last much longer. I get weaker and weaker every day. (360)

As he says this, we note that he is dressed in a '*black coat*' and wears '*a white cravat*' (357); this 'funeral dress' is not only suited to his sombre mood; it also 'forewarns us of his approaching death'.[4]

Brovik wants Solness to recognize his son's talents as an architect by letting Ragnar do some independent work:

> BROVIK: (*after sitting down with difficulty*) Well, it's this question of Ragnar. This is what's worrying me most. What's to become of him? (360)

While we are reminded visually, in this passage, of Brovik's illness, we are informed verbally that what worries him is not so much his own precarious situation as his son's future. Brovik's illness, we begin to realize, is not only a symbol of his 'enslavement' under Solness; it is also a sign that he is suffering from his son's 'enslavement'.[5]

Soon yet another aspect of Brovik's illness is introduced:

> SOLNESS: But he [Ragnar] hasn't really learnt anything ... thoroughly, I mean. Except how to draw.
> BROVIK: (*looks at him with suppressed hatred and says hoarsely*) You hadn't learnt much about the business either, when you were working for me. But that didn't stop you from launching out. (*Breathing with difficulty.*) Or from getting on. You went and left me standing ... and a lot of other people as well. (361)

Again, Ibsen is careful to remind us of Brovik's illness – again he has the old man breathe '*tungt*' (SV 37) – as he lets him reveal circumstances in the past, which must still be a source of pain to him; Brovik's 'enslavement' takes on a grimmer appearance as we learn that he has earlier been Solness' master and that Solness, in part at least, is responsible for his social decline and the reversal of roles between them.

Brovik's appeal to Solness is in the manner of a dying man's last. wish:

...surely you haven't the heart to let me die... without seeing something of what Ragnar can do. And I also very much want to see them married ... before I go. (361)

Ibsen is clearly using Brovik's illness to put moral and emotional pressure upon the dominant master builder. But Solness does not yield:

SOLNESS: [–] I'll never give way to anybody! [–]
BROVIK: (*rises with difficulty*) Have I to die like this? An unhappy man, without any proof that I was right to have faith and confidence in Ragnar? Without ever seeing a single example of his work? [–] Must I die so miserably?
[–]
SOLNESS: (*seems to battle with himself, then says in a low but firm voice*) You must die as best you can. (363)

Again Ibsen stresses the fact that Brovik does not fear to die; what he fears is rather that he must end his days in the conviction that his life has been meaningless, a futile struggle; his time soon being up, he is desperately looking for a 'faith' that can reconcile him with life – and death. But Solness, as we have seen, refuses to give him this faith.

At this point we are perhaps ready to redeflne the significance of Brovik's illness: it is obviously related not only to the past but also to the future; the man is emotionally trapped between his bitterness against the former and fear of the latter; his difficulties to breathe is an appropriate metaphor for his spiritual dilemma.

With all hope shut out his illness rapidly takes a serious turn:

BROVIK: [–] (*sways and stops beside the sofa table*) Could I have a glass of water? (363)

After his fatal talk with Solness, Brovik disappears from the office – never to return. Through the other characters we hear of his gradual physical decline. In the beginning of Act II we learn that he is in bed and that the doctor is coming to see him. Shortly after this we come across some startling lines:

MRS SOLNESS: (*over by the plants*) I shouldn't wonder if he, too, died.
SOLNESS: (*looks at her*) He too? Who else do you mean?
MRS SOLNESS: (*without answering*) Ah yes. Old Mr Brovik – he's also going to die now, Halvard. You'll see. (392)

We have earlier seen how Ibsen has given depth to Brovik's illness; now he seems intent to give it scope as well. But who does Aline Solness refer to? Ibsen does not make this clear – and for good reasons. For as they stand, Aline's words point in several directions.

She may well be thinking of her dead children; we note that she is watering (i.e. giving life to) the plants as she speaks these lines; the plants are presumably of a high and stately kind – Ibsen uses the word '*blomsteropsatser*' (SV 68)[6] in the stage directions; later in the act Solness refers to Aline's talent for 'building children's souls' so 'that they might grow straight and fine, nobly and beautifully formed, to their full human stature' (406f.) – a phrasing which certainly suggests that Aline's concern with the plants symbolizes her concern with the dead children.

But Aline may also be thinking of herself; 'now she is dead', Solness is later to state about her (428), and as a living dead she noiselessly moves around the house, '*thin and drawn*' and dressed '*in black*' (36s) – not unlike Brovik, whose anguish she shares: 'I don't think I can bear it any longer' (394), she exclaims, meaning the burden of guilt that weighs her down.

Finally, Aline may be referring to Solness; the mere fact that she mentions his name – Halvard – in a speech announcing the death of someone besides Brovik may be cited in support of this view. Such an interpretation means, of course, that we furnish Aline with second sight, but this is wholly in agreement with the mysterious note Ibsen frequently strikes in this play; moreover, Dr Herdal has earlier observed, with reference to Aline, that 'women have a damned keen intuition about certain things' (369).

By keeping Aline's statement vague, Ibsen is able to link the 'deaths' of Brovik, the children, Aline and Solness in a suggestive way; through those little words 'too' and 'also' he manages to give scope to Brovik's illness and a sense of fatal connection between the past, the present and the future.

Later in Act II we get a new message concerning Brovik's health:

SOLNESS: Your father's no better, I hear.
RAGNAR: Father is sinking fast now. That's why I beg of you... please write something nice on one of my drawings. Something for Father to read before he... (407)

Earlier the father has appealed for his son; now the son appeals for his father. But Solness still refuses. When he finally yields, it is significantly because Hilde orders him to do so. But his change of mind comes too late: in Act III we learn that when Kaja finally returned the drawings to Brovik with Solness' positive comment on them, the old man had already 'had a stroke' and 'was no longer conscious' (432). When the play closes it stands clear that Brovik is, or will shortly be, dead; this is what Ragnar's remark that the father no longer needs him amounts to, spoken as he carries '*a large green wreath with flowers and silk ribbons*' in his hands (432).

Brovik's physical decline seems psychologically motivated by the adversities his son and his fiancée suffer; it is significant that he has his stroke shortly after he (presumably) has learnt that Solness has dismissed Kaja and Ragnar and when he realizes that there is no reason to believe that Ragnar will ever prove himself or that the two will ever marry, since Kaja's passion concerns Solness, not Ragnar. Considering this, it is hardly an exaggeration to say that Solness is directly responsible for Brovik's death. The message that could have restored the old man to health or at least let him die in peace ironically arrives too late.

Brovik is decidedly a minor character in the play and his importance is largely indirect. His existence seems determined primarily by Ibsen's need (1) to place his protagonist in a social context, (2) to have him outlined as a character before the main action gets under way, (3) to provide him with a conflict and (4) with a flaw. These functions, which Brovik shares with many minor dramatis personae, do not, however, explain why Ibsen has chosen to make the man sickly.

Has Ibsen, then, burdened him with his illness in order to elicit our compassion for the old man, thereby securing an interest for him and his fate? Although I would not totally exclude this possibility,[7] it is obvious that Brovik's illness, like Brovik himself, has primarily an indirect function: it is not an isolated phenomenon; rather, it is the most realistic part of a largely metaphoric pattern.

We have already noted certain similarities between Brovik and Aline Solness. An obvious link between the two we find in their illness: while Brovik has breathing difficulties, Aline has spent some time 'på sanatoriet' (SV 53),[8] and the family doctor has now come to see her. But, as in Brovik's case, Aline's physical illness is merely an image for her true illness, which is of a spiritual nature. Like Brovik, she has suffered a decline concomitant with Solness' rise: her creative functions have been cut short; she too is a 'slave' nourishing smouldering aggressions under a surface of obedience and loyalty. The dying man clearly parallels the spiritually dead woman.

There is, however, one fundamental difference between Brovik and Aline: her traumatic self-reproaches have no counterpart in him. This difference is important, since it means that with the introduction of Aline, Ibsen enriches the illness motif with a new aspect: illness from now on comes to signify not just suffering caused by outward pressure (social suffering), but also suffering caused by a pressure from within (moral suffering).[9]

For all his contrasting outward appearance, Halvard Solness too is not altogether unlike Brovik and a number of minor resemblances indicate that Ibsen has intended them as parallels – up to a point. They differ somewhat in age but not significantly: while Brovik is '*old*', Solness is '*a man of mature years*' (358), '*en noget ældre mand*' (SV 34). Both men are '*impatient*' (357, 359, 360). Solness' contemptuous dismissal of Brovik's talk about material compensation – 'That isn't what I mean at all' (359), 'Det er jo slet ikke *det*, jeg mener' (SV 35) – is even verbally echoed in Brovik's dismissal of Solness' suggestion that he recompense Ragnar: 'It's not that at all' (360), 'Det er slet ikke *det*' (SV 36).

Also by their stage positions Brovik and Solness are linked. During his conversation with Solness, Brovik sits in the armchair while Solness, demonstrating his superiority, apparently remains standing. When Brovik has left him, Solness stands '*with bowed head by the armchair*' (364), recognizing, as it were, that his guilt feelings toward the old man are weighing him down. Shortly afterwards, during his confessions to Dr Herdal, his confidant, he places himself in the armchair. The point of this position becomes clear toward the end of their conversation, when it appears that Solness too is 'ill':

SOLNESS: [–] I somehow... enjoy the mortification of letting Aline do me an injustice. [–] You see it's rather like paying off a tiny instalment on a huge immeasurable debt. ... [–] And that always eases one's mind a little. One can breathe more freely for a while, you understand. [–] (*Flaring up*) Well, damn it, you think the same about me as Aline does. [–] She's begun to think I'm... so to speak... ill.

DR HERDAL: Ill! You! She's never said a single word about that to me. What's supposed to be wrong with you, my dear fellow?

SOLNESS: (*leans over the back of the chair and whispers*) Aline thinks I'm mad. That's what she thinks.

DR HERDAL: (*rising*) But my dear Mr Solness...!

> SOLNESS: Yes, she does, by thunder! That's how it is. And she's got you to believe it, too. Oh, I assure you, Doctor, it's quite plain to me you do... quite plain. I'm not so easily fooled, let me tell you. (372f.)

In this passage, which could have been taken out of Strindberg's *The Father*,[10] Solness ironically proves his precarious mental state in his very attempt to dis-prove it: his exaggerated suspiciousness at this point must inevitably warn the Doctor that he is not well. Like Brovik – but in a somewhat different way – Solness feels confined, trapped between the past he cannot rid himself of and the future which he fears. Like Aline, he suffers from an insurmountable feeling of guilt. In the lines just quoted Solness indicates that he normally suffers from 'breathing difficulties'; when speaking to Hilde about the ordinary human happiness he has had to abstain from as an artist, he actually '*breathes heavily*', '*ånder tungt*' (SV 82).[11] Brovik and Solness find it hard to breathe; Aline spends some time in a sanatorium. Their suffering is clearly related.

The parallel between Brovik and Solness is suggested also in the later reports concerning Brovik's declining health. 'Father is sinking fast now' ('Med far gar det fort nedad nu', SV 84), Ragnar tells Solness; soon he is to witness Solness 'sinking fast' from his tower. The wreath, which Ragnar in the final act hands over to Solness, is not only an emblem of Solness' ultimate triumph but also a reminder of the death that awaits both him and Brovik. Even by the manner of their death Ibsen links the two: while Brovik suffers a stroke,[12] Solness' 'head is all smashed in' (445).

Our impression that Solness suffers from pangs of conscience is confirmed by his confession to his wife in Act II:

> SOLNESS: [–] I've never done you any wrong. Never knowingly, never deliberately, that is. And yet – I feel weighed down by a great crushing sense of guilt.
> MRS SOLNESS: Guilt... on my account?
> SOLNESS: Mainly on your account.
> MRS SOLNESS: Then you are... sick after all, Halvard.
> SOLNESS: (*heavily*) I suppose I must be. Or something of the kind. (396)

While Solness has earlier tried to tell the Doctor – and above all himself – that he is not ill, that his 'illness' is merely a product of his wife's sick mind, he now admits to her that he is indeed 'sick'. We have already defined his 'illness' as an image of his intense guilt feelings; now we are inclined to define it more precisely as: a strong sense of guilt without any rational basis. The root of Solness' trouble is still obscure to us; when he is presumably about to reveal it to Aline – and to us – Ibsen cuts their conversation short by letting Hilde enter. It is by such interruptions that Ibsen secures a dramatically effective distribution of his gradual revelation.

Not until later in the act, in his confessions to Hilde, does Solness indicate why. he feels particularly guilty toward Aline. The reasons he gives are intimately connected with his occupation. On one hand he feels responsible for the fire, which reduced Aline's home to ashes and meant the start of his successful career, because he had secretly wished this to happen. On the other he feels that as an artist he deprives those close to him – and notably his wife – of their right to happiness and independent growth:

> SOLNESS: [–] You see Aline had her vocation in life too. Quite as much as I had mine. (*His voice trembles*) But her vocation had to be ruined... crushed, smashed to pieces... so that mine could go marching on to... to some kind of great victory. (406)

Solness' 'illness', we now realize, does indeed have a real basis. The two reasons he presents have a common denominator; in both cases he blames his own egotism, an egotism whose fatal consequences we have already experienced with regard to the Brovik family. It is, to be sure, an egotism of a sophisticated kind, and the moral dilemma Ibsen's master builder finds himself in is clearly the artist's archetypal dilemma: to what extent does he have loyalties not only to his art but also to his surroundings? To put it in terms of the imagery of *The Master Builder*: to what extent is it possible to build both church spires and homes for men? Solness' illness, we can now see, is incurable, because it is directly related to his function as an artist; to give up his vocational egotism would mean to give up what ultimately is his justification in life: to build high; to cure himself Solness would need to become someone else; but, as he tells Brovik in the beginning: 'I am what I am! And I can't change myself!' (363).

While Aline and the Brovik family would welcome a softer Solness, a man more concerned with homes than spires, Hilde pulls him in the opposite direction:

> HILDE: In your case I should want to see a conscience that was... well, thoroughly robust.
> SOLNESS: Robust, eh? Well. Have you a robust conscience, I wonder?
> HILDE: Yes, I think so. I've never noticed it wasn't. (412)

Hilde's appearance contrasts strongly with those of the master builder's 'slaves':

> *She is of medium height, lithe, of slim build. Slightly tanned by the sun. She wears walking clothes [–], a sailor's collar open at the neck, and a small sailor hat on her head. She has a rucksack on her back, a plaid in a strap, and a long alpenstock.* (375)

Here, it would seem, we find incarnated both a healthy, robust conscience and a predilection for soaring heights. Yet we must not judge too much by appearances. When Hilde claims that she has a robust conscience, Solness sceptically replies: 'Probably hasn't been particularly tested, I imagine' (412). In the final act it is tested, when Hilde partakes of Aline's secret sorrows. And now she too, momentarily, shows signs of a 'fragile conscience': 'I can't hurt someone I know', she says (428), and a little later she voices a brief Hamletian soliloquy:

> Oh, if only one could fall asleep and leave the whole sorry business behind! (*She lays her arms flat down upon the table, rests the left side of her head on her hands and shuts her eyes*) (429)

Hilde dreams of resting her head – in death; for death is the only real solution to the dilemma she too now experiences, the pull between opposite loyalties; her words and illustrative action point forward to Solness' 'suicidal' solution of his dilemma at the end.

An indication that Solness is not as strong as he looks we find in his inability to stand altitudes. While Aline only sees his dizziness as a physical shortcoming, Hilde interprets it symbolically:

HILDE: (*looks intently at him*) Is it true, or isn't it?
SOLNESS: That I get dizzy [svimmel]?
HILDE: That *my* master builder dare not... cannot climb as high as he builds. (421)

And a little later:

HILDE (*bursts out gaily*). You could never be dizzy [svimmel]!
SOLNESS. Tonight we'll put up the wreath... Princess Hilde. (421)

Hilde's hero, then, is a man who not only has high aspirations but also dares to live up to them; she is as extreme in her demands as Brand. While Aline's master builder cannot climb the tower, Hilde's can, because Hilde, who can give him the support of a robust, non-compromising conscience, wills him to do it; this is why Solness can figuratively speak about their putting up the wreath together.

Ten years earlier, we learn, Solness nearly fell from the tower of the Lysanger church, when he grew dizzy at the sight of Hilde waving her flag (381). At the end we witness how he falls from his tower immediately after Hilde has snatched Aline's white shawl and waved it about (444). The implication is evident: Hilde is directly responsible for Solness' fall – as she is responsible for his climb. Both the wreath and the white shawl carry double connotations: on one hand they may be associated with death,[13] on the other with the bridal ceremony. Hilde's snatching of Aline's shawl is a demonstration of her 'robust conscience', her decision not to let Aline stand in her way, her desire to be wedded to *her* master builder. Solness, whose conscience is 'fragile', cannot wholeheartedly rid himself of the wife, of the past; he grows dizzy and falls, a victim of what Hilde has earlier called his 'dizzy conscience' (svimmel samvittighed, SV 110).[14]

As we have seen, illness in one form or another plays an important part in *The Master Builder*; far from appearing in a random manner the motif is structured according to the dramatic laws of gradual revelation and rising suspense; it is for this reason that we can better speak of a 'pattern' than of a 'motif'. To indicate how Ibsen has composed this pattern, I shall isolate those aspects of it which concern Brovik and Solness; in the order of presentation they are:

Act I
1. Brovik is old and seriously ill.
2. Solness is healthy and strong in appearance.
3. Brovik is 'enslaved' by Solness.
4. He is soon to die.
5. He suffers from his son Ragnar's "enslavement".
6. He suffers from his own social decline.
7. He suffers from Ragnar's incapability of marrying Kaja.
8. He suffers from his lacking faith in Ragnar.
9. Solness has grown dizzy ten years earlier when climbing a tower.
Act II
10. Solness is 'ill', he suffers from exaggerated suspiciousness.
11. He suffers from guilt feelings toward Aline, without obvious reason.
12. His guilt feelings are due to his 'vocational egotism'.
13. Brovik, affected by what befalls Kaja and Ragnar, is 'sinking fast'.

14. Solness suffers from a 'fragile conscience'.
15. He still gets dizzy.
16. His dizziness is a result of his compromising spirit.
17. He is going to climb his own tower, will not get dizzy.

Act III

18. Brovik suffers a stroke and is dying.
19. Solness gets dizzy and falls from his tower, his head is 'smashed in'.

It is easy to see from this scheme how Ibsen progresses from a realistic to a symbolic level, from description of a situation to a description of a state of mind. Brovik's illness is rapidly transposed from a physical to a spiritual level; also among the reasons for his suffering we can distinguish a progression from surface to depth: we move from socially determined reasons (5-7) to a religiously tinted one (8). Once the nature of Brovik's illness is fully established, Ibsen can part with him; in the following acts we merely receive brief reports about his decline (13, 18).

In Solness' case we start out with impressions of health and strength (2), partly demolished at the end of Act I, when we hear of his dizziness (9); so far Ibsen sticks to the realistic level. In Act II we are transposed first to a mental, then to a spiritual one. In three stages we witness his battle with himself, his denial to the Doctor that he is 'ill' (10), his admission to his wife of his guilt feelings but denial of personal responsibility (11), his final acceptance, when speaking to Hilde, of his personal responsibility (12). Once we realize that Solness suffers from a 'fragile conscience' (14), his dizziness transcends its realistic meaning and be-comes an image of his sensitivity and compromising spirit (16). By gradually enriching the meaning of Solness' 'illness' in this way, Ibsen can finally, when he has Solness climb his tower, present us with a highly complex action, which we are now ripe to accept on a wholly symbolic level.

But what is really the significance of the Brovik-Solness parallel? To state that, dramaturgically, Brovik's illness serves to prepare for Solness', is not saying very much. A better way of putting it is to say that it is Brovik's function to foreshadow Solness' fate, to cast a shadow over his future, for by putting it this way we have indicated that Ibsen's technique is based on his wish to create a sense of nemesis: it is Solness' fate to suffer himself what he has caused Brovik to suffer. But the parallel also has another significance: it helps to underline the contrasting nature of Brovik's and Solness' illnesses: while the former is largely situational, the latter is moral; Aline actually combines the two aspects: her illness is an image both of her 'enslaved' existence and her strong sense of guilt.

The fact that the two men follow a similar development and die more or less simultaneously may raise the question whether Brovik cannot, in fact, be regarded as an aspect of Solness' self. Solness' attitude to Brovik appears to be ambivalent: on one hand he needs him, because 'he's so extraordinarily clever at working out stresses and strains and cubic contents' (371), on the other he seems to despise him, because he keeps himself busy with such 'damned rigmarole' (371) and because he lacks inspiration and will-power (411). Brovik thus appears to represent the petty aspects of Solness' occupation; while he can certainly draw ordinary houses, he cannot build high towers, much less climb them; in this sense old Brovik may be viewed as an incarnation of a stage – building homes for men – which Solness wants to outgrow. In line with this, the end can be interpreted symbolically as a struggle between Solness' two selves, a struggle in which his compromising self, associated with the dying Brovik as well as with the fainting Mrs Solness (444) whose vocation he had 'smashed to pieces' (406), plunges to its death, while his aspiring self triumphs.

In *The Master Builder* illness appears, as it were, in three different guises: we deal, in turn, with physical, mental and spiritual illness. This progression is highly significant for Ibsen's technique of gradual revelation; the closer we come to the end, the wider and deeper the significance of the motif becomes; what ultimately concerns the playwright-and us-is not the mental illness, as Weigand seems to believe,[15] but the spiritual one. The mental stage – Solness' suspiciousness, for example – is merely a transient one, a link between the physical and the spiritual ones. In his struggle with his own sense of guilt, Solness cannot be reduced to a mental case; his 'illness' is not at all a psychiatric phenomenon; it is an image of his sensitivity to his own moral and metaphysical dilemma; if his sensitivity in one sense constitutes his 'illness' – it tears him apart – it is in another sense a sign of his being truly alive, a sign, that is, of his 'health'. It is precisely Solness' sensitivity to his archetypal situation which explains why we on one hand can identify ourselves with his struggle and on the other feel that he is – as a tragic hero ought to be – at once more sickly and yet healthier than we, everyday creatures, are.

Notes

1. If not otherwise indicated, page references in the following are to J. W. McFarlane's translation of the play in *The Oxford Ibsen*, VII (London, 1966); page references to the Norwegian original are to *Hundreårsutgave. Henrik Ibsens Samlede Verker*, ed. F. Bull, H. Koht and D. A. Seip, XII, here abbreviated SV.
2. J. Northam, *Ibsen's Dramatic Method* (London, 1953), p. 174.
3. The expression is Northam's, *loc. cit.*
4. Northam, *loc. cit.*
5. The connection between Brovik's illness and his worry for Ragnar appears more clearly in the Norwegian original, where it says, in the directions for the first speech, that Brovik '*ånder tungt*' (SV 33), while he later complains that his worry for Ragnar 'er det tyngste' (SV 36).
6. McFarlane translates this with 'plant-holders' (391).
7. In a letter to Edvard Brandes, Ibsen indicated that the characters – and he presumably meant all of them – deserve our interest in their own right. Cf. *The Oxford Ibsen*, VII, p. 533.
8. McFarlane's free rendering – 'I [Hilde] met her when she was spending a few days up in the mountains for her health' (377) – obscures this connection; when Solness in the following speech says 'up *there*', he need not necessarily mean 'up in the mountains'; he might just as well mean 'up north' (cf. the expression 'up at Lysanger', 376); besides, the translation is absurd in its implication that Aline could be cured in a few days; a literal translation of Ibsen's sentence should read: 'We were together a few days at the sanatorium – '.

9. The often expressed idea that Aline is more concerned with her dolls than with her dead children, i.e. more concerned with the wrong done to her than with her own guilt, reveals a superficial reading of the play. It is precisely because the memory of the children is so painful to her that she has to repress it; her preoccupation with the lost dolls is a sign of her unsuccessful attempt to do this; disguised as dolls the dead infants keep coming back to her.

10. In his letters Ibsen frequently makes positive comments on *The Father*. Cf. G. R. Reistad,'Om Ibsens lesning', *Ibsenårbok 1968-69* (Oslo, 1969), p. 54.

11. McFarlane translates this actor's direction freely: '*With a heavy sigh*' (405).

12. The connection between Brovik's breathing difficulties and his final stroke is not easy to see; the lacking coherence seems to be an indication of Ibsen's disinterestedness in the realistic aspects of Brovik's illness.

13. Cf. Northam, *op. cit.*, p. 183.

14. McFarlane obscures the connection by substituting a banal expression – 'weak nerves' (432) – for Ibsen's metaphoric one.

15. H. J. Weigand, *The Modern Ibsen*, 2nd ed. (New York, 1960), p. 274ff.

Originally published May 1972 (Vol. 11, No. 1).

Myth and Modernity: Henrik Ibsen's Double Drama

Erik Østerud

Introduction

Ibsen is considered one of the fathers of the theatre of naturalism. This theatre is 'a theatre of illusion'. It intends to put 'life as it is' on stage. It presents ordinary people, people in real rooms, speaking and behaving like the rest of us.

There has been a tendency to consider the theatre of naturalism with its narrow rooms of everyday life as a medium too poor and restricted to stage the problem of human destiny.[1] In Ibsen's case, however, the confrontation with the narrow spaces and the myopic perspective seems to have represented an enormous – and happy – challenge to his scenic imagination. In fact he turned it to his advantage, developing the expressive capacity of naturalism to a level few playwrights since have approached. How did he achieve this?

Some forty years ago John Northam opened up a new field among Ibsen scholars.[2] Speaking of 'visual suggestions' he demonstrated how a specific layer of significance could be revealed by a close reading of the visual details in Ibsen's stage-directions. Northam considered the visual communication between stage and audience as a privileged access to a knowledge of the higher world that Ibsen's characters were *also* exploring. Beneath the surface of everyday life the Ibsen hero was confronted with problems equal to those known by the heroes in Greek or Shakespearean theatre. Northam's view added grandeur to Ibsen's protagonists and was a convincing argument for ranging Ibsen's tragedies alongside the classics. He asserted that 'great reckonings' could take place even 'in little rooms'.[3]

Like Northam I consider Ibsen's realistic setting to be transparent, carrying meaning above and beyond the simple 'effect of the real'. But I assume the double meaning to be expressed in quite another way. Ibsen allows a sacred drama, a drama of myth and ritual ceremonies, to be housed within another drama, a drama of modernity.

A sacred drama presents the current of events within a framework of myth, magic and religion. It expresses its values in repeating ritual performances within mythological patterns. Rites are celebrated and performed within a cosmic space. This cosmic space is structured in contrasts between what is sacred and what is profane, what is inside and what is outside, what is up and what is down, what is pure and what is contagious, what is centre and what is periphery. The qualitative differences in which space is organized leave places open for man's encounter with invisible spirits, with gods and demons. Through the ritual acts the faith and the moral values of sacred tradition are kept alive and carried from the past into the present situation. Imbued with the sacred the present moment is rescued from the chaos of floating time. The rite is an act performed again and again, year after year, cyclically celebrating and renewing the same social and cultural order. The magical effect of the ritual procedure depends on the performer's ability to carry it through correctly, to repeat the steps and acts known by the cultural community for centuries. The characters are more 'gods' than 'personalities', in the sense of being objects of cults with a specific imagery and ritual attached to them. As myths are looked upon as archetypical events in a distant past, of which events in ordinary life are repetitions, the link between present and past can be described as metaphorical, not metonymic. The structure of the mythology is synchronic, not diachronic.

We must now ask where the ritual acts and magic are to be found in Ibsen's plays.

The answer is: in Nora's Tarantella-dance imitating the death-struggle of the victim of a spider's poison; in Mrs Alving's celebration of her dead husband, who will not stay in his grave and leave her in peace; in Rebekka's and Rosmer's wedding celebration carried out as a common suicide, an act which can also be regarded as a magic-mimetic repetition of the exit from life that the lunatic Beate had chosen; in Hedda Gabler's symbolic burning of the child, and in her attempt to stage the vine-leaf dream, first through Løvborg, and then carried out by herself; in the Master Builder's ritual climbing up to the top of the tower to argue with God; in the Rat-Wife's enchanting playing on her Jew's harp; and finally in Irene's and Rubek's apocalyptic ascent to the top of the mountain.

Turning to the drama of modernity we find the experience best defined by Marshal Berman in his book *All That is Solid Melts into Air*: 'All that is solid melts into air, all that is holy is profaned, and men at last are forced to face with sober senses the real condition of their lives and their relations with their fellow men'.[4] The man of modernity is cut off from the normative past with its fixed rules and criteria. Tradition has no legitimate claim on him. There are no examples to imitate, no directions to follow. Man has to create his own present – and his own future. The awareness of the present, of its inevitable transitoriness appears as his main source of inspiration and creativity. Modernity is linked to the conquest of rationality and individual autonomy; it starts where the sacred world of myth and religion has been finally defeated and destroyed. 'Personality' can only emerge within a historical context.

Diachrony, historical change, transgression and a *metonymic narrative* are key concepts for modernity. Modernity cultivates the utopian perspective, it wants the new, even the shockingly new, to be released from the present moment. The sacred drama on the other hand works with a different set of concepts. Among them are *synchrony, tradition, mimetic repetition* (*metaphorical narrative*) and *cosmic space*. In Ibsen's plays the two types of drama confront each other. As they have opposite conceptions of the present moment, they fight each other. The sacred drama attacks the actual flux of life from behind in an attempt to link what *is* to what *has been*: time should not change! The drama of modernity puts a strong and never-ending effort into freeing the present moment from the tyranny of tradition in order to change what *is* to what *shall be*: to be is to become!

Both types of drama contribute to a widening of the arena of the theatre of naturalism, the sacred drama by linking the bourgeois parlour to a cosmic space, the drama of modernity by putting the events of everyday life into a temporal perspective of historical existence.

The theme of modernity is introduced in *Ghosts* as a social and political goal for the protagonist, Mrs Alving. In her famous lines about the presence of ghosts in Norwegian society she takes up the torch from the enlightenment movement, and gives herself an identity as a fighter for knowledge, freedom and progression. 'I am half inclined to think we are all ghosts, Mr Manders,' she says, and continues: 'It is not only what we have inherited from our fathers and mothers that exists again in us, but all sorts of old dead ideas and all kinds of old dead beliefs and things of that kind. They are not actually alive in us; but there they are dormant, all the same, and we can never be rid of them'.[5]

These lines suggest how the qualities of modernity (rationality and autonomy) have to be conquered by a bold wrestling with forces rooted in a sacred world. Although the mythical worldview expressed in these forces is outdated, it nevertheless works upon our character. It does not influence the rational part of our mind: its effect has much more to do with what Freud calls 'the uncanny'. It attacks the 'archaic' layer of the psyche. Karl Heinz Bohrer talks about 'die Furcht vor dem Unbekannten' as a 'Vermittlungs-Struktur von Tradition und Moderne'. 'Das Unbekannte' is to him 'wenn nicht mehr das Erlebnis, so doch noch immer das Wort, verbirgt einen mythischen Rest, den die Aufklärung nicht aufzulösen vermochte'.[6]

It is possible to interpret the closing scene in *A Doll's House* from a similar perspective. Breaking out of her marriage Nora has liberated herself from the slavery of illusions and conventions which tradition had imposed upon her. In this reading the oft-repeated question about where she is now heading, can easily be answered. She has embarked for the future. Her exit represents a transition from a closed world of myths, rituals and endless repetitions – in which her own growth as a human being has been brought to a standstill – into an open world of dynamic and historical change. Nora has become *another* – 'a new', 'a modern'.

In her new identity private and public life are closely knit together. Through a series of uncompromising deeds she will be challenging a society heavily dominated by prejudice. Her deeds may have – indeed will have – an eye-opening effect on other women. She has become an instrument for progress, not primarily by putting women's liberation on her agenda and discussing it publicly, but by being free and expressing this freedom through her behaviour – by *doing* more than *saying*. Nora has made – and makes – history move. In her action the historical movement involves much more than just women's emancipation. It has to be taken in the broadest meaning of the word. It covers human progress in general, that is: the utopian movement. Utopia is to Ibsen more the way to the goal than the goal itself. Utopia is already announced when *some* members of society start to question values which have been considered self-evident and eternally valid.[7]

This clash between a sacred drama and a drama of modernity, between a drama of spatial patterns and a drama of temporal order, is perhaps most clearly visible in the key-scene in *When We Dead Awaken*, as will be seen in the following. Here are some remarks to this topic:

The Gaze

This key scene – the moment of creation between Irene and Rubek in which the masterpiece, The Resurrection Day, was completed – is a scene of mythological-spatial pattern. It is a repeated tableau in which Irene every time strikes the same pose before the eyes of the artist. She poses as 'a young, naked woman, untouched by worldly experience – awakening to the light and the glory, with nothing ugly or unclean to cast off'.[8]

As they meet daily in his studio and with energy and self-sacrifice indulge in their common mission, which Rubek conceives of as a religious ceremony, they happen to fall in love with each other. Their love is not declared, yet the tacit affection they both feel cannot help influencing their collaboration in the studio, which gives rise to extremely complicated emotional situations. In the highly intensified atmosphere there is a speechless communication between them, a visual interaction between *his* gaze and *her* body, between his viewing and her showing.

To Rubek Irene becomes a sacred creature, to be touched only by worshipful thoughts. He has the conviction that if he touches her, or desires her in sensual terms, his spirit will be profaned so that he cannot create what he is striving for. Thus he conceptualizes 'the tableau of creation', the tableau between the viewing artist and the exposing model in the image of The Resurrection Day. What he wants to express in his art, is imitated in the artistic procedure.

This tableau scene dates as far back as Rubek's youth. Years have passed since then, but Rubek cannot forget what he once achieved as an artist, having been unable to surpass it. However, the memory of the masterpiece fills him with mixed feelings, as it also reminds him of an incomplete – or rather barely initiated – love story. Irene left immediately after their sessions in the studio were over, and later she is nowhere to be found.

Now they meet again. This time they both know what they have been missing since they separated, and they do not hesitate to tell each other. Rubek admits that there were days on end when her beauty nearly drove him out of his senses. And she for her part reveals that she too was sexually possessed. She blames him for not having touched her.

The way they express their love shows how the tableau can be seen as an arena in which two different perspectives are employed at the same time. We have already spoken of the visual communication between the artist's gaze and the model's body united in a common effort to complete their high mission. But these roles are coupled with the roles of the voyeur and the exhibitionist. Focusing on this hidden, tacit – and only semi-conscious – game, the arena now also resembles a 'peep-show'. At one level every effort is made to express and expose visual chastity. At the other level the picture of the chaste, attractive young woman struggling against her own impulse to 'sin', by no means discourages the watcher's gaze. On the contrary, it increases his desire. Even his own resistance to 'sin' enhances his excitement. Artistic creation is mixed up with pornography. The artist cannot help celebrating his own secret sensuous feast while watching his model. In this feast fantasy conquers what he is not allowed to have in real life. Looking becomes a metonymic substitute for touching.

Visual consummation takes place where bodies are not allowed to meet.

The pornographic duplicate of 'the tableau of creation' is also expressed in Irene's practice as a model later in life. When Rubek asks her about her living, how she managed to live, she answers:

> Bi lidt; lad mig sé – . Jo, nu har jeg det. Jeg har stået på drejeskiven i varietéer. Stået som nøgen statue i levende billeder. Strøget mange penge ind. Det var jeg ikke vant til hos dig; for du havde ingen.[9]

> Wait, now, let me see – Yes, now I know. I've stood on revolving platforms in cabarets, as a naked statue in living tableau. Raked in reams of money that way. That's more than I ever did with you; you never had it.[10]

There is a power of extreme violence in Rubek's gaze. Legitimated by the myth the gaze splits the emotions into accepted and denied passions. It establishes a fissure in Irene between the madonna and the whore, between the girl who always had a sharp needle hidden in her hair while she stood for him, and the girl who wanted to be touched. This experience generates hysterical symptoms which can be located in her mental life ever after. The hysterical trauma has the power of reproducing itself in the future. What she explores from now on are nothing but repetitions or copies of this 'Ur-Szene' from her youth.

As this traumatic fissure is strictly linked to scenes in which the gaze is involved, we may fairly call the unconscious in *When We Dead Awaken* 'the optical unconscious'.[11] Since Freud was simultaneously working on the same trauma, under the 'Ur-Szene' theory, a comparison between Ibsen and Freud might prove beneficial.[12]

The 'Ur-Szene'

The Freudian 'Ur-Szene' has to do with the shocking experience of sexuality in early infancy. The consequence of the 'Ur-Szene'– whether it really happened or is merely a product of fantasy – is traumatized sexuality, which can, however, be treated by therapy later in life. The conflicting emotions and desires that Irene and Rubek experience during the hey days of their artistic creation, are – as we have seen – also of a traumatic character. What happened to them then has never been really forgotten since. Traces of the strong emotional split they were subject to, can be located in almost everything that happens to them later.

If we compare Rubek's (or Irene's) 'Ur-Szene' to that of Freud, we have to emphasize that Ibsen does not locate his 'Ur-Szene' in early infancy. For Ibsen the crucial moment in the life of a human being is to be found on the threshold between youth and adolescence. At this point the young and unsettled man or woman can free themselves from the dependency on the parental family and establish a life on their own. The transformation from youth to adolescence in Ibsen's plays might be described as a 'rite of passage'.[13] This is the moment when Rubek and Irene meet and decide to work together.

Personal autonomy does not come without further ado in Ibsen's plays. It has to be grasped. Since freedom frightens as much as it attracts, the act of transgression demands courage.[14] The transgression could be called an initiation into adult life and a supplanting of the traditional values which the fathers honour.

This is why the Ibsenite 'Ur-Szene' always points forward to the future. In Rubek and Irene's case their biological age has kept them away from the freedom of adolescence, the paradise they have been longing for in their juvenile hopes and fantasies. The 'Ur-Szene' appears when the waiting-time is over and life can be grasped in all its richness and happiness. Now, finally, fantasy can be transformed into reality. The total engagement with which they approach each other reveals how they are designed to support and complement each other in future life. There is a neat symmetry in their relation, a reciprocity which makes it quite obvious to unite in art and love, in freedom and joy.

But the perfection of the situation is exactly what causes problems. The unlimited freedom expressed in the challenge coming from Irene, the extremely high temperature of the feeling of life at this very moment, is frightening. Rubek cannot face it. This is where the myth comes into his life. The project he launches, wrapped in mythical packing, grants him the right to lay the freedom out in lots and take possession of only one part of it. He grabs what art offers him and leaves love untouched. The myth can justify: it depicts his great artistic victory, the monument of The Resurrection Day, as a product brought forth by a necessary sacrifice of love. At the same time the pathetic sacrifice adds grandeur to the artistic victory, making it appear as a result of a great inner struggle. This subtle manoeuvre of arguments, in which it becomes obscure even to Rubek himself what is cause and what effect, is the actual beginning of a career totally dominated by self-deception. From this very moment the myth makes Rubek's life congeal into a pose, into a position of existential immobility. From now on his life revolves around the same 'Ur-Szene', which he perpetually repeats. He cannot cross the gap between youth and adult life; he cannot grow; he cannot renew himself.

The Retrospective Technique

Comparing Ibsen's drama to Freudian therapy, there is one further consideration to be made. The Freudian procedure of recalling the 'Ur-Szene' has been associated with what the Greeks called *anamnesis* or recognition. Knowledge is acquired by identifying what happens to us now with something else that happened once in the past. We take hold of our lives by looking backwards. Life turns forwards, but can only be explained backwards, as the logic of time is causal.

Ibsen scholars normally put the retrospective technique, which the play-wright is known to have cultivated with such success, into this framework. In his reflections on the historical change within the drama genre from the renaissance to modern times Peter Szondi blames Ibsen for not having been able to put 'the actual time', 'the dramatic presence' on the stage.[15] In Ibsen's theatre the audience is permitted to witness only the effects of actions which took place years ago, he writes. In *John Gabriel Borkman* the past is not, as in Sophocles' *Oedipus*, a function of the present, according to Szondi; the present is rather an occasion for conjuring up the past.[16] The past lives on in Ibsen's leitmotivs, conjured up where they are mentioned. Szondi emphasizes how Beate Rosmer's suicide becomes 'an eternal presence' because of the millpond in *Rosmersholm*, and he claims that the motif of genetic inheritance in *Ghosts* serves more to make the past present than it does to embody the antique notion of fate. The fact that the past itself has invaded the stage in Ibsen's plays expresses for Szondi a crisis in the history of the dramatic genre, a tendency to let the dramatic genre interfere with the novel. Time can only be reported *about* in the drama; its direct presentation is possible solely in an art form that includes it 'among its constitutive principles'. This art form is the novel.

In my presentation of the Ibsenite 'Ur-Szene', however, it has been suggested how Ibsen puts the emphasis not on what has happened in the past but on what has *not* happened. Ibsen's 'Ur-Szene' is a moment in the past pregnant with freedom and possibilities, which his characters did not grasp in due time. But having failed once does not prevent them from getting the chance again later in life. That is why the retrospection has a *prospective* function in Ibsen. Recalling the fatal moments in the past is like being confronted with dreams and hopes which are still unfulfilled.

Put into this perspective the Ibsenite 'Ur-Szene' appears more to be a prefiguration of something that is ahead of the Ibsen hero. It is of course painful to be constantly reminded of past failure, but at the same time it is comforting to realize that everything can be changed. There is still time.

The difference between a past-directed causality and a future-directed finality is expressed in Northrop Frye's *The Great Code. The Bible and Literature* by a short excursion to Kierkegaard's *Repetition*.[17] There are in Kierkegaard's book two types of repetition, one related to causality, the other to finality. The first one represents 'the mere attempt to repeat a past experience'. In Frye's presentation this is associated with a Platonic recollection or anamnesis. The second type is 'the Christian antithesis (or complement) of Platonic recollection, which finds its focus in the Biblical promise: 'Behold, I make all things new' (Revelation 21:5).[18] Kierkegaard's own 'repetition' is in Frye's view derived from, or even identifiable with, this forward-moving thinking of the Bible.

The two types of repetition lead us back to the Ibsenite double-drama presented at the beginning of this paper: the first points to the metaphorical world of myth and ritual, the other to the metonymical world of history and modernity. The first type of repetition keeps the world fixed in spatial immobility, the other makes the world move in temporal instability.

The world of myth and spatial immobility, the world of the sculptor's congealed human beings – the existential mode of the statue – will be explored in the following.

A Moving Statue

In his article 'Moving Statues, Talking Statues' Kenneth Gross discusses the fantasy of an animated statue, of a piece of sculpture which moves, speaks, shows signs of awareness, responds to a gesture – coming to life as oracle, lover, enemy, avenger, monster, demon or angel.[19] He describes this fantasy as one of the oldest examples of the work of magic in European culture and places it in the theatrical traditions of masque, pantomime and *tableau vivant* games.

Gross asks: What does it mean for a statue to step down from a pedestal, to enter the sphere of the human or natural, to lose its isolation and aura?

> It can seem both a fall and a resurrection, a descent and a transcendence into the human, both an enchantment and a disenchantment. It can be an image of the most profound, gratuitous restitution, a figure for a recovery of the world, a return of objects themselves from their alienation. And yet in numerous texts the life which a statue takes on is partial, daemonic, unnatural, a violation rather than a recovery of the world – calling into question our naively benign pictures of metamorphosis.[20]

The key-word in Gross's reflections is 'metamorphosis'. The word recalls Ovid's *Metamorphoses*, in which the story of Pygmalion is one of the figures. Each metamorphosis is a description of how the terrible performative power of the gods intervenes in human history, transforming boys into flowers, girls into trees. Each metamorphosis is a change of shape, in which justice is done, an account paid off. The fulfilment of the destiny of a human being expressed in his or her metamorphosis is not exile from the human community, nor is it the ultimate separation of death. It is halfway between the two, neither death nor life. The one who has been transformed remains as a memorial example still present within the human community – in the form of a tree, a fountain, a flower. The halfway state of the victim of a metamorphosis is a sign that his or her fault has not been completely punished or expiated. The changed state may be read as life-giving or death-dealing, depending on how it is viewed.

The story of Pygmalion differs from most of the stories in the *Metamorphoses*. It is a tale in which something inanimate comes alive, rather than the other way around. To punish the loathsome Propoetides Venus in her wrath makes them the first women to become public prostitutes. The blood hardens in their cheeks as they become shameless, spiritually hard. Then Venus punishes them again. She makes them literally stone. Pygmalion's horror at these wicked, stony-hearted women leads him to remain celibate. To make up for women who have become painted ladies with hearts of stone, Pygmalion creates another painted lady out of stone. This statue had all the appearance of a real girl, so that it seemed to be alive, to want to move. Pygmalion gazed in wonder, and in his heart there rose a passionate love for this image of a human form.

Thus the coming alive of Galatea in this story can be considered as an inverted metamorphosis. The word metamorphosis acquires a double meaning: a transformation from life to death or from death to life.

The two kinds of metamorphosis intersect in *When We Dead Awaken*. From one perspective the creation of The Resurrection Day can be looked upon as the sculptor's self-asserting statement pointing to the magic life-giving force of the artist. In that case Irene appears as Rubek's Galatea. From another perspective – and this is Irene's view – the art of creation is a transformation of life to death, human to inhuman, animate to inanimate.

The whole play is full of references to similar acts of transformation in which life- and death-metaphors are contrasted and opposite meanings of the action appear. The bear-hunter Ulfhejm compares his own job to Rubek's artistic work in this way:

'We both like working with hard material, ma'am – both I and your husband. He likes wrestling with blocks of marble, I imagine – and I wrestle with the hard, straining sinews of bears. And both of us force our material down under control at last. Become lord and master over it. We never give up till we've overcome it, no matter how much it fights back'.[21] And this description of the hard work ends in a life-giving myth. He adds: 'Yes, because the stone has something to fight for too, I'm sure. It's dead, and it resists with all its strength being hammered into life. Exactly like a bear when you sneak up and prod it out of its den'.[22] In this case the underlying reversed meaning of the life-giving procedure is obvious: the bear-hunter is first of all a killer of life.

The ambiguous meaning of Rubek and Ulfhejm's magic procedures is due to their act of liberation being based on an act of suppression as well. One aspect of life is released by subduing another. That is why it is so dangerous to raise three fingers in the air and swear to go with this 'lord and master'. The pact with the redeemer is a pact with the devil as well. In this type of metamorphosis the knife seems to be the magic weapon. But the knife is more an instrument for splitting up or tearing apart than for healing. Being the object of the magician's knife, as Irene has been and Maja becomes – and here I am speaking in a more metaphorical sense about the expression – causes suppression and agony more than happiness and freedom. It *looks* like self-expansion, but underneath the surface there are these untouched and half-recognized needs and desires, which provoke dissatisfaction and a feeling of emptiness. The existence of these feelings is a permanent threat to the mythic self-interpretation of 'the two great artists'.

In the opening scene of the play when Irene turns up once again in Rubek's life after having disappeared without trace, her visual appearance makes Rubek immediately recognize her as the model for his statue. And indeed, she is that in more than one meaning of the word. She has adopted all the properties of a statue: its stiffness, its coldness, and its lack of gaze. She is like the uncanny phenomenon of a statue Kenneth Gross talks about, which has stepped down from a pedestal to wander around in the sphere of the human.

To Rubek her visual appearance is a strong argument for the grandiose vision he celebrated in his earlier days: the myth of the magic life-giving force of the artist. As he sees her now, she *is* the incarnate Resurrection. She *has* been transformed by his art. She *is* exactly what *he* identifies with life.

Her view is the opposite. She is unhappy. She feels her life destroyed. She feels as if she has been locked up within a cold statue of marble. From the deep inside of this cold marble her oppressed human voice is complaining. She asks to be set free. Imprisoned within the statue she feels as if she is asleep or dead. She wants to 'awaken', to 'come to life' again.

As described earlier, Ibsen pays very much attention to what has been called 'the rite of passage' or the transformation from' youth to adolescence. Modernity has to be conquered by a crossing of the border between youth and adolescence. What have been described here as metamorphoses, pretend to be this sort of movement, but in fact they are not. They are faked 'rites of passage'; they keep the characters linked to the existential position *before* the transition, exploring life only in dreams, hallucinations and inner visions. Irene and Rubek's interaction is reduced to an exchange of images, to visual communication, to *her* physical appearance and *his* gaze. Behind the visual communication there is a reciprocal feeling of emptiness, of unlived life. Life has become a wasteland.

The Wasteland

This experience is emphasized in the title 'When We Dead Awaken', but it is also expressed in a short dialogue between them at the end of the second act:

> PROFESSOR RUBEK: (*gentager drømmende*) Sommernat på vidden. Med dig. Med dig.
> (*hans øjne møder hendes*)
> Å Irene, – det kunde ha' været livet. – Og *det* har vi forspildt, – vi to.
> IRENE: Det uoprettelige sér vi først, når –
> (*bryder kort af*)
> PROFESSOR RUBEK: (*sér spørgende på hende*) Når – ?
> IRENE: Når vi døde vågner.
> PROFESSOR RUBEK: (*ryster tungsindig på hodet*) Ja, hvad sér vi så egentlig?
> IRENE: Vi sér at vi aldrig har levet.[23]

> RUBEK: (*repeats, as if dreaming*) A summer's night on the moors. With you. With you.
> (*His eyes meeting hers*) Oh, Irene, – that might have been our life – and we lost it, you and I.
> IRENE: We'll see what we've lost only when – (*breaking off*)
> RUBEK: (*with an inquiring look*) When – ?
> IRENE: When we dead awaken.
> RUBEK: (*shakes his head sorrowfully*) Yes, and what, really, do we see then? Irene. We see that we've never lived.[24]

In the history of the reception of *When We Dead Awaken* the interpretation seems to have taken two different directions. As the play carries the sub-title *A Dramatic Epilogue*, there are good reasons for taking the play as a comment on *some* of Ibsen's previous plays, or on *all* of them. Thus, the different phases in Rubek's life and art have been read as allegories over different stages the authorship has passed through. More common is perhaps the view that *When We Dead Awaken* expresses an irreconcilable conflict between art and life – painfully experienced in Ibsen's own life.

This article emphasizes how life with all its richness and possibilities for love and art has been rejected by the main character in the play. Art and love can be, and should be, conquered together. Anxiety, however, prevents the young artist from doing so. In the final act of *Peer Gynt* after the shipwreck a mysterious passenger pops up when Peer is clinging to the keel. He asks Peer: 'My friend, have you even once in your life / Known the victory only dread can give?' Peer has not, and neither has Rubek. Rubek's career after the fatal meeting with Irene describes a double inner retreat from the world: retreat from life on the pretext of what art demands; and retreat from art using life as the excuse. The drying up of inner feelings and emotions is compensated for and camouflaged by outer successes.

Art as such is not responsible for this tragic discrepancy between outer appearance and inner realities. The artist is only *one* of Ibsen's *many* illusionists who knows how to let images dug up from the fantasy enter into the physical world and play their roles there. This kind of visual spell is expressed in *A Doll's House* by Nora's masquerade, in *The Wild Duck*, by Hjalmar's photography, in *The Master Builder* by Solness' architecture and so on.

There is generally a tendency to theatricality among Ibsen's many self-deceptionists. From one point of view these characters can be described as terribly weak and evasive ('soft and lazy and full of self-forgiveness', as Irene expresses it in her critique of Rubek). From another point of view they can be considered as individuals in possession of a great hunger for life, of great expectations and aspirations. However, this aspect of the personality – also called the identity – is tragically and painfully kept imprisoned in the material/ immaterial image of the character. How can this prison of images and performances and poses be blown up, so that the identity can come free?

This is the crucial question in the last part of *When We Dead Awaken*. How can the existential border between youth and adolescence that Rubek and Irene during their young days never passed, now – when finally recognized – be crossed? How can Rubek and Irene in an existential meaning of the words 'move forward' together? How can they change their lifestyle from a simple repetition of tradition to a total renewal that releases modernity and gives them what they have never had: access to their own identities?

In the opening scene we learn that Maja and Rubek are lodging in a luxurious spa hotel. On the one hand the hotel appears as a residence for pleasures and gratifications. Here every need seems to be met, every service to be available. As there is no lack, there can be no yearning for other places to be. This seems to be heaven, or eternity! The symbolic meaning of the stage-set seems to correspond to Maja and Rubek's self-complacent depiction of their marriage and social success. They seem to have achieved everything they aimed for. They know of nothing more to ask for.

This is *one* symbolic meaning the opening set offers us. There is another and opposite one too: not only healthy people frequent the hotel. Sickness and death are there. If the spa is a place for rich people to enjoy life at their leisure, it is at the same time a sanatorium for sick people fighting for their lives, a kind of wasteland.[25]

The symbolic meaning of the sickness we meet among the people at the spa has to be found in the hidden sterility of Rubek and Maja's marriage. The superficial satisfaction obtained from the luxurious life they spend together, is being denied by a restless and desperate quest for something else, something they suspect they don't have. This quest turns heaven into hell, life into death:

PROFESSOR RUBEK: (*sér op fra sin avis*) Nå Maja? Hvad er der i vejen med dig?
FRU MAJA: Hør bare hvor lydløst her er.
PROFESSOR RUBEK: (*smiler overbærende*) Og det kan du høre?
FRU MAJA: Hvilket?
PROFESSOR RUBEK: Det lydløse?
FRU MAJA: Ja, det kan jeg da rigtignok.
PROFESSOR RUBEK: Nu, du har kanske ret, mein Kind. Man kan virkeligt høre lydløsheden.
FRU MAJA: Ja, det skal gud vide en kan. Når den er så rent overvældende som her, så –

PROFESSOR RUBEK: Som her ved badet, mener du?
FRU MAJA: Overalt her hjemme, mener jeg. Inde i byen var der jo larm og uro nok. Men alligevel, – jeg syntes at selve larmen og uroen havde noget dødt over sig.[26]

RUBEK: (*looking up from the paper*) Well, Maja? What's the matter?
MAJA: Just listen, how silent it is here.
RUBEK: (*smiling indulgently*) Can you hear that?
MAJA: What?
RUBEK: The silence?
MAJA: Yes. Definitely.
RUBEK: Well, mein Kind, maybe you're right. Undoubtedly, one can hear silence.
MAJA: Yes, God knows anyone can. When it's as overpowering as it is here –
RUBEK: At the spa, you mean?
MAJA: I mean, everywhere in this country. Down in the city there was plenty of noise and activity. But nevertheless – I felt that even that noise and activity had something dead about it.[27]

The discrepancy between outer prosperity and inner sterility is everywhere on the stage and in the characters.

The play moves on from this point zero. Irene's reappearance makes Rubek immediately feel how his life has been degraded from the moment she left, and he tries to re-establish the kind of relation they once had:

PROFESSOR RUBEK: (*afledende*) Kunde du ikke ha' lyst til at rejse med og ho hos os i villaen dernede?
IRENE: (*sér hånligt smilende på ham*) Sammen med dig og den anden dame?
PROFESSOR RUBEK: (*indtrængende*) Sammen med *mig* – ligesom i de skabende dage. Lukke op alt det, som er vredet i baglås i mig. Kunde du ikke ville det, Irene?
IRENE: (*ryster pa hodet*) Jeg har ikke nøglen til dig længer, Arnold.
PROFESSOR RUBEK: Du *har* nøglen. Ingen uden du har den!
.   (*trygler og beder*)
Hjælp mig, – så jeg kan komme til at leve livet om igen!
IRENE: (*ubevægelig som før*) Tomme drømme. Ørkesløse – døde drømme. Vort samliv har ingen opstandelse efter sig.[28]

RUBEK: Wouldn't you like to come down and live with us, in the villa by the lake?
IRENE: (*looking at him with a disdainful smile*) With you – and the other woman?
RUBEK: (*importunately*) With me – just like the days when we created together. You could open up everything that's locked away in me. Couldn't you do that, Irene?
IRENE: (*shakes her head*) I don't have the key to you any longer, Arnold.
RUBEK: You have the key! You alone have it! (*beseeching her*) Help me – so I can try to live my life over again!
IRENE: (*impassively as before*) Empty dreams. Aimless – dead dreams. *Our* life together can never be resurrected.[29]

Mere repetition is not enough. It will only take them back into the painful split of the 'Ur-Szene'. But here Irene's critique leads him to new insight. How this happens requires a comment.

Insight – and New Blindness

In reply to Irene's question, Rubek has to tell her what has happened to the
masterpiece – their common child, as she expresses it – after she left. He enlarged the
composition. The little round pedestal on which her statue stood; erect and isolated,
no longer had room for everything he saw with his own eyes in the world around him.
He extended the pedestal, moved back the statue of her, and set a piece of the curving,
bursting earth on it. Out of the cracks in the earth he let human beings swarm up, with
disguised animal faces.

Irene is shocked and reacts with unrestrained accusations against him. Her self-
sacrifice turned out to be without any meaning! she says. The dialogue continues:

> PROFESSOR RUBEK: (*ivrig, river hatten af sig og tørrer sveddråberne af panden*) Ja
> men hør nu også, hvorledes jeg har stillet *mig selv* hen i gruppen. Foran ved en kilde,
> ligesom her, sidder en skyldbetynget mand, som ikke kan komme helt løs fra
> jordskorpen. Jeg kalder ham angeren over et forbrudt liv. Han sidder der og dypper
> sine fingre i det rislende vand – for at skylle dem rene, – og han nages og martres ved
> tanken på at det aldrig, aldrig lykkes ham. Han når i al evighed ikke fri op til
> opstandelsens liv. Blir evindelig siddende igen i sit helvede.
>
> IRENE (*hårdt og koldt*) Digter!
>
> PROFESSOR RUBEK: Hvorfor digter?
>
> IRENE: Fordi du er slap og sløv og fuld af syndsforladelse for alle dit livs gerninger og
> for alle dine tanker. Du har dræbt min sjæl, – og så modellerer du dig selv i anger og
> bod og bekendelse, – (*smiler*) – og dermed er dit regnskab opgjort, mener du.
>
> PROFESSOR RUBEK: (*trodsende*) Jeg er kunstner, Irene. Og jeg skammer mig ikke over
> den skrøbelighed, som kanske klæber ved mig. For jeg er *født* til kunstner, sér du. Og
> blir så aldrig andet end kunstner alligevel.
>
> IRENE: (*sér på ham med et fordulgt smil og siger mildt og blødt*) Digter er du, Arnold.
> (*stryger ham lindt over håret*)
>
> Du kære, store, aldrende barn, – at du ikke kan sé *det*![30]

> RUBEK: (*ardently, pulling off his hat and mopping his forehead*) Yes, but listen now, how
> I've introduced myself in the composition. In front, by a spring – it could be here – a
> man sits bowed down by guilt, as if he can't quite detach himself from the earth's
> crust. I call him remorse for a lapsed life. He sits there and dips his fingers in the
> flowing water – to rinse them clean – and he's wrung and harrowed by the thought
> that he'll never, never succeed. In all eternity he'll never be free to experience
> resurrection. He'll sit there perpetually in his own hell.
>
> IRENE: (*cold and harsh*) Poet!
>
> RUBEK: Why poet?
>
> IRENE: Because you're soft and lazy and full of self-forgiveness for every sin of your life,
> the acts you've done and the thoughts you've had. You killed my soul – and then you
> model yourself in remorse and penance and contrition – (*smiles*) – and you think that
> settles the score.
>
> RUBEK: (*defiantly*) I'm an artist, Irene. And I'm not ashamed of the human frailties I
> might carry around with me. Because, you see, I was *born* to be an artist. And no
> matter what, I'll never be anything else.
>
> IRENE: (*regards him with a veiled, evil smile and speaks softly and gently*) You're a poet,
> Arnold. (*lightly, stroking his hair*) You're a big, dear, overgrown child, not to see it.[31]

219

'I call him remorse for a lapsed life'. This is Rubek's self-portrait, his self-understanding framed as an allegory over the guilt. Every element in this sculpture contributes to the depiction of the repenting artist, every part of the work of art – the flowing water, heaven and earth – is here used as props and stage setting for staging the image. But this is first of all a theatrical pose. The pain is there, or rather: the pain is *visually* there and can be watched, but the *feeling* of remorse is not therefore necessarily present. The motif chosen for the self-portrait is a situation in which the depicted character should be deeply introspective and self-absorbed.[32] But Rubek transforms the content into form, the feeling to theatrical make-believe. Irene immediately recognizes it as a cover-up for a *lack of introspection*. The picture of the thing is not like the thing itself. That is what she expresses by disdainfully calling him 'Poet'. To her the poet does not live life; he only pretends to do so.

Irene's reproaches and clear-sighted perspective on their common misery open Rubek's eyes. As soon as the insight is absorbed, they agree to embark upon a new adventure together – this time to complete the love affair they started a number of years earlier, and which they now know is the way to their own identities.

In the last act we find them advancing in the snow-landscape firmly resolved to reach a level of existence where life can be lived 'to the full for once'. They conceive of this fullness of life as an ecstatic bridal embrace in which they are totally absorbed in each other. At the very end of the play, .however, their plans are dramatically crossed by an avalanche that tumbles them in the masses of snow and buries them. This is the tragic conclusion of the play.

How is this dramatic intervention from nature to be explained? What has nature to do with Rubek's fear of life, erotic frustration, and self-deception?

When Rubek explains to Irene in the second act how he had changed the masterpiece, enlarged the composition, and introduced himself into it, he makes an interesting comment on the setting of the picture. '(...) listen now, how I've introduced myself in the composition,' he says. 'In front, by a spring – it could be here – (...)'. 'By a spring – it could be here.' This statement reveals how the traditional procedure to transform the environment to theatrical remedies in order to build up a more convincing and impressive self-portrait, is extended from Rubek's work of art to the scenic reality. Even the real mountain landscape of hard rocks, steep walls and snow-mantled peaks can be deprived of their identity as factual 'beingness' to serve the artist in his mental vision. Reality is changed into picture.

As Rubek and Irene advance in the dangerous mountain landscape on their way to celebrate their marriage feast, there are alarming omens from the heavy storm, and they are also warned by Ulfhejm and Maja, who have tried to reach the top, but are now on their way down again.

Warnings do not stop them. On the contrary, the wind's blowing its trumpet is like soft music in their ears, urging them to continue. For one moment Irene hesitates. She does not know if the premises are what they should be. Therefore she asks him: 'Have you forgotten what I am now?' His answer is: 'For me you can be whoever and whatever you want! For me you're the woman I dream of seeing in you.' Once again his inner vision is more real to him than outer reality; once again he seems to prefer the image to the real thing. The exceedingly strong expressions he uses to convince

Irene of the force of his love and of his firm decision to realize it, are melodramatic self-exposure. Once more the scenic performance serves as a cover-up for the emptiness of the inner feeling and energy. The sounds from the roaring tempest compete with his exaggerated voice and the rhetoric to make this performance look like an audacious plunging into life.

Earlier in his life Rubek's playing and acting could continue without any risk of his being revealed – by others or by himself. This is not the case any more. Through Irene's reappearance Rubek learned to look into his own emptiness and deception. After having learnt 'to see', his way back to blindness is hampered. More melodramatic effects have to be invested, stronger effects are needed to drown out his own self-critical consciousness and soothe his growing desperation. The increasing intensity of the drama taking place in nature, seems to give Rubek access to splendid visual and acoustic effects for this purpose.

There is, however, a limit. The more Rubek struggles to submit reality to his own illusions, the more he risks reality striking back and insisting on its own autonomy. Seen from this perspective it gives meaning to let Irene and Rubek be buried in the masses of snow.

Conclusions

The intention of this close reading has been to show how two types of drama, 'the spatial drama of myths and rituals' and 'the modern drama of time', are intertwined in *When We Dead Awaken*.

The act of liberation (the conquest of the self) which Ibsen prescribes has been mapped as a passage (transformation or metamorphosis) from fantasy to reality, from youthful play to the seriousness of adolescence (containing individual freedom and responsibility). Through an analysis of the artist-model scenes this paper has tried to reveal how such scenes could be identified as a 'rite of passage'. The Ibsenite 'rite of passage' has then been compared to the Freudian 'Ur-Szene', and the trauma experienced in the Ibsenite 'Ur-Szene' explained as a result of a split in the main character, a confrontation between a strong 'will to life' and a similarly strong 'fear of life'. This conflict prevents the protagonist from genuinely crossing the borderline between youth and adolescence. He has submitted to continuing his life in the playground of infancy, and to shaping it as repetitive imitations of the 'Ur-Szene'. Life does not move any more. Time does not affect it. The character has locked himself up in a mythical space, in an illusionary world without any interaction with real life.

For a short moment the main character succeeds in making this mythical space translucent for himself. A moment later he turns his momentary insight into a new, and fatal, blindness.

Notes

1. The problem of naturalism on the stage is discussed in Bert O. States, *Great Reckonings in Little Rooms. On the Phenomenology of Theater*, Berkeley, Los Angeles, London, 1985.
2. John Northam, *Ibsen's Dramatic Method. A Study of the Prose Dramas*, London, 1953, 2nd ed. Oslo, 1971.
3. Bert O. States' expressions. Northam's problem is also discussed by Francis Fergusson in his well-known study of *Ghosts* in *The Idea of a Theater*, Princeton, 1949.
4. Marshall Berman, *All That Is Solid Melts Into Air. The Experience Of Modernity*, New York, 1982, p.99, quoting from Marx's *Communist Manifesto*.
5. The translation is Rolf Fjelde's in *The Complete Major Prose Plays*, New York, 1965, p.238.
6. Karl Heinz Bohrer, *Plötzlichkeit. Zum Augenblick des ästhetischen Scheins*, Frankfurt 1981, p.68.
7. Dr Stockman's statement at the end of *An Enemy of the People* can be regarded as an illustration of this viewpoint. A reading of *A Doll's House* as a double drama in which myth and modernity confront each other is found in Erik Østerud, 'Henrik Ibsens italienske karneval. Visualitet og teatralitet i *Et dukkehjem*', *Agora*, 2-3/93. Also printed in *Masken som repræsentation*, edited by Jørgen Østergård Andersen and Charlotte Engberg, Aarhus, 1994.
8. Fjelde, 1965, p.1072.
9. *Hundreårsutgave. Henrik Ibsens samlede verker* (ved Francis Bull, Halvdan Koht og Didrik Arup Seip), Bind XI, Oslo 1936, p.233f.
10. *Ibid.*, p.1048.
11. This expression is taken from Rosalind E. Krauss, *The Optical Unconscious*, Massachusetts, 1993. Vision and visuality have been discussed vividly in studies about film, photo, painting, sculpture and texts during the last 10-15 years by critics such as Susan Sontag, Roland Barthes, Laura Mulvay, Kaja Silverman, Jonathan Crary, Barbara Freedman, Martin Jay, Martin Bryson, Michael Fried and Mieke Bal, besides Krauss. Some of these names have played a role for the perspective chosen in this study.
12. Freud has treated Ibsen's *Rosmersholm* in 'Einige Charactertypen aus der psychoanalytischen Arbeit', *Studienausgabe*, X. See Gunnar Brandell, *Freud og hans tid*, København 1963, and Lis Møller, 'Det analytiske teater: Freud og Ibsen', *Nytt Norsk Tidsskrift*, 1/1990.
13. A. van Gennep, *Les rites de passage*, Paris, 1909.
14. Anxiety looked upon as an anthropological condition is expressed in almost every one of Ibsen's plays. The influence of Søren Kierkegaard's *Begrebet Angest* is obvious.
15. Peter Szondi, *Theory of the Modern Drama*, A Critical Edition. Edited and Translated by Michael Hays. Foreword by Jochen Schulte-Sasse, Cambridge, 1987.
16. *Ibid.*, p.16.
17. Northrop Frye, *The Great Code – The Bible and Literature*, London, 1982, p.82.
18. *Ibid.*, p.82.
19. Kenneth Gross, 'Moving Statues, Talking Statues', *Raritan. A Quarterly Review*, IX:2, Fall 1989, New Jersey.
20. *Ibid.*, p.5. Gross's theme is also discussed in Carsten Thau, 'Menneske-automaten', *Kritik* 105, København, 1993.
21. Fjelde, 1965, p.1044.
22. *Ibid.*, p.1044.
23. *Hundreårsutg.* Bind XIII, p.271.
24. Fjelde, 1965, p.1080.

25. The Wasteland metaphor has a central position in the myth of the Holy Grail. In an article in the Ibsen Year-book for 1963-64, '"Når vi døde vågner" på mytologisk bakgrunn', I have pointed out intertextual relations to this myth.
26. *Hundreårsutg.* Bind.XIII, s.215f.
27. Fjelde, 1965, p.1032.
28. *Hundreårsutg.* Bind XIII, p.268.
29. Fjelde, 1965, p.1077.
30. *Hundreårsutg.* Bind XIII, p.263f.
31. Fjelde, 1965, p.1073f.
32. For an understanding of the contrast between 'absorption' and 'theatricality' see Michael Fried, *Absorption and Theatricality. Painting and Beholder in the Age of Diderot*, Chicago 1980. See also Erik Østerud: 'Henrik Ibsens teatermaske. Tablå, absorpsjon og teatralitet i *Vildanden*', *Edda*, 3/93.

Originally published November 1994 (Vol. 33, No. 2).

PAUL BINDING

With Vine-Leaves in His Hair
The Role of the Artist in Ibsen's Plays

The title of this study of the artist in Ibsen's work is taken from Hedda Gabler's ambitions for the heroic death of her former lover, Ejlert Løvborg, and points to a cultural inheritance from both Greek tragedy and Romanticism's concept of the artist-as-rebel. In his great sequence of prose plays the figure of the artist (or would-be artist) is of the greatest importance to Ibsen in his presentation of the tensions inside contemporary society. His empathy with his dramatis personae and his exact and scrupulously accurate placing of them in context means that we need to appreciate his artist-characters in relation to their respective pursuits if we are to see those plays in which they appear in all their depth.

This study focuses particularly on *Gengangere* (*Ghosts*), *Fruen fra havet* (*The Lady From the Sea*), *Hedda Gabler*, *Bygmester Solness* (*The Master Builder*), and *Når vi døde vågner* (*When We Dead Awaken*). Osvald in *Ghosts*, for example, opposes the spirit of modern French painters to his Norwegian milieu, yet how far are we to admire him for this? In this personal reflection, Paul Binding examines the idea that Ibsen's understanding of his people and situations here is of immeasurable help to us now in our search for values on which to build our lives.

'There is much in this book which ... leaves you longing to reread Ibsen, and keen to see him properly performed.' (*Independent on Sunday*)

ISBN 978 1 870041 67 6

UK £14.95
(2006, paperback)

For further information, or to request a catalogue, please contact:
Norvik Press, University of East Anglia (LLT), Norwich NR4 7TJ, England
or visit our website at www.norvikpress.com